E. H. HARRIMAN

A Biography

IN TWO VOLUMES

VOLUME II

E. H. Harriman
At a Tuxedo Horse-Show

E. H. HARRIMAN

A Biography

BY
GEORGE KENNAN

WITH ILLUSTRATIONS

VOLUME II

Select Bibliographies Reprint Series

BOOKS FOR LIBRARIES PRESS
FREEPORT, NEW YORK

First Published 1922
Reprinted 1969

STANDARD BOOK NUMBER:

8369-5092-5

LIBRARY OF CONGRESS CATALOG CARD NUMBER:

77-99663

PRINTED IN THE UNITED STATES OF AMERICA

CONTENTS

CONTENTS

ILLUSTRATIONS

E. H. HARRIMAN

CHAPTER XVIII

FAR EASTERN PLANS

MR. HARRIMAN'S direct business relations with the Far East began in the year 1905. The aid given by Kuhn, Loeb & Co. to the Japanese Government in floating its war bonds, as well as Mr. Harriman's own interest in China and Japan, based on his connection with the Pacific Mail Steamship Company, early attracted his attention to that part of the world, and when in the spring of 1905, he received an urgent invitation to visit Japan, from the American Minister in Tokyo, Mr. Lloyd C. Griscom, he determined to suspend for a time his financial and railroad activities in the United States and look over personally the Oriental field, with a view to ascertaining what could be done for the extension of American commerce in Far Eastern countries.

"It is important," he said in a letter to Mr. Griscom, "to save the commercial interests of the United States from being entirely wiped from the Pacific Ocean in the future," and "the way to find out what is best to be done is to start something."

This proposal to "start something" was characteristic of Mr. Harriman's methods. He did not think it necessary to perfect all the details of a plan before going to work. When he had clearly defined the object to be attained, his policy was to "start something," and then work out the scheme in accordance with circumstances and conditions as they might arise. The clearly defined object that he had in view in this case was the extension of American influence and the promotion of American commerce in the Far East; but beyond this, with the details not yet worked out, was a plan for a round-the-world transportation line, under unified American control, by way of Japan, Manchuria, Siberia, European Russia, and the Atlantic Ocean. Such a railroad and steamship line, if successfully established, would unite for commercial purposes four of the most populous countries on the globe; and would enable the United States not only to take a commanding position in the Orient, but to supply the wants and direct in some measure the commercial activities of hundreds of millions of people in the least developed parts of Europe and Asia.

To most observers at that time a round-the-world transportation line, under American management, would have seemed an unrealizable dream; but Mr. Harriman had made many of his visions come true,

and he believed that he could give objective reality
to this one. His plan was, first, to secure control
of the South Manchuria Railway, which Japan,
through the fortunes of war, had just acquired from
Russia. This road was then in a very unsatisfactory
physical condition; but Mr. Harriman proposed to
reconstruct and reëquip it, with American capital,
and make it the eastern part of his proposed trans-
Asiatic line. Having secured this essential link, he
intended to buy the Chinese Eastern, which he
thought the Russians, having lost Port Arthur,
would gladly sell, and then acquire transportation or
trackage rights over the trans-Siberian and the
Russian Government roads from North Manchuria
to the coast of the Baltic Sea. These acquisitions, in
connection with the Pacific Mail Steamship Company and the American railroad systems that he
already controlled, wholly or in part, would give
him a continuous line more than three quarters of
the way around the globe, and it would be a comparatively easy matter, thereafter, to connect up the
termini by establishing a line of steamers across the
Atlantic from the United States to Russia. He anticipated most difficulty in persuading the Japanese
to surrender or share the control of the South Manchuria road, which, with the Fushun coal-fields adjacent thereto and the southern part of the island

of Saghalin, were all that they had been able to get from Russia, by way of indemnity, to cover their colossal war expenditures. However, he had strong hope of success, for the reason that the Japanese were heavily in debt and urgently in need of capital for the improvement of their transportation facilities and the development of their recently acquired territory on the Asiatic mainland. The purchase of the Chinese Eastern and the acquirement of the necessary rights over the trans-Siberian he regarded as comparatively easy. Russia had allowed a Baltimore capitalist to build and manage her first railroad, from St. Petersburg to Moscow, and had even asked an American engineer to finance and construct the great road from the Urals to the Pacific.[1] It seemed probable, therefore, that the Czar would gladly make concessions to American capitalists if, with their aid, he could have the trans-Siberian line double-tracked, properly equipped, and efficiently managed.

Preparations for the trip to the Orient were begun

[1] The proposal to finance and build the trans-Siberian railway was made by the Russian Government to a well-known railroad engineer in the United States. The terms offered were liberal, but the amount of capital required was so great that it could not be obtained without the aid, or at least the good-will, of the Jewish bankers and financiers in Europe. They, incensed by the treatment of their people in Russia, declined to coöperate, and the American engineer found it impossible to organize a syndicate that would be strong enough to finance the enterprise.

in July and were soon completed. The party as made up consisted of Mr. and Mrs. Harriman, with their daughters Cornelia, Mary, and Carol and their sons Averell and Roland; Mr. and Mrs. Robert Goelet; Mr. R. P. Schwerin, vice-president of the Pacific Mail Steamship Company; and Dr. W. G. Lyle, Mr. Harriman's personal physician. They sailed from San Francisco on the steamship Siberia August 16th and, after short stops at Honolulu and Midway Island, arrived in Yokohama on the evening of August 31st.

The reception given to Mr. Harriman by Japanese officials, financiers, and business men was extremely cordial. Representatives of the Bank of Japan and the famous Mitsui Company boarded the steamer as soon as the anchor was down, and when the party had landed and taken quarters at the Grand Hotel, calls and assurances of welcome were received from the president and vice-president of the Yokohama Specie Bank; the president of the Industrial Bank of Japan; the manager of the Japan Steamship Company; Count K. Inouye, one of the "Elder Statesmen"; Baron Iwasaki, Senator Watenabe, and Mr. K. Mori, a personal representative of the Minister of Finance.

In Tokyo on the following day, calls from distinguished Japanese continued, and invitations to dinners, lunches, garden parties, and other hospitable entertainments were received from Prince Fushimi, Prime Minister Katsura, the Minister of Finance, Count Inouye, Baron Iwasaki, Baron Shibusawa, and many prominent business men. On the 4th of September, Minister Griscom gave a dinner at the Legation, in honor of Mr. Harriman and his party, which was attended by the most eminent officials and statesmen in the Japanese capital, including the Premier, the Minister of the Imperial Household, the Minister of Communications, the Vice-Minister of Foreign Affairs, the Vice-Grand Master of Ceremonies, Count Inouye, Count Toda, and Viscount Inaba. In responding to a toast at this banquet, Mr. Harriman hinted at the plans that he had in mind and prepared the way for future negotiations by saying to the Japanese guests:

You have made great strides in the art of war; but you must look to the arts of peace for those greater achievements which mean prosperity, contentment, and happiness. Your people will advance their material welfare still further and more rapidly as they realize the advantages which follow concentration of effort and harmony of operation in their industrial and commercial affairs. From New York to the Pacific Coast, and from there to Japan, about ten thousand miles, the railroad and steamship lines are practically under one control and one management. The economies of operation, the comfort to the traveling public, and the advantages to shippers of this concentrated control can be readily appreciated. The benefits to the people of the United States which follow, directly and indirectly are incalculable. The same policy, if followed in Japan, is bound to produce the same results. I hope the day may not be far distant when Japanese business men and American business men, realizing that their interests are common, may be brought into closer relationship.

This was a sufficiently clear indication of Mr. Harriman's purpose to unite, if possible, the transportation systems of America and the Far East; but, unfortunately, circumstances at that time were such as to make the accomplishment of this purpose unusually difficult. The general outlines of the Portsmouth Treaty had just been published in Japan, and the common people, ignorant of their Government's real situation, were intensely dissatisfied with the terms of peace. Their armies, they reasoned, had won every battle in which they had been engaged, and their country was clearly entitled to exact an indemnity from Russia, and to demand the restoration of the whole of the island of Saghalin. The action of their Government in making peace, apparently at the suggestion of President Roosevelt, without securing the legitimate fruits of victory, was an unpardonable exhibition of weakness for which it deserved to be condemned and punished.

No hostile demonstrations were made against Americans, but on the fourth day after Mr. Harriman's arrival, an immense mob of patriotic rioters attacked the residence of the Home Minister, and when they were opposed by the police, began destroying police stations, police kiosks, and street cars in all parts of the city. Dr. Lyle and Mr. Harriman's private secretary, while on their way to dinner at the residence of the Finance Minister, attempted to pass in jinrikishas through the crowd and quickly became involved in difficulties. The rioters were in a mood to resent almost anything, and raising the cry of "Russians!" they began hooting and throwing stones. Dr. Lyle was struck on the shoulder and slightly hurt, but he and his companion, after some delay, succeeded in reaching safely the Finance Minister's house. Although this attack did not seem to be directed against Dr. Lyle and Secretary McKnight as Americans — it was too dark to see who they were — the Government thought it prudent, at the end of the dinner, to send Mr. Harriman and his party back to the Legation under the protection of an armed escort, and to post guards in the Legation grounds.

On the following evening, September 6th, as the street disorder still continued, a dinner in honor of Mr. Harriman at the Nobles' Club was abandoned, for the reason that the Club happened to be situated near the residence of the Home Minister, which was the storm center of mob violence. Fearing that the known agency of President Roosevelt as an intermediary in the peace negotiations might turn the hostility of the uninformed but excited populace toward Americans in general, and wishing to relieve Minister Griscom as far as possible from anxiety and responsibility, Mr. Harriman decided to take his party to Nikko for a few days, and to return to Tokyo when the Government should have suppressed the disorder and reëstablished normal conditions. On the afternoon of September 7th, in a special train furnished by the Nippon Railway Company, the Harriman party proceeded to Nikko, where they arrived about 7 P.M. In the course of the two days that they spent in this famous resort, they visited the ancient temples and the mausolea of Ieyasu and Iemitsu; rode through the celebrated avenue of giant cryptomeria trees, and ascended the wild and romantic gorge which leads, at a height of forty-three hundred feet, to the beautiful mountain lake of Chuzenji. Learning by telegraph that the disorder in Tokyo had ceased, they returned, September 11th, to the American Legation, and on the following day Mr. Harriman, Mr. Goelet, and Mr. Schwerin were received in audience by the Emperor.

As Mr. Harriman could spend only a limited time in the Far East, and as he desired, before his return, to visit China and Korea, he was obliged to promote his round-the-world-line enterprise, as far as it could be promoted in Tokyo, by a "whirlwind campaign" of visits and interviews. Between the 1st and 13th of September, he made the acquaintance of all the prominent statesmen in Japan, including Marquis Ito, Count Okuma, the Premier, and most of the Ministers; and succeeded in awakening the interest and enlisting the support of several eminent financiers, including especially Mr. J. Soyeda, president of the Japanese Industrial Bank. Having thus accomplished all that it was possible to accomplish in a few days, he and his party started on the 13th of September for Kyoto and Kobe, leaving further negotiations for the acquirement of the South Manchuria Railway in the capable hands of Minister Griscom and President Soyeda.

As Mr. Harriman's visit to China and Korea in the latter part of September and the first part of October had no decisive bearing upon the negotiations that chiefly engaged his thoughts, it need not be fully described. Chartering for his party at Kobe the commodious steamer Ohio III, he sailed through the Inland Sea and across Korea Bay to Port Arthur; visited the battle-fields that had given to the fortress its world-wide fame, and then proceeded to Tientsin and Peking. Leaving the Chinese capital on the

PORT ARTHUR, MANCHURIA

P. R. Schwerin   Roland Harriman   E. H. Harriman

28th of September, the party again crossed the Gulf
of Pechili and Korea Bay, landed at Chemulpo, and
went by rail to Seoul, where they attended a luncheon given in their honor at the Imperial Palace and a
garden party arranged by Mr. T. Megata, financial
adviser of the Korean Government. On the 8th of
October they took a special train to Fusan, at the
end of the peninsula, where the Ohio III met them
and carried them to Nagasaki. After inspecting the
shipbuilding plant and dry-docks in this famous seaport, they sailed again for Kobe, proceeded thence
by rail to Yokohama, and on the 9th of October
finally returned to Tokyo, thus completing a jour-
ney that covered about three thousand miles and occupied twenty-six days.

During Mr. Harriman's absence, Minister Griscom did all that could be done to promote what
seemed to him the best interests of the United States
in the Orient by persuading the higher Japanese
authorities to consider favorably Mr. Harriman's
plans. In his interviews with Premier Katsura,
Count Inouye, and the Minister of Finance, he took
the ground that coöperation with America would be
in every way profitable to Japan, by strengthening
her credit, furnishing her with capital for the improvement of her transportation system, facilitat-
ing her trade, and enabling her to develop quickly

and fully the material resources of her recently acquired territory on the Asiatic mainland. The South
Manchuria Railway was urgently in need of reconstruction and reëquipment, and there was no man in
America, perhaps in the world, better qualified by
experience and ability to direct such work than the
rebuilder of the Union Pacific. Mr. Harriman's relations, moreover, with American bankers and financiers were such that he could secure at once the pecuniary support which Japan needed, but which she
alone might not be able to get quickly enough to
meet the emergencies of the situation. The suggested project would bring Japan and the United
States into much closer relations, both commercially
and politically, and if successful it would furnish a
large revenue to the Japanese Government and thus
compensate the Japanese people for their failure to
get a pecuniary indemnity from Russia.

In his negotiations with the higher authorities,
Mr. Griscom was ably assisted by Mr. Durham W.
Stevens, who had been in the service of the Japanese
Government for more than twenty years, and who
had earned the respect and trust of all the Emperor's
statesmen and officials.[1] The result of their joint

[1] Mr. Stevens entered the service of the Japanese Government in
1883, as counsellor of its Legation in Washington. He was soon afterward transferred to Tokyo, where he became a member of the Bureau
du Protocol of the Conference for the Revision of Treaties between

efforts was in every way encouraging. Premier Katsura said that he would give the matter immediate and serious consideration, and Count Inouye, one of the most influential of the Elder Statesmen, promised that he would call a meeting of the Minister of Finance, the Minister of Communications, and other high officials directly interested, and would try to reach a decision at once. Count Inouye himself was very favorably impressed and said to Mr. Griscom: "We would be very foolish to let such a great chance slip."

When Mr. Harriman returned to Tokyo, on the 8th of October, negotiations were so far advanced that the imperial authorities were ready to consider promptly, if not to accept, a definite proposition; and in three or four days of strenuous activity he succeeded in getting the details settled and reduced to writing in the following memorandum of agreement:

MEMORANDUM of a preliminary understanding, dated October 12, 1905, between His Excellency Count Katsura Taro, representing the Japanese Government, and Mr. E. H. Harriman, representing himself and associates.

Japan and foreign Powers. Between 1887 and 1904 he was engaged in various diplomatic negotiations, and in the latter year he was appointed adviser to the Korean Government at Seoul. He was assassinated in San Francisco in 1908 by a misguided Korean fanatic who regarded him as an enemy of the Korean people, although, in reality, he had always been their sincere friend.

A syndicate to be formed to provide capital for the purchase of the South Manchuria Railway, acquired by the Japanese Government, and its appurtenances; the rehabilitation, equipment, reconstruction and extension of the same, and the completion and improvement of the terminals at Tairen (Dalny); and it is understood that the two parties are to have joint and equal ownership in the properties acquired. Permission to work coal mines (in connection with the railroad) to be given to a corporation by special agreement, in which there shall be joint interest and representation.

The principle of development of all industrial enterprises in Manchuria shall be such that each party shall have the right to an equal interest with the other. The Manchurian railroad, with its appurtenances, rails, cross-ties, bridges, superstructure of all character, stations, buildings, platforms, warehouses, docks, wharves, etc., to be taken at their true value, to be determined by joint representation of each party.

The organization to be made on basis that will meet exigencies and conditions as they may exist at the time. As it is deemed advisable to meet the conditions in Japan, the corporation is to be operated with Japanese control. Changes are, however, to be made therein from time to time, as far as circumstances will permit, looking toward a final equalization of representation and control. The corporation is to be organized under Japanese law. Mr. Harriman, having agreed for himself to operation through a Japanese company, the only open question is as to his associates agreeing thereto, which he believes they will.

To provide for an arbitrator, it is agreed that Mr. Henry W. Denison shall be appointed to fill that place.[1]

[1] Mr. Denison, at that time, had been legal adviser of the Japanese Foreign Office for about a quarter of a century. He had been re-

In case of war between Japan and China, or Japan and Russia, the railroad shall at all times obey the instructions of the Japanese Government in the matter of the conveyance of troops and war materials, and the Japanese Government is to compensate the railroad for services rendered and protect it against aggressions at all times.

It is agreed that Mr. J. Soyeda, President of the Industrial Bank of Japan, shall be the medium of communication between the parties hereto.

The including of any outside interests (other) than the parties hereto shall be done only after conference and mutual agreement.

With this memorandum of agreement in his possession, Mr. Harriman sailed from Yokohama in the steamship Siberia on the afternoon of Friday, October 12th. He had not accomplished all that he desired to accomplish, but he had at least "started something," and there seemed to be a fair prospect that the concession thus obtained would ultimately lead to the consolidation of Japanese and American transportation interests on the Asiatic mainland, and greatly extend and promote the commerce of the United States in that part of the Orient.

Unfortunately, while Mr. Harriman was at sea, on his way to San Francisco, all his Far Eastern plans were suddenly blocked by an obstacle that he

peatedly decorated by the Emperor for distinguished service, and enjoyed the implicit trust of both Government and people. He was born in Guildhall, Vermont, in 1846 and received his higher education in the Columbian (now George Washington) University.

had neither foreseen nor considered. Three days
after he sailed from Yokohama, Baron Komura, the
Japanese Minister of Foreign Affairs, returned to
Tokyo from the United States, bringing the treaty
that he and Minister Takahira had just negotiated
with the Russian plenipotentiaries at Portsmouth.
As soon as the Harriman-Katsura agreement for
joint control of the South Manchuria Railway was
shown him, he said: "It cannot possibly be carried
out, because it is inconsistent with Article VI of the
treaty that we have just made with Russia." The
article in question provided that the transfer of the
South Manchurian road from Russia to Japan should
be made only with the consent of the Chinese Government. Until, therefore, such consent should be
obtained, Japan had no legal rights that could be
shared with Mr. Harriman. Aside from this, Baron
Komura was opposed to the Harriman-Katsura
agreement on its merits. The Japanese people were
already so dissatisfied with the Portsmouth Treaty
that they had resorted to mob violence as a protest
against it, and their discontent would be greatly increased if they should learn that their Government
had sold to a Japanese-American syndicate nearly
all that they had gained in two years of successful
war. To have made peace without securing a pecuniary indemnity was bad enough; but to sell more

than half the fruits of their victory to the Americans, and thus throw open to foreign competition the commercial field which they had bought with their treasure and blood would seem to them intolerable.

Baron Komura's arguments and influence were too strong for the supporters of the Japanese-American agreement, and in less than a week a change of policy was decided upon. When Mr. Harriman, with his mind full of plans for the future, arrived in San Francisco, he received from the Japanese consul there the following note:

I beg to inform you that I have been instructed by Count Katsura, of my Government, to deliver the following message to you immediately upon your arrival in San Francisco:

"The Japanese Government have found it necessary to institute a more thorough investigation and examination of the questions which are the subject of memorandum of October 12, 1905, and they consequently request you to regard the memorandum as in abeyance until they are able to communicate with you more fully regarding the matter."

Ten days later, when Mr. Harriman had reached New York, he received the following cable message from Mr. J. Soyeda, president of the Industrial Bank of Japan:

Tokyo, October 30, 1905

E. H. HARRIMAN, New York

Prime minister requests to forward following confidential message to you explanatory message handed you by Japanese consul San Francisco.

"Having considered detailed report made by Minister Foreign Affairs on his return home, and having in view pacific attitude Chinese Government on railroad question, Japanese Government has come to conclusion that question embodied in memorandum, October 12th, requires more thorough and complete examination than possible at present time. As you are aware, Portsmouth Treaty provides for consent of China regarding transfer to Japan of railroad property, and for agreement with Russia regulating connecting railroad service. Until agreements with China and Russia are concluded, impossible to determine precisely what rights and properties are included in the transfer, or what earning capacity of railroad is likely to be. Without full knowledge on these points impossible to make definite arrangements for working railroad and property which would prove satisfactory to either Japanese Government or E. H. Harriman. Consequently Japanese Government deem wise request E. H. Harriman to regard said memorandum as in abeyance for the time being. Japanese Government will proceed, as soon as possible, to conclude necessary international agreement. Such agreement will probably necessitate some essential change in proposed arrangement with Mr. Harriman. But in any event, Japanese Government will consult him before making arrangement with private capital."

SOYEDA

This cable message was the result of a compromise between Baron Komura and the supporters of the Harriman-Katsura memorandum. The former advocated immediate cancellation of the agreement, for the reason that it was inconsistent with Article VI of the Portsmouth Treaty. In view, however, of all the circumstances, and especially of Katsura's ignorance of the stipulation regarding Chinese consent, Baron Komura agreed to regard the memorandum as "in abeyance," and to leave open the possibility of confirmation at a later time, provided no objection should be raised by the Government of China.

If the Japanese Minister of Foreign Affairs had been previously consulted, and had favored the agreement on its merits, he might possibly have found some means of dealing with the Chinese complication; but he had never met Mr. Harriman and had not been impressed, as had his colleagues, by the latter's forceful personality; he doubted the expediency of sharing control of the South Manchurian road with a syndicate about which he knew little or nothing; and he believed that the agreement, if allowed to go into effect at that time, would increase his own unpopularity in Japan, and would render extremely difficult, if not wholly impossible, the negotiation of the treaty with China that he then had in contemplation. He therefore insisted upon postponement, at least, and the other members of the Ministry yielded.

In this thwarting of Mr. Harriman's plans there seems to have been no intentional breach of faith on the part of the Tokyo authorities. It was simply

a case in which one branch of the Government, acting independently, concluded a treaty that nullified
action taken almost simultaneously by another
branch. Count Katsura did not know that Baron
Komura had agreed in Portsmouth to make the
transfer of the railroad conditional upon Chinese
consent, while Komura, in concluding such agreement with Russia, was ignorant of the Tokyo memorandum. One compact or the other had to be set
aside, and in holding the Harriman agreement "in
abeyance" while he negotiated with China, Baron
Komura thought, perhaps, that he was making the
best of an accidental and unfortunate situation.
But be that as it may, he started for Peking with
Mr. Denison, on the 6th of November, leaving the
railroad matter in this unsettled state.

Negotiations with the Government of China for
a new treaty occupied more than a month, and Mr.
Harriman was not informed of the result until the
15th of January, 1906, when he received from Mr.
Soyeda the following cable message:

Tokyo, January 15, 1906

E. H. HARRIMAN
New York
Baron Komura returned on the 1st of January and the
new Cabinet was formed on the 7th. I have been urging
the necessity of informing you what to be done, and am
now asked to wire you. Count Katsura requests me to

let you know that obtaining from China consent contemplated by Article VI Portsmouth, N.H., Treaty it was necessary to provide that Manchurian railway should be worked by company composed exclusively of Japanese and Chinese shareholders, following in that respect terms of original concession to Russia. Count desires me to convey expression of regret that, in view of above circumstance, he is compelled to ask you regard memorandum of October 12, 1905, as of no effect, as it is manifestly impossible to make any arrangement based on it. He adds, however, that the Japanese Government entertain a doubt as to possibility of Japanese and Chinese capital alone being sufficient to meet requirements of necessary improvements and extension of Manchurian railway, and that therefore should an occasion arise in future enabling them to open negotiations with foreign capitalists, on a different basis, a fresh consultation may be held with you. I desire to add Court has been relieved of his position as Prime Minister, and send this telegram after consulting with Marquis Saionji, his successor.

SOYEDA

In a letter written to Minister Griscom in January, 1906, Mr. H. W. Denison, legal adviser of the Japanese Foreign Office, gave the following explanation of Baron Komura's failure to get the consent of China to the Harriman-Katsura agreement:

The Japanese Government have secured the consent of China to the assignment of the railroad [the South Manchurian] between Port Arthur and Chang-chun, subject to the same terms and conditions that attached to the original grant to Russia; that is to say, the railroad is to be worked by a company composed exclusively

of Japanese and Chinese shareholders. You will find
the original concession to Russia in Rockhill's book
"Treaties and Conventions with and concerning China
and Korea," pp. 207–224, and I enclose a newspaper
copy of the official version of Baron Komura's agreements with China. . . . If the Chinese avail themselves
of the opportunity of taking half a share in the Manchurian enterprises, a definite understanding on the
basis of the memorandum of October 12th is impracticable. There is at the present time a very strong anti-
concession wave sweeping over China. The Government are endeavoring, by hook or by crook, to get back
the grants already made. They cancel the concessions
in case of default in any direction, and they buy back
the grants if no grounds for cancellation exist. In this
frame of mind, and being unable to cancel or repurchase
the Manchurian concessions, it is more than likely that
China will gladly take the one half interest in the enterprise. In that case I believe some arrangement on new
lines will be possible, but only if the negotiations are
undertaken by a man of force and prestige like Mr.
Harriman.

In the spring of 1906, Mr. Jacob H. Schiff, of the
firm of Kuhn, Loeb & Co., happened to visit the
Far East, and, at the request of his old friend and
associate, Mr. Harriman, made an attempt to revive
the 1905 agreement; but Baron Komura was as much
opposed to it as ever, and after a number of conferences the negotiations were again dropped.

Thus ended Mr. Harriman's attempt to get control, or partial control, of the South Manchuria Railway, as an essential link in his projected round-the-

world transportation line. His ill success, however, did not shake his faith in the practicability of the enterprise, but merely led him to consider other means of bridging the gap between the Gulf of Pechili and the trans-Siberian road. The difficulties in the way were very great. A new and independent line through Manchuria or Mongolia could not be built without Chinese consent, and the Chinese, at that time, were strongly opposed to the granting of any more railroad concessions to foreign syndicates. So far, moreover, as a line through Manchuria was concerned, they themselves were almost powerless, for the reason that, in the treaty of December, 1905, with Japan, they had agreed "not to construct any main line in the neighborhood of and parallel to the South Manchuria Railway." Even, therefore, if they had been willing to let Mr. Harriman build a road from the Gulf of Pechili to the terminus of the Chinese Eastern, they could not do so, because it would necessarily be a "main line in the neighborhood of and parallel to the South Manchurian."

Mr. Harriman thought, at one time, of building a road across the Gobi Desert by the old caravan route, passing through Kalgan and Urga and connecting with the trans-Siberian near Irkutsk; but as the distance would be great — twelve hundred miles or more — and as most of the country to be

traversed was so barren as to promise little in the
way of agricultural development, this scheme was
soon dismissed as impracticable.[1] The only alter-
native was a new line, about four hundred and fifty
miles in length, from the Gulf of Pechili to the trans-
Siberian Railway at Tsitsihar. This road, although
nearly parallel with the South Manchurian, would
be separated from it by an average distance of one
hundred and seventy miles, and consequently would
not be in the prohibited "neighborhood."

In the early part of 1906, Mr. Harriman received
full reports on the trade, industry, and resources of
northeastern China from Colonel Holabird and Mr.
Wallace, two experts whom he had sent to make
investigations in the Far East; and in that and the
following year he was kept fully informed with regard to railroad affairs in Siberia and Manchuria by
Willard D. Straight, Consul General of the United
States at Mukden.[2]

[1] It is not certain, however, that even this line would have been
unprofitable. The Chinese themselves afterward began the construction of four hundred miles of railway along this route, and on the
Peking-Kalgan section, which was completed in 1912, the net profits
of operation in 1913 were twenty per cent on the investment.

[2] Mr. Straight was a young graduate of Cornell University whose
acquaintance Mr. Harriman made in October, 1905, at the house of
Edward Vernon Morgan, American Minister to Korea. Mr. Straight
was then Vice-Consul-General in Seoul, but he had previously been
correspondent of Reuter's Agency and the Associated Press in Korea
and Manchuria and had spent two years in the service of the Chinese
Imperial Maritime Customs at Nanking and Peking. He impressed

For a year or more, no opportunity to promote the Far Eastern enterprise presented itself, but in September, 1907, Lord Ffrench, representing Pauling & Co., of London, and Mr. J. O. P. Bland, representing the "British and Chinese Corporation," secured from the Chinese Government the right to extend the Chinese Imperial Railway from Hsin-min-tun to Fakumen, with the privilege of building, ultimately, to the trans-Siberian at Tsitsihar. As this seemed to open the way for such a Russian connection as Mr. Harriman had in view, Mr. Straight wrote him, in September, 1907, suggesting an alliance with the British syndicate, as a means of securing the essential link in the projected round-the-world line without the coöperation of the Japanese. Mr. Harriman replied by cable, however, in October 1907, that, owing to the panic of that year, financial conditions were such as to prevent the raising of the necessary funds.

Mr. Harriman as a young man of character and force, and one whose ability and experience might make him a valuable assistant in such an enterprise as that which was then in contemplation. When the American Legation in Seoul was closed, in the fall of 1905, Mr. Straight went with Minister Morgan as private secretary, and when Mr. Morgan was appointed Minister to Cuba in 1906, he accompanied him to Havana. A few months later the State Department transferred him to China and made him Consul-General at Mukden. On his way back to the Far East, in the summer of 1906, he spent a week-end at Arden, where Mr. Harriman discussed with him the railroad situation in Manchuria and arranged to keep in touch with him by means of correspondence.

In the summer of 1908, when the financial situation in the United States had somewhat improved, Mr. Harriman decided to make another move in the Far East, and requested Secretary Root to recall Consul-General Straight, in order that American capitalists might discuss with him the expediency of making a loan to China for agricultural development and railroad construction in Manchuria. Meanwhile Mr. Straight had secured from Tang Shao-yi, the Chinese Governor at Mukden, a signed memorandum of agreement which was to form the basis of negotiations for a loan of $20,000,000. With this sum it was proposed to establish a Manchurian Bank, which should coöperate with American and Chinese interests in the construction of a railway from Tsitsihar to Aigun. Then, if the bank and the American capitalists could come to an agreement with Pauling & Co. who had the right to build a road southward from Tsitsihar to Hsin-min-tun, it would be possible to construct a trunk-line from the Gulf of Pechili to the Amur, and thus bridge the gap between the Pacific Ocean and the trans-Siberian road.

In September, 1908, Consul-General Straight returned to the United States, bringing with him the memorandum of agreement with Tang Shao-yi for the $20,000,000 loan. Through the influence of Mr.

Harriman, and with the cognizance and approval of the Secretary of State, Kuhn, Loeb & Co. agreed to undertake this loan, provided all the details thereof could be satisfactorily arranged. Late in November, Tang Shao-yi came to Washington, ostensibly to thank President Roosevelt for the remission of part of the Boxer indemnity, but really, in great part, to negotiate the proposed loan for the establishment of the Manchurian Bank.

Here again, however, Mr. Harriman's plans were blocked by events that could not possibly have been foreseen. Tang Shao-yi's appointment had been made through the influence of his friend Yuan Shi-kai, who was then Grand Councillor and head of the Chinese Foreign Office, and who was greatly interested in securing American capital for the development of Manchurian resources. About the middle of November, 1908, both the Emperor and the Empress Dowager of China died, and Prince Chun, an enemy of Yuan Shi-kai, became regent. This undermined Yuan's power, and led, a few weeks later, to his dismissal from office. Tang Shao-yi, thus left without support at home, became discouraged, and the matter of the loan was allowed to drop.

Mr. Harriman, however, continued his negotiations for the acquirement of a Manchurian line, both

with Russia and again with Japan. In the summer
of 1909, after he was stricken with mortal illness, he
secured a promise from the Russian Minister of
Foreign Affairs, Mr. Kokovtsef, that upon the latter's return from a trip that he was about to make
to the Far East, he would recommend the sale of the
Chinese Eastern Railway to American interests.
But even this partial success came too late. On the
9th of September, Mr. Harriman died, and there
was no one left in America capable of undertaking,
much less of carrying through, such a colossal enterprise as the establishment of a round-the-world
American transportation line. Whether the "Master
Builder" himself could have accomplished it, if he
had lived, it is impossible to say; but the results of
successful accomplishment might have influenced
profoundly the world's history. No one who has
studied Mr. Harriman's constructive and admin-
istrative methods can doubt that if he had ever
acquired even partial control of the trans-Siberian
railway, he would have doubled or trebled its carrying capacity. Then, when the great war of 1914
came, Russia would have been able to draw heavy
artillery and ammunition from Japan and America
over an efficient through line of great capacity, and
would not have been reduced to such straits as she
was when her troops, largely without proper weapons

and almost wholly without reserves of ammunition, were forced out of Poland and driven halfway to Petrograd. Her defeats in the war with Japan in 1904–05 were mainly due to the inadequacy of the trans-Siberian road as a means of speedy transportation, and her reverses on the German frontier, ten years later, were due, in part at least, to the same cause. During the winter and spring of every year, the railroad to the Pacific was her only open line of communication with the outside world, and it never was in physical condition to meet the demands made upon it. If, reconstructed and reëquipped by Mr. Harriman and the American syndicate, it had been made part of a great international transportation system, it might have become the decisive factor in the struggle with Germany in 1914–15, and might thus have changed the earlier stages, if not the whole course, of the great World War.

CHAPTER XIX

LIFE AND WORK AT ARDEN

DURING the ten years of hard work and mental strain that followed the reorganization of the Union Pacific, Mr. Harriman found diversion and relaxation in the management and development of his great country estate in Orange County, New York. This property, when he bought it at an auction sale of the Parrott holdings in 1885, comprised 7863 acres. It was situated on the western side of the Hudson River, five or six miles north of Tuxedo Park, and could be reached from New York City by the Erie Railroad in about an hour and a half. It consisted, for the most part, of wild forest land, broken and diversified by the picturesque hills of the Ramapo Highlands, which rise out of the valley of the Ramapo River, near the present station of Harriman, and extend eastward through Orange and Rockland Counties to the Hudson.

Not far from the western boundary of the estate, in a deep ravine between two parallel ranges of wooded hills, nestled a small mountain tarn called Forest Lake, and in a spacious clearing near it stood the homestead of the Parrott family, together with

THE ORIGINAL HOUSE AT ARDEN

a smaller cottage occupied at one time by a married daughter. When the estate was sold, the old Parrott homestead was reserved; but the reservation did not include the cottage, and in this, after enlarging and improving it, Mr. and Mrs. Harriman took up their residence, making it their permanent summer home and giving to the estate as a whole the name of Mrs. Parrott's family — "Arden."

In acquiring this property Mr. Harriman acted largely upon impulse. He attended the auction sale because his old friends, the Parrotts, invited him to do so; but he had no definite intention of buying until he found that most of the prospective bidders were lumbermen, or timber speculators, who proposed to ruin the beautiful Ramapo hills by stripping them of trees. To prevent such devastation he determined to purchase the whole estate himself. He was an ardent lover of nature, and especially of forests, and he could not bear to see the woods through which he had so often roamed as a boy turned by the lumberman's axe into a shadeless waste of underbrush and stumps. So, partly for the sake of old association and partly for the sake of the people of Orange County, he bought the property.

When he went there to live, he felt more strongly than ever that he ought to save from denudation and destruction as much of this beautiful region as possible; so, year after year, as he had opportunity, he added to his holdings by making further purchases. First and last, between 1888 and 1900, he bought about forty different farms, or wooded tracts, which adjoined his property on one side or another, so that eventually the estate came to have an area of about twenty thousand acres, or thirty square miles.

For several years after Mr. Harriman began to spend his summers at Arden, he amused himself by giving personal attention to the details of farming and dairying; but in 1896 he organized a corporation known as the Arden Farms Dairy Company and entrusted to it the agricultural development of the property, together with the keeping of the accounts and the management of a general store which had been opened for the accommodation of the employees. About the same time he engaged a civil engineer to make a topographical survey and a map of the estate, and to lay out and open through the forest a system of bridle-paths which could eventually be widened and made into permanent roads.

Two years later he began to extend and develop the dairy industry in the Ramapo Valley. By dredging out the channel of the river for a distance of four or five miles, he obtained fall enough for an extensive system of lateral ditches to empty into it, and on the land thus improved by proper drainage he created pasturage and raised hay enough for a herd of Guernsey, Jersey, and Holstein cows. He then put up a spacious barn for them and built near it a well-equipped modern dairy, which supplied pure milk in large quantities, not only to people in the immediate neighborhood, but to the residents of Tuxedo Park and later to the United States Military Academy at West Point. In the movement to improve the quality of the milk supply, which afterward extended to all parts of the country, Mr. Harriman was one of the pioneers and employed scientific methods.

To the conservation and management of the forests, which covered about six sevenths of the estate, equal attention was given. For some years Mr. Harriman directed this work personally, selecting the trees, or the kinds of trees, to be preserved, and cutting away the old or imperfect timber so as to leave the younger growth properly spaced. A few years later, in 1900 or 1901, he secured expert assistance by bringing several trained foresters from the Department of Agriculture in Washington, and after that time the work of selection and conservation was carried on under their supervision. One summer a number of students from the Yale School of Forestry in New Haven came to Arden and camped out on the estate for the purpose of studying conditions and methods and getting practical experience under competent instruction.

In the welfare of the large body of workmen employed on the estate Mr. Harriman took an active personal interest. He was often misjudged by those who saw him in business relations only. When dealing with great problems of transportation or finance, he seemed to be cold, reticent, and austere. His manner was never effusive, and often brusque, and his character, on its business side, had a certain hardness of fiber that made him seem unimpressible and unresponsive. All who came in contact with him felt the dynamic force of his energetic personality; but few gave him credit for kindliness or sympathetic feeling. A newspaper man who was familiar with his work and achievements and who had profound admiration and respect for his intellectual ability, once said of him: "He would be a wonderful character if he only had a heart." But this was a misjudgment based on incomplete knowledge of his many-sided nature. Mr. Harriman had a heart, and a warm one, even if he did not wear it on his sleeve in the field of great business affairs.

To his neighbors at Arden, who saw him in a very different environment, kindliness, sympathy, and regard for the needs and welfare of others seemed to be among the salient features of his character. His relations with his employees were intimate and cordial, and when they were sick or in trouble he never forgot them or failed to give them help. Rev. J. H. McGuinness, rector of the little Episcopal Church at Arden, has given many striking illustrations of Mr. Harriman's personal interest in the welfare and happiness of all the people on his estate.

Christmas at Arden [Mr. McGuinness says] was always an especially festive holiday. A census was taken annually of every man, woman, and child on the estate, and the list was carefully studied, so that a suitable gift might be provided for each. Mrs. Harriman herself made the presentations, while her husband stood beside her, and it was an absolute rule with them that no one should be forgotten. But mistakes would occur. One evening, at the close of the distribution, somebody asked, "Where's Tom?" Tom, a half orphan, was the most forlorn boy on the place — a poor little heartbroken chap who lived with a drunken father in a shack four miles from the house. The question went around, where was Tom? And immediately Mr. Harriman took it up. Investigation proved that by some mistake the boy's name had been omitted from the list. Soon after this was discovered, Mr. Harriman himself, accompanied by Averell, went to the little shack in the woods, with a sled — a fine sturdy sled, such as every boy longs for — and gave it to Tom as a proof that, although his name had been accidentally omitted from the Christmas list, he had not been forgotten.

The belief that a good time is necessary to the right kind of living was a marked trait of Mr. Harriman's character. He enjoyed his horses, as well as games and sports of all kinds, and he wanted others to have their recreation too. Convinced that all work and no play makes Jack a dull boy — if not something worse — he arranged at Arden a hall for social purposes, where parties were held and amateur plays given. He was immensely fond of riding, swimming, and all athletic sports. He had been a baseball player himself as a lad, and he kept up his skill at tennis as a man. One summer he arranged for the boys of Arden and Southfield to meet in a series of baseball matches, and promised a complete set of new uniforms to the team that made the better record. As it turned out, the home team won. They received their uniforms, but the Southfield boys had played their best and, to their surprise, they met one morning to find a set of new uniforms awaiting them as well.

Mr. Harriman had been a boy himself — some men never have been — and not a boy came his way that he did not constitute himself a guardian, almost a father, to him. He took a great many young men West in his business expeditions and started them, where there seemed to be better openings, in a newer world. He secured an appointment for one Arden boy at West Point and for another at Annapolis, and to all whom he thus helped he said, by way of encouragement, "Keep on moving up, up!"

I am speaking last of Mr. Harriman as a church member, for the reason that this phase of his life seems to me to sum up the whole. He believed in God and he believed in worshiping God. Nothing but an extraordinary emergency, such as serious illness in his family, could interfere with his attendance at church. Not only was he active in all the work of the parish, but also in the circuit of little missions which I organized throughout the country near by. Every Sunday, after service,

I would walk home with him to lunch and during these walks he would ply me with questions about the mission work and about those of my parishioners who were in trouble.

It struck his attention that the men of Arden were not coming to church, and as this fact impressed itself upon him he began a series of letters to them urging attendance. A quotation from one of these letters will show his attitude more clearly than any comment.

"Religious work," he said, "cannot be carried on permanently without active and continued help from the men. Women and children must not be left to do it all. Boys attend Sunday school and church and are, no doubt, benefited thereby; but by the example of the men they only expect to do so while boys. Under the influence of your indifference they get to believe that when they grow up it is unmanly to attend church and show any interest in religion. You should change this. Make it a pleasure as well as a benefit and do the thing in a whole-souled way."

Mr. Harriman had a right to preach this to others if ever a man had, for never was a practical religious life lived in a more whole-souled way than his own.[1]

When Mr. Harriman bought and enlarged the Parrott estate and thus saved thirty square miles of the beautiful Ramapo Highlands from timber speculators and lumbermen, he rendered a great service to the people of Orange County; but this was by no means the only benefit that he conferred upon them. In every movement that had for its object the bet-

[1] "The Personal Side of E. H. Harriman," by Rev. J. H. McGuinness, rector of the Arden parish. (An unpublished manuscript.)

terment of local conditions he took an active and generally a leading part. "It was solely through his influence," says the "Goshen Democrat," "that the saloons and dives were obliterated from certain sections which lay adjacent to the Erie Railroad in the towns of Woodbury and Tuxedo, and which were formerly infested with lawless and shiftless men. It was through his influence, too, that the practically obsolete industry of breeding and raising light harness-horses was revived in Orange County. In the movement for road improvement he was a leader, an educator and a pioneer." [1]

When, in 1895, Mr. Harriman first attacked the problem of getting better county roads, he met with objections and opposition on various grounds and from all sorts of people. Some thought that his proposals involved too much expense and would lead to a great increase in taxation; some did not care to have the county made more accessible, while others, by reason of inertia or natural conservatism, were hostile to innovations generally. He then began a campaign of education. At large expense to himself he built several miles of improved modern road; invited private citizens and public officials to inspect the work; explained the method of construction, and showed by argument and illustration how better

[1] *The Goshen Democrat*, Goshen, New York, June 20, 1907.

means of intercommunication would benefit the people by giving quicker and easier access to markets and thus enhancing the value of farm products and farm lands. But he did not meet with much encouragement. Not more than half a dozen men were with him in the earlier days of the movement, and these were won over by his earnestness, the fairness of his arguments, and the evident sincerity of his desire to improve and benefit the county in which he had made his home. For two or three years his proposals had little popular support, but he was not at all discouraged.

In 1896, he organized the Orange County Horse and Road Improvement Association, whose objects were "to stimulate the horse interests of the county of Orange; to give and supervise horse shows and public exhibitions of speed; to furnish entertainment and recreation for the people, and to forward the improvement of the roads in said county."

Here, again, was manifested Mr. Harriman's practical wisdom. His primary and ultimate purpose really was to secure good roads; but in organizing the association he put the horse first, simply because more persons were interested in horses, horse shows, and races than in better means of intercommunication. Very few, at that time, appreciated the great benefits that would come to the county through road improvement, and many, even of those who favored it, were deterred by public opinion from openly advocating it.[1]

On the 23rd of April, 1897, Mr. Harriman secured the enactment of what was known as the Orange County Road Law, which was a comprehensive scheme for the construction of county roads, and which also provided for raising the necessary funds by an issue of bonds. This measure became a law nearly twelve months before the general State law was passed, and more than a year before the supervisors of Orange County took any action. Meanwhile, Mr. Harriman, with the coöperation of the Horse and Road Improvement Association, caused detailed maps to be made of what were thought to be the best routes for the proposed roads, and when, on the 20th of May, 1898, the supervisors took the subject up for consideration, these maps were presented to the board and formed the basis for a resolution authorizing the construction of eight different lines of improved road. This resolution, after full discussion, was adopted by a vote of eighteen to twelve. Thus, after nearly three years of persistent effort, Mr. Harriman had the satisfaction of seeing the complete success of a movement which eventu-

[1] Address of the president of the Horse and Road Improvement Association at Goshen, New York, February 25, 1911.

WITH A FAVORITE TROTTER (RIVAL)

ally gave to Orange County more good roads, in proportion to its area and population, than any other county in the State.

In recognition of this public-spirited work, the Horse and Road Improvement Association erected in the public square at Goshen, Orange County, New York, a beautiful granite and bronze drinking fountain, dedicated to Mr. Harriman, which was unveiled by his youngest son, Roland, and was formally presented to the village authorities by the president of the association February 25, 1911. The granite bowl, which serves as a base for an eighteen-foot, electrically lighted shaft of bronze, bears the inscription:

IN MEMORY
of
EDWARD HENRY HARRIMAN
Erected by the Horse and Road Improvement Association
and
Dedicated February 25, 1911
HE LIVES IN THE MEMORY OF HIS FRIENDS

CHAPTER XX

CHANGES IN THE ILLINOIS CENTRAL

THE year 1906 was a trying and harassing one to Mr. Harriman, for the reason that it brought him into open and active conflict with his old friend and associate, Stuyvesant Fish.

In the board of directors of the Illinois Central there had long been a feeling of dissatisfaction with certain features of President Fish's administration; and in the latter part of 1906 it culminated in a movement to oust him from his position. Mr. Harriman, as chairman of the finance committee, was virtually compelled to become the leader of this movement, partly because he was largely responsible for the management of the company's finances, and partly because he shared the feeling upon which the opposition to Fish was based. Owing, however, to the fact that he was president of the Union Pacific, as well as a director of the Illinois Central, his actions were generally misjudged and his motives misconstrued. It was said, for example, that he opposed Fish and tried to oust him from the presidency, not because he thought a change would promote the interests of the Illinois Central, but because he believed that if he could remove Fish and replace him with a man of his own, he could get control of the road and virtually turn it over to the Union Pacific. This charge was repeatedly made, not only by Fish's friends, but by Fish himself.[1] Then, of course, Harriman's enemies took the matter up, accused him of disloyalty to his old friend as well as treachery to the road that he pretended to serve, and asserted that his sole motive was an unscrupulous determination to bring the Illinois Central under the domination of the Union Pacific and thus extend and increase his own power. The press and the public generally, ignorant of the reasons for the opposition to Fish, regarded the effort to displace him as a movement engineered by Harriman personally for his own aggrandizement and for the benefit of the Pacific railway systems that he controlled. Even in Europe, sympathy was generally with Fish, and in a cartoon widely circulated in England Harriman was represented as a black-masked bandit holding up, at the muzzle of a pistol, an Illinois Central train.[2]

The facts in the case, however, which were for a long time concealed in order to save the credit of the

---

[1] Statement read by President Fish at the meeting of stockholders of the Illinois Central in Chicago, October 17, 1906.

[2] *Edward H. Harriman and the Union Pacific*, by Alexander Millar, p. 15. See also "The Harriman Group and the Illinois Central," in the *Economist* (London), vol. 64, November 24, 1906.

company, throw a very different light upon Harriman's motives and behavior.

The trouble with Fish, and the opposition to him in the board of directors, began in 1903. Early in the spring of that year, when Mr. Harriman returned from a trip to California, certain directors of the company came to him and informed him that Mr. Fish had deposited more than half a million dollars of Illinois Central money in the Trust Company of the Republic, a small and weak concern in which Fish was one of the trustees. The directors, who had not been consulted in the matter, doubted both the propriety of the transaction and the safety of the money so deposited, and asked Mr. Harriman what action should be taken with regard to it. As Mr. Fish, meanwhile, had gone to Europe, all that Harriman could do was to order a withdrawal of the deposit. When, however, the secretary of the Illinois Central went after the money, he was told by the officers of the Trust Company that withdrawal of the deposit at that time would force them into bankruptcy. Mr. Harriman thereupon directed that the $500,000 be drawn out gradually, a little at a time, and eventually it was all recovered.

On the 15th of June, 1903, after Mr. Harriman had gone to Europe to recover from an illness and a surgical operation, Mr. Fish, who had meanwhile returned, again deposited a large sum of Illinois Central money in the Trust Company of the Republic, withdrew it, and a month later again deposited it, for the purpose, apparently, of aiding the Trust Company at times when the latter happened to be financially embarrassed.[1]

In the course of the same summer, without the approval or consent of the board of directors, Mr. Fish loaned $1,500,000 of Illinois Central money to himself, upon collateral security which was then regarded, and which afterward proved to be, wholly inadequate.

When Mr. Harriman returned from Europe, in the fall of 1903, some of the directors laid these facts before him and asked him to join them in bringing the matter to the attention of the whole board, with a view to having the president deposed. Mr. Harriman, however, would not consent to this; interceded for Mr. Fish, and finally, at a considerable personal sacrifice, loaned to the latter $1,200,000 of his own money, in order to enable him to take up his obligations to the company and straighten out his financial affairs.

Two years later, while this loan was still unknown

[1] It was said that the Trust Company had become involved in difficulties through its efforts to finance an industrial corporation known as the United States Shipbuilding Company, in which Fish was also interested.

to a majority of the directors, and while a large part of it was still outstanding, it became the subject of the following correspondence between the borrower and the lender:

I

At Hot Springs, Va.
October 2, 1905

MY DEAR MR. HARRIMAN:

I have to-day paid a bill rendered by Mr. Tegethoff for interest on $449,735, July 1 to October 1, $5,746.61, which is figured at the rate of 5 per cent. Of course I have said nothing to him about it, but it strikes me that the rate is rather high, considering those that have prevailed in New York within the last week or two.

Very truly yours

STUYVESANT FISH

II

November 2, 1905

STUYVESANT FISH, ESQ.
135 Broadway
New York

DEAR MR. FISH:

On my way from San Francisco I received your letter from Hot Springs regarding interest rate, 5 per cent, on your loan. The original loan, $1,200,000, was made to you about two years ago at a time when it was very inconvenient for me, and had it not been made, the amount would have been invested in some good security at much less price than now prevails, such as Illinois Central, about 125, or Union Pacific, say about 85. At the time I was also lending money to and using my credit in financing Railroad Securities Company. Making the loan to you necessitated selling some of the Illinois Central stock at the low price to liquidate some of the amount due me and thus provide part of the amount loaned to you. I was influenced at the time by the desire to keep the Illinois credit untarnished, as it would not have been had the circumstances become known to the whole board of directors and thus made public. I was Chairman of the Finance Committee, and although illness and an operation had made several months' absence necessary, during which period you borrowed from the Illinois Central, I felt some responsibility. The old association with you was another inducement for me to come to your rescue. It has resulted in your being able to retrieve yourself, and I am glad of it.

Another matter which you might remember is the Shipbuilding Syndicate subscription, which I made at your request, and, as you stated, "Will you do me the favor?" Afterwards you asked me to take $50,000 additional, stating you would take it off my hands later on. When you talked about it again, appreciating your financial condition, I told you not to give it another thought.

Very truly yours

E. H. HARRIMAN [1]

III

New York, Nov. 29, 1905

MY DEAR MR. HARRIMAN:

Since receiving your letter written in reply to mine of October 2 to you, I have, as you know, been more than busy. In so far as the rate of interest on loan to me is concerned, that matter is for you to determine and I accept what you have written as final. I was only in-

---

[1] The "Shipbuilding Syndicate" to which Mr. Harriman referred was the industrial corporation which was being financed by Mr. Fish's Trust Company of the Republic.

duced to write you as I did on October 2 from the fact that I had been carrying for a long while other loans at three and three and a half, and one at four, and had then recently renewed them at those rates for further periods of six months.

Very truly yours
STUYVESANT FISH

If, after receiving this help from Harriman, Fish had ceased to use the money of the Illinois Central without the consent of the board, his past offenses might have been condoned; but six or eight months later, in January, 1904, he again drew upon the treasury of the Illinois Central in order to increase the deposits of another banking concern in which he was interested, namely, the Commonwealth Trust Company.[1] His persistence in thus using the money of the company without authority greatly intensified the dissatisfaction of the few directors who were acquainted with the facts, because, as one of them said, "it indicated that he looked upon the Illinois Central as his personal property, to be used as he personally saw fit." So strong, in fact, was the disapproval of his methods, that if it had not been for the advice and intercession of Mr. Harriman, the movement to oust him from the presidency would probably have begun long before it did. Actuated by friendship for Fish, as well as by a desire to "keep

[1] Successor to the Trust Company of the Republic.

the credit of the Illinois Central untarnished," Mr. Harriman counseled patience, forbearance, and secrecy. He, himself, said nothing to anyone about the loan that he had made to Fish, and he strongly advised the dissatisfied directors not to create a scandal by laying the matter formally before the whole board. For two years, therefore, the public, the stockholders, and many of the directors were wholly ignorant of the facts in the case.

But such a state of affairs could not continue indefinitely. In the summer of 1906, the relations between Fish and a majority of the directors became still more strained, as the result of a conflict that occurred over the nomination of a candidate to fill a vacancy in the board caused by the death of William Morton Grinnell. Mr. Fish was desirous of electing a man of his own choice, and for various reasons. In the first place, he sincerely believed, no doubt, that the influence of the Union Pacific in the Illinois Central directorate was becoming too strong. Mr. Harriman had recently bought $28,000,000 of Illinois Central stock, and Mr. Fish apparently thought that this indicated an intention to dominate or control the company in the interest of the Union Pacific.[1] Then, too, three members of the Illinois

[1] When Mr. Harriman was examined as a witness before the Interstate Commerce Commission, a year and a half later, he was asked the direct question whether the acquirement by the Union Pacific of

Central board were directors also of the Union Pacific, and as the average attendance at board meetings was only seven or eight, the addition of a fourth representative of Union Pacific interests might imperil Illinois Central supremacy.

In the second place, Fish was well aware that his unauthorized use of the funds of the company was known to several of the directors as well as to Harriman, and he naturally wanted to get into the board

a large block of Illinois Central stock had any connection with the movement to oust Fish from the presidency. "Not an iota!" replied Harriman. "It had nothing whatever to do with it." The relation of one event to the other was "only a coincidence. If the Union Pacific had not disposed of a certain amount of its holdings of securities, and had not had money to invest in other like securities, it never would have acquired the Illinois Central stock." ("Hearings before the Interstate Commerce Commission in the Matter of Combination and Consolidation of Carriers"; testimony of Mr. Harriman, pp. 150–52.)

The surplus money thus used came into the Union Pacific treasury through the distribution of the assets of the Northern Securities Company after that corporation was dissolved by order of the United States Supreme Court. In pursuance of a policy which he regarded as wise and judicious, Mr. Harriman reinvested this money in the securities of various railroad companies, of which the Illinois Central was only one. He bought on behalf of the Union Pacific, for instance, 10,000 shares of Atchison, Topeka & Santa Fé; 19,000 shares of New York Central, and more than 45,000 shares of Baltimore & Ohio; but none of the presidents of these roads ever contended that his purpose was to dominate them or to turn them over to the Union Pacific. At the beginning of 1907, he controlled large blocks of stock in eight different railroad corporations, and his holdings in some of them — the Baltimore & Ohio, for example — were considerably greater than in the Illinois Central. His investment in the latter was made chiefly because that was the line over which grain was shipped from Union Pacific territory to the Gulf ports. ("Hearings before the Interstate Commerce Commission," etc., pp. 280 and 290–94.)

a friend of his own who would be likely to stand by him in case of trouble.

Finally, an election of officers for the ensuing term was near at hand, and he may have feared that the addition of another member to the ranks of the dissatisfied would endanger his position as president.

All of these considerations probably had weight with him, but he made public avowal of only one of them — the alleged danger of alien control. He was fighting, he said, to save the Illinois Central from the domination of the Union Pacific.

The date for the annual meeting of shareholders was the 17th of October, 1906, and as early as June of that year, President Fish sent a circular letter to all owners of the company's stock, requesting them to forward their proxies to him, to be voted by him, or by certain other representatives of the existing administration whom he designated. In all previous lists of alternates, Mr. Harriman, as chairman of the finance committee, had been included; but from the latest list his name was dropped. This indicated, of course, that the proxies sent to Fish would be voted against the Harriman group and in favor of candidates approved by the president and his supporters. The Harriman party met this move by proposing that all proxies be solicited and received by a specially appointed committee, and when Mr.

Fish declined to agree to this, Director Peabody,[1] at the next meeting of the board, offered the following resolutions:

Resolved: that Messrs. Astor, Auchincloss, Goelet, Luttgen, and Vanderbilt be appointed a committee to communicate with the shareholders and request their proxies for the next annual meeting.

Resolved: that the committee, if appointed, in its discretion consult counsel as to any legal questions that may arise.

In due course of parliamentary procedure these resolutions would have been put to a vote; but Mr. Fish, as chairman of the board, would not allow them to be acted upon, and after denouncing them as part of a plan to turn the Illinois Central over to the Union Pacific, he broke the quorum by withdrawing from the meeting and leaving the room.[2]

Some time after this disruption of the board meeting, President Fish, who perhaps felt uneasy with regard to the possible outcome of his action, went to Melville E. Stone,[3] explained to him the

[1] Charles A. Peabody, president of the Mutual Life Insurance Company of New York, who was one of the dissatisfied directors.

[2] The board at that time consisted of thirteen directors, seven of whom constituted a quorum. There were seven present at the outset, but the withdrawal of President Fish left only six. The directors opposed to Fish were Cornelius Vanderbilt, J. T. Harahan (vice-president of the company), Charles A. Peabody, John W. Auchincloss, Robert W. Goelet, Walter Luttgen, and E. H. Harriman.

[3] Melville E. Stone had long been a friend of Mr. Fish, as well as of Mr. Harriman, and it was for that reason that Fish went to him for advice.

situation, and solicited his advice and assistance. Stone asked him if he knew Henry H. Rogers of the Standard Oil Company. Fish replied that he did not, although they had been neighbors in Seventy-Eighth Street for many years. Stone suggested that inasmuch as Rogers had influence with Harriman, it might be well to consult him, and he offered to go with Fish to call upon him. As a result of the interview, Rogers consented to take the matter up with Harriman, and a few days later he informed Stone that Harriman and Peabody were willing to confer with Fish and to discuss with him the question of proxies for the forthcoming annual meeting. The conference, which was arranged by Rogers and Stone, was held in Mr. Rogers' office, on the 27th of July, and resulted in the following agreement:

Agreed July 27, 1906, 10 A.M.

1. Three outgoing directors to be reëlected, Messrs. Beach, Harahan, and Vanderbilt.

2. Mr. Grinnell's successor to be selected by a majority of the several directors acting.

3. Mr. Peabody's resolution of July 18, the one calling for a new proxy committee, to be withdrawn and not to be revived this year.

4. Mr. Harriman will ask that the Harriman-Kuhn-Loeb proxies be given to Mr. Fish.

STUYVESANT FISH
CHARLES A. PEABODY
E. H. HARRIMAN

This seemed to be a final and satisfactory settlement of the question in dispute; but when it came to a test, Fish refused to abide by the agreement. On the 10th of October a majority of the directors sent to him the following note:

New York, October 9, 1906

STUYVESANT FISH, ESQ.
DEAR SIR:
We select Henry W. De Forest of New York City to fill the vacancy caused by the death of Mr. William Morton Grinnell and request that he be elected to fill such vacancy at the stockholders' meeting to be held on October 17th.

CHARLES A. PEABODY
CORNELIUS VANDERBILT
J. T. HARAHAN
JOHN W. AUCHINCLOSS
E. H. HARRIMAN
ROBERT W. GOELET
WALTER LUTTGEN

Henry W. De Forest, the man selected by a majority of the board to fill the vacancy, was a New York lawyer of high reputation and unimpeachable integrity. He happened, however, to be a director in one of Mr. Harriman's companies — the Southern Pacific — and this fact alone was enough to make him a *persona non grata* to Mr. Fish. At a meeting of the board on the 10th of October, Fish made a vigorous protest against the selection; asserted that it would make him a party to the plan to turn over the control of the Illinois Central to those controlling the Union Pacific, and declared that he would not help to promote any such scheme. He was willing, he said, to vote the proxies of Harriman and his associates in accordance with their wishes; but he should use the other proxies that he held as seemed to him best in the interest of the stockholders who had confided them to him. He defended his course by saying that when he signed the agreement of July 27th, he was verbally assured by Harriman and Peabody that there was "no intention or plan to turn over the control of the company to those controlling any other corporation," and that "the vacancy resulting from the death of Mr. Grinnell would be filled by the selection of a man of character, independent of any clique, who would represent the whole body of stockholders without regard to any outside interest." That assurance, he said, had not been fulfilled.

Mr. Harriman, on the other hand, denied that any verbal promise had been made which would abrogate or restrict the discretionary power of a majority of the board. "It passes the bounds of credulity," he said, "to suppose that we would give Mr. Fish the right to nullify the very agreement we were signing, and to veto the selection to be made by a majority of the directors." [1]

[1] Statement given to the press by Mr. Harriman about October 18th.

Mr. Harriman's view of the transaction was subsequently made still more clear in the following letter
to Melville E. Stone:

New York, Oct. 25, 1906

DEAR MR. STONE:

I would like to remind you of the circumstances which
led up to the agreement with Mr. Fish, made last July.

In June last, more than a month before the usual
meeting of the Illinois Central Board to take action
upon the closing of the books and arranging for the
usual annual meeting to take place in October, Mr.
Fish sent out proxies in his name in an unusual way and
at such an unusual time. At the July meeting of the
Board, a resolution was introduced to appoint a proxy
committee of four members of the Board. Mr. Fish,
who was present and presiding, declined to put the
motion and left the room, in that way breaking a quorum, thus preventing action by the Board. The Board
thereupon adjourned for one week. Just at the end of
the week I met Mr. Fish at your solicitation, on his
behalf, the outcome of which was the following agreement:

[Agreement quoted]

This agreement was faithfully carried out on our
part, and all proxies were sent to Mr. Fish as therein
agreed. On Friday, October 12th, five days before the
stockholders' meeting, Mr. Fish sold me his one third
interest in the Railroad Securities stock, agreeing to
take, and I agreeing to pay him therefor 8769 shares
of the Illinois Central and $1,537,020.49 in cash. Of
course had I known of his intention to break faith, I
would not have made this transaction.

Mr. Fish is quoted as stating at the stockholders'

meeting that there was a condition as to the nominee to be selected by the Board. Nothing ever occurred to justify the inference of any understanding or agreement other than that embodied in the agreement, nor was there any intimation by Mr. Fish, from the date of the agreement until after he was notified of Mr. De Forest's selection, that he had any understanding himself that there was any such qualification.

I give you this information inasmuch as it was through your action on behalf of Mr. Fish that negotiations were entered into which ended in the agreement.

Very truly yours

E. H. HARRIMAN

October 16, 1906, on the eve of the annual meeting of stockholders, Mr. Harriman called up Mr. Stone by telephone, reminded him that he was largely responsible for the conference which resulted in the agreement of July 27th, and asked him to hold Mr. Fish to his pledge. Stone thereupon consulted Rogers, and the two together drafted the following telegram, which was sent to Fish over Stone's name:

New York, October 17, 1906

STUYVESANT FISH
New York

Have seen Mr. Rogers who says that in the talk in his office which led to your meeting with Mr. Harriman, he understood you to say distinctly that you would be satisfied with any one whom the board should select to fill Mr. Grinnell's place; that he was authorized by you to say that to Mr. Harriman, and that he did say it to Mr. Harriman. I now remember the statement

myself. In the light of this fact, do you not feel bound
by that pledge?

MELVILLE E. STONE

Notwithstanding the pressure thus brought to
bear upon Mr. Fish, he adhered to his determination
to vote in favor of a candidate of his own selection
all the proxies in his possession except those given to
him by Harriman, Kuhn, Loeb & Co., and their
associates. These latter proxies he offered to let
Director Welling vote for De Forest, or any one else
whom Harriman might designate. To this Harriman replied by telegraph: "Of course I cannot assent
to any departure from the agreement."

The annual meeting, October 17th, was attended
by about two hundred and fifty stockholders, most
of whom owned only a few shares each. Fish had
proxies for 690,657 shares, or nearly two thirds of
the whole number outstanding. After reading a long
statement in justification of his course, Mr. Fish
nominated as his candidate for Mr. Grinnell's place
James De Wolfe Cutting, of New York, and voted
for him proxies representing 594,741 shares. Proxies
for about 96,000 shares, which, Fish said, he had
received from Harriman and Kuhn, Loeb & Co.,
were not used at all. Inasmuch as the proxies voted
in support of Mr. De Forest represented only 2100
shares, Mr. Cutting was declared elected.

Of course the 96,000 shares, which Fish held proxies for but did not vote, fell far short of representing the real strength of the Harriman-Peabody group. Mr. Cromwell pointed out this fact before the vote was taken, and said to Mr. Fish:

All the proxies you have received have been influenced, in part, by the coöperation, as well as by the non-interference, of Messrs. Peabody and Harriman under the agreement that they signed with you. It is, therefore, utterly impossible to distinguish what proxies you have received through the benefit and influence of this agreement. It is mere fiction to select a few that came through one particular channel. These proxies came from all over, by our suggestion and often from those who came to Mr. Harriman's office and were directed to you.[1]

According to a statement published by Mr. Cromwell in the "New York Tribune" on the day after the meeting, the Harriman-Peabody proxies that were actually turned over to Mr. Fish, under the agreement, represented more than 300,000 shares, two thirds of which Fish voted for his own candidate.[2]

The repudiation by Fish of his written agreement with a majority of the directors, and his subsequent action in voting against them two thirds of the

---

[1] Stenographic report of the annual meeting, pp. 21–22. Mr. Cromwell was Mr. Harriman's representative.

[2] *New York Tribune*, October 18, 1906, and *Commercial & Financial Chronicle*, October 20, 1906.

proxies that they themselves had caused to be sent to him, strained to the breaking point the forbearance of his opponents in the board. On the 7th of November, just prior to the meeting for the election of officers, eight directors — a majority of the board — sent to him a communication in which, after reciting the circumstances which brought about the conference of July 27th, they said:

In violating the agreement and electing your own personal nominee, you assumed to treat as a personal affair the proxies given to you upon the faith of the agreement. Furthermore, notwithstanding the positive agreement that the three directors, Messrs. Beach, Harahan, and Vanderbilt, whose terms were expiring, should be reëlected, we have good reason to believe that up to the last moment you seriously planned a breach of that promise also.

We are quite aware that you gave reasons at the meeting for your refusal to fill the vacancy as agreed, and you are reported as going so far as to claim that you had some understanding to the effect that the person selected should be satisfactory to you, thus submitting yourself as the sole judge, whereas the entire purpose of the agreement, in respect of the vacancy, was to eliminate you as the person to select and substitute the judgment and action of a majority of the directors.

The simple fact appears to be that, regardless of your written promise, on the faith of which you were entrusted with the proxies, you found no difficulty in satisfying yourself that your personal interest and the interest of the company are identical, and that any action was justifiable to assist in securing your own control.

The situation is solely of your own creating; but, in view of what has taken place, of your deliberate violation of an agreement intended to produce peace in the board, and of your attitude toward your fellow members, we are convinced that you have rendered impossible that harmony which must exist between the president of the company and individual members of the board, and that you have so seriously impaired your usefulness as an officer of the company as to compel us to refuse to vote in favor of your reëlection.

Late in October, or early in November, when it had become apparent to Fish that his position as president was extremely insecure, he again sought the intercession of his friend, Melville E. Stone. The latter, a day or two later, had an interview with Harriman in the course of which he told him that Fish really needed the salary he received as president, and that he was hoping to be retained. Harriman spoke kindly of Fish, as he always had done, but said he doubted whether anything could save him, because the directors were determined to remove him. In view, however, of Fish's need of money, and of his long and useful service as president, he (Harriman) was willing to propose to the directors that they make him chairman of the board. When this offer was made known to Fish, he declined to consider it, and the outcome of the struggle then became inevitable. At the meeting of the board on the 7th of November, Fish was deposed and J. T.

Harahan, second vice-president, was elected in his place.

Fish was greatly embittered by what he regarded as the injustice done him, but, aside from talking freely on the subject, he took no action until the summer of 1907, when, at a regular meeting of the board, he filed a series of resolutions criticizing the management of the company's affairs by President Harahan and calling for an investigation. Without considering the resolutions on their merits, the board referred them to the accounting and traffic officers of the company for a report.[1] Meanwhile, Mr. Fish sent a circular letter to all the shareholders, in which he accused the company's officers of manipulating their accounts, and declared that the affairs of the Illinois Central were, "to all intents and purposes, managed from the offices of the Union Pacific Company, No. 120 Broadway." When, a week or two later, this letter was published, President Harahan addressed to the stockholders the following communication:

The statement in the circular letter issued by Mr. Fish to the stockholders and published to-day that the Illinois Central accounts have been "padded," or in any way manipulated, is absolutely untrue. He knows that there has been no change whatever in the relations of the Illinois Central with the Union Pacific and Southern Pacific. The resolutions presented by him some weeks

[1] *New York Herald*, August 29, 1907.

ago to the board of directors, making these charges, were referred to the accounting and traffic officers, and their reports, which were transmitted by me to the board of directors, show that the charges were utterly groundless; that the accounts have been kept precisely as they were under Mr. Fish's administration, and that the relations with all connecting lines are the same as before his retirement. His reference to alleged domination by the Union Pacific is merely an effort to play upon what he supposes to be current prejudice, and it should not deceive any one.

The attack made by Mr. Fish on the character of his fellow directors and upon the operating, accounting, and traffic officers of the company, warrants a full statement to the stockholders of the reasons why Mr. Fish was not entrusted with the continued management of the property. I enclose herewith a copy of a letter addressed by eight directors of the company to Mr. Fish, under date of November 7, 1906, setting forth specifically some of the reasons why they would not vote for his reelection as president.

There were other reasons of a controlling character, which were referred to in general terms, but, out of consideration for Mr. Fish, were not specifically mentioned in that letter. The most conspicuous of these is that while Mr. Fish was president of the company, and, as such, the virtual custodian of its treasury, he loaned to himself, as an individual, about $1,500,000 from the treasury of the company, upon security of his own selection which proved to be inadequate and unmarketable. Mr. Fish being unable to repay the loan, or to satisfactorily secure it, there were various consultations among his friends on the board of directors, and negotiations designed for the payment of the indebtedness and the protection of the credit of the company, as well as of Mr. Fish's reputation.

After it was demonstrated that Mr. Fish was unable to reimburse the company, a director, individually, loaned him the money necessary to repay the company. In order to secure this loan, Mr. Fish pledged not only the unmarketable collateral above mentioned, but also conveyed his residence in the city of New York and his individual interest in the estate of the late Hamilton Fish. Out of consideration for Mr. Fish such conveyances were not placed on record. The director making this loan carried it for several years until Mr. Fish was able to liquidate it.[1]

Furthermore, Mr. Fish, who was a member of the executive committee of the Trust Company of the Republic and was very active in its affairs, deposited a large amount of money of the Illinois Central Railroad Company in that company after its credit was seriously impaired; and although this sum was ultimately collected, the process required several months, and during that time the risk was a cause of great anxiety to the directors. Moreover, he loaned to the president of the Trust Company of the Republic, individually, money of the Illinois Central Railroad Company upon inadequate security, with the result that the railroad company was unable to collect the entire amount and suffered a loss.

It is due to the officers and directors whose motives and conduct have been impugned, and to the stockholders to whom Mr. Fish has addressed an appeal based on his charges, that these facts should be known.[2]

[1] It is a significant fact that although Mr. Harriman, actuated by loyalty and friendship, made this loan to Mr. Fish in 1903, his identity as the lender was not disclosed until February, 1907, when he was examined as a witness before the Interstate Commerce Commission. Even six months after that, when President Harahan made the above statement to the stockholders, the name of the "director" who had extricated Mr. Fish from his difficulties and saved his reputation was not mentioned.

[2] *New York Herald,* September 25, 1907.

In the controversy between Mr. Fish and his successor, final judgment was rendered by the owners of the road. At the annual meeting of stockholders on the 3d of March, 1908, when Mr. Fish appeared as a candidate for reëlection as director, he was defeated by proxies representing 583,161 shares, all of which were voted for his opponent, Mr. J. F. Titus.[1] Thus ended the official connection of Mr. Fish with the Illinois Central Railroad Company, which had continued without interruption for more than thirty years.

In view of all the facts revealed by the documentary evidence in the case, it would seem that Mr. Harriman's treatment of Mr. Fish was not only just, but generous. He did all that he could to protect him, even when he wholly disapproved of his conduct; and if he turned against him at the last, it was only because Mr. Fish himself, by his repudiation of the agreement of July 27th, had made further defense of him impossible.

[1] Mr. Titus was assistant to President Harahan. It was understood, however, at the time of the election, that he took the directorship only temporarily as *locum-tenens* for Mr. J. Ogden Armour. (*Commercial & Financial Chronicle*, March 7, 1908.)

CHAPTER XXI

SAN FRANCISCO EARTHQUAKE AND FIRE

HARRIMAN, in the earlier part of his career, showed his ability and resourcefulness mainly in the successful accomplishment of colossal tasks that he voluntarily set for himself; but toward the close of his life he had to deal not only with self-imposed tasks, but with great and sudden emergencies created by the titanic forces of Nature. Among the most calamitous of such emergencies were the destruction of the city of San Francisco by earthquake and fire in April, 1906, and the inundation of one of the most fertile parts of southern California, by an unprecedented overflow of the Colorado River in June of the same year. Neither of these mishaps greatly affected Harriman's personal fortunes, nor did either of them threaten disastrous loss to the railroads that he managed; but in time of public calamity he was, first of all, a patriotic citizen, and he never failed to respond promptly to any call for public service.

The almost complete destruction of San Francisco by earthquake and fire in 1906 was one of the great catastrophes of history. It began about five o'clock on the morning of Wednesday, April 18th, with a series of violent earth tremors which affected more or less perceptibly the whole Pacific Coast from Oregon to Mexico, but which were most severe in the vicinity of San Francisco Bay. The earthquake alone would not have destroyed the city, nor any considerable part of it; but, unfortunately, it started fires in a number of buildings that had been thrown down by the shocks and, at the same time, killed the chief of the fire department in his bed, and fractured or dislocated the pipes that supplied the city with water, so that the fire fighters were left without an official head to direct their operations and without any adequate means of combating the flames. In less than five hours, the small separate fires united in a great conflagration which soon got wholly beyond control and raged, almost unchecked, for three days and nights. Attempts were made to limit it by back-firing and by blowing up buildings in the line of its advance; but these efforts were only partially successful, and the flames were finally stopped at Broadway, Franklin, and Gough Streets by means of water from the bay pumped through a tandem string of fire engines connected by long sections of hose. Meanwhile, however, the whole business part of the city and some of the residential part, covering an area of more than five square miles, had been reduced to heaps of smoking ruins.

General A. W. Greely, who then commanded the Pacific Division of the United States Army, made a special report to the War Department on the disaster in which he said:

On April 18th, San Francisco was a city of 500,000 inhabitants; the commercial emporium of the Pacific Coast; a great industrial and manufacturing center, adorned with magnificent buildings, equipped with extensive local transportation, provided with the most sanitary appliances, and having an abundant water supply. On April 21st, these triumphs of human effort, this center of civilization, had become a scene of indescribable desolation, more than 200,000 residents having fled from the burnt district, leaving several hundred dead under its smoldering ashes. Even buildings spared by the fire were damaged as to chimneys, so that all the food of the entire city was cooked over camp-fires in the open streets. Two hundred and twenty-five thousand people were not only without shelter, losing homes and all personal property, but were also deprived of their means of present sustenance and future livelihood. Food, water, shelter, clothing, medicines, and sewerage were all lacking.

The news of the disaster reached Mr. Harriman in New York on the afternoon of April 19th. He immediately telegraphed the general managers of the Union Pacific and Southern Pacific systems to put all the resources of the two roads at the service of the stricken city. But this did not seem to him enough. He wanted to be on the ground, where he could see what was happening and direct personally the work of relief so far as it was dependent on transportation. On the morning of Thursday, April 19th, before he even knew the extent of the disaster, he started for San Francisco in a special train. In New York and all along the road he kept constantly in touch, by telegraph, with the operating officials of the Union Pacific and Southern Pacific systems and impressed upon them the importance of getting supplies — especially foodstuffs — into San Francisco at the earliest possible moment. At every important station between the Great Lakes and the Pacific he received reports on the situation and wired instructions with regard to the loading and movement of relief trains. Action on these instructions was prompt and effectual. On the very first day of the disaster, E. E. Calvin, vice-president and general manager of the Southern Pacific, bought nearly twenty thousand dollars' worth of food in Los Angeles and Sacramento and hurried it to San Francisco in special freight trains running on passenger schedule. As a result of this efficient work, the burned-out inhabitants of the city were not compelled to go hungry, even for a single day. But the problem of feeding them was greatly simplified by carrying scores of thousands of them either to neighboring towns where food was plentiful, or to the homes of their relatives in the East. On Thursday,

April 19th, the next day after the earthquake, the Harriman lines moved 1073 carloads of refugees out of the city, and nearly as many more on the 20th.

Fortunately the water front of the city was not injured, either by earthquake or by fire, so that the Pacific roads were able to use the ferry house as their headquarters after their offices in the Merchants' Exchange Building and their terminal at Third and Townsend Streets had been burned. Vice-President Calvin put at the disposal of the municipal authorities not only all the ferryboats of the Harriman lines, but also their three river steamers Apache, Modoc, and Fruto, which carried thousands of refugees to Oakland, Berkeley, Alameda, and other places on the bay, and brought back hundreds of tons of food-stuffs and miscellaneous supplies.

But the Harriman lines did not confine their helpful work to transportation alone. When explosives were needed to blow up houses in the line of the fire's advance, they were furnished by the railroad authorities. When gasoline was wanted for the automobiles and motor cars that were carrying officials, physicians, nurses, or supplies, only the railroad companies had an adequate supply. Their hospital at Fourteenth and Mission Streets was thrown open to the injured and their surgeons and nurses gave first aid to more than two hundred and fifty wounded people. Their employees assisted the police in guarding supplies and putting a stop to looting, and thirty of their heavy wagons, which were being used in the construction of the Bay Shore cut-off, were turned over, with their teamsters, to the military authorities and utilized in the hauling of supplies. In short, Vice-President Calvin, in compliance with Mr. Harriman's telegraphic instructions, put "all the resources" of the two great Pacific systems at the service of the city, and it is doubtful whether any other single agency did more to alleviate distress in the first week after the fire began.

At ten o'clock Sunday morning, only a few hours after his arrival, Mr. Harriman, accompanied by Vice-President Calvin, attended a conference of the citizens' "Committee of One Hundred" which had been organized to deal with the emergency, and which was then meeting every day at Fort Mason where General Funston had his headquarters. At this conference, after listening to the various plans that were proposed, Harriman

suggested that an immediate start be made by putting men at work clearing the streets of débris; that citizens in the unburned area be urged to resume their usual occupations; and that an effort be made to get all the people to doing something that would occupy their minds and restore them as soon as possible to a normal condition. He offered free transportation to all who wished to go to their relatives or friends where they could be cared for. In the matter of restoring conditions and confidence, he, himself, set the example by directing us to immediately secure an office building, repair it ourselves and occupy it with our forces at the earliest possible moment. All of his suggestions were accepted and put into effect, and from that time on his resourcefulness and energy inspired the people to intelligent and continued action.[1]

The most urgent need, at first, was transportation for the relief supplies that California and the country at large were ready to furnish, and this need Mr. Harriman, with his two great railway systems, was abundantly able to meet. He immediately ordered operating officials throughout the Union Pacific and Southern Pacific systems to give relief trains and refugee trains right of way over all other traffic, and to carry both people and supplies without charge. Food, clothing, and tents, from various parts of the Pacific Coast, were already pouring into the city, and they were quickly supplemented by similar supplies from the East, where they were bought with $2,500,000 appropriated by Congress and more than $10,000,000 subscribed by the people of the United States. In the thirty-five days between April 18th and May 23d, the Union Pacific and Southern Pacific Railways brought into San Francisco, free of charge 1603 carloads of supplies, at a cost of

[1] Statement by Vice-President Calvin.

$445,410, and carried out of the city 224,069 refugees whose fares, if they had been paid, would have amounted to $500,831.[1]

But the Harriman lines helped the people of San Francisco in many other less important ways. There was great uncertainty and confusion at first on account of the impossibility of quickly disseminating information. All of the newspaper buildings had been burned, and the homeless thousands in the streets had no means of knowing what was going on and what they could do or were expected to do. This great need was promptly met by the passenger department of the Southern Pacific Company, which established information bureaus at nine different places in the burnt district and kept them supplied with news by means of horseback riders and automobiles sent out from the company's temporary headquarters in the ferry building. The news thus carried was printed on half-sheets and posted up at every bureau, together with bulletins of train service, information as to relief work, inquiries with regard to missing people, and orders from the civil and military authorities. These bureaus were maintained for three weeks and were of the greatest possible use to thousands of people who, in the absence of newspapers, telephones, and street cars, could get in-

[1] Report of Vice-President Calvin, June 18, 1906.

formation in no other way. The passenger department of the Southern Pacific also helped to restore
confidence and hope by publishing and distributing
a folder entitled "Imperishable San Francisco,"
and by printing and circulating a weekly journal
called "Progress" which contained not only current
news but encouraging and inspiring articles written
by Governor Pardee, Professor Omori, of Japan, the
city officials, and other prominent men. These publications were sent to leading newspapers, maga-
zines, clubs, and railroad agencies throughout the
United States.

The Southern Pacific also rendered valuable
service to the city in other ways by laying temporary tracks in the street; by lending the use of
their railroad wires to the Western Union Telegraph
Company — in some cases furnishing operators as
well — and by finding work in other towns of the
State for hundreds of laborers and mechanics
thrown out of employment by the disaster. All of
this service Mr. Harriman planned or approved,
while, at the same time, he gave his personal attention and assistance in many individual cases of distress that happened to come to his knowledge.

Late one evening [says Mr. Calvin], as we stood on the
after deck of a ferryboat returning to Oakland Pier, a
stranger approached me and stated that his wife had

died from shock; that he had no acquaintances in the
city from whom he could secure help, and requested that
I give him transportation for himself and the remains of
his wife to their former home in the East, as he had only
money enough on hand to pay his traveling expenses.
After I had written out an order for the necessary transportation and turned away from him, Mr. Harriman inquired of me how I knew the man's story was correct. I
told him that I did not know, but that I felt it better to
take chances in a case of that kind than to run the risk of
denying help to a deserving man. He replied: "It is well
that you reached that conclusion, because if you had
not done so, I should have taken the case out of your
hands and given him the money myself."

A catastrophe which destroyed in three days
property valued at $325,000,000 might perhaps
have discouraged — at least temporarily — the most
hopeful spirit; but it could not daunt for a moment
a man like E. H. Harriman, who, on his own personal judgment and initiative, was spending an even
greater sum than that in the reconstruction and re-
equipment of the two great Pacific railway systems.
He took a sanguine and optimistic view of the situation from the very first, and before the embers of the
great conflagration had completely cooled, he said
to the world in a published statement:

California was never more prosperous than now. All
business interests are on a sound basis and the banks
are strong in resources. San Francisco's commanding
position in relation to the commerce of the world is un-
affected, and its facilities, in the shape of transportation

lines, wharves, and docks, are intact. It will astonish
the world with the quickness of its reconstruction.
Rapidly the city is becoming a beehive of activity,
and ere long the imperishable spirit of San Francisco,
clothed anew, will invite you within the gates of the new
and greater metropolis of the Pacific.

Two and a half years later, the "Railway World"
said editorially:

When San Francisco was laid in ashes, it was Mr.
Harriman who took personal charge of the situation;
his railroads rushed supplies into the city and carried
thousands of refugees away from the city, without
charge for either service. It was primarily due to his
organizing genius and energy that San Francisco so
quickly rallied from its great disaster.[1]

\[1\] *Railway World*, September 3, 1909.

CHAPTER XXII

THE UNION PACIFIC DIVIDEND IN 1906

THE Harriman lines, in the spring of 1906, could well afford to give a million dollars' worth of free transportation to the burned-out and destitute citizens of San Francisco, because the roads had never before been as prosperous as they were that year. In 1898, when Harriman took hold of the Union Pacific, very few financiers thought that his plans for the reconstruction of it and his anticipation of profit to be made out of it would ever be realized. "Not many believed that the company's preferred stock would ever pay a dividend, and a large proportion of the Wall Street contingent predicted that it would prove a difficult matter to continuously meet the interest charges on the bonds." [1] But the financiers and the Wall Street brokers were mistaken. Mr. Harriman's plans and anticipations were not visionary and the realization of some of them came very soon. The Union Pacific Company began paying a one-and-a-half per cent dividend on its preferred stock in October, 1898, and the same

[1] "The Growth of the Harriman Lines," by John Moody, *Moody's Magazine* (New York), October, 1906, p. 546.

amount on its common stock in April, 1900. Year
after year, as the reconstruction of the road pro-
gressed and Mr. Harriman's plans developed, the
income of the company steadily increased. In 1897,
it was less than $15,000,000; in 1900, it was $39,-
000,000, and at the end of the fiscal year 1906, it
had grown to $47,000,000. The net earnings of the
Harriman lines in 1906 were $69,674,089, while in-
come from other sources amounted to $18,500,000,
so that the total net receipts for that year were more
than $88,000,000. The Union Pacific then had, prac-
tically in cash, a surplus of $100,000,000, and Mr.
Harriman and his associates could command $500,-
000,000 for any enterprise that they might wish to
undertake.[1] About one fourth of the net income of
the Union Pacific Company in 1906 was derived from
investments, so that it might have paid all of its
fixed charges and four per cent on its preferred stock
without running a single train.[2]

Owing to vast expenditures for betterments on
both the Union Pacific and Southern Pacific systems, dividends, for some years, did not keep pace
with earnings; but the dividend on the Union Pacific stock was increased from four per cent to five

[1] "The Growth of the Harriman Lines," *Moody's Magazine*,
October, 1906, pp. 547–49.
[2] *Quarterly Journal of Economics*, vol. 21, p. 672; *Railroads:
Finance and Organization*, by W. Z. Ripley, pp. 66 and 508.

per cent in 1905, and from five per cent to six per cent in 1906, while the earnings of the Southern Pacific had become great enough to justify a first dividend of four or five percent on the stock of that company also.

In the spring of 1906, Harriman became convinced that the time had come for the adoption of a more liberal dividend policy. He did not publicly state the reasons that had brought him to this conclusion, but to one of the directors he said confidentially in May: "We have got to increase the dividends in the Union Pacific and pay a good round dividend in the Southern Pacific. The dividend in the Southern Pacific should be five per cent. I do not know just what the Union Pacific dividend ought to be, but it ought to be a good big increase. The amendment to the Interstate Commerce Law makes me change my views regarding the general policy of dividend disbursements. The time has come when instead of putting most of our money back into the property, we should give a larger share to the stockholders. If we don't, the Government will take it away from us." [1]

[1] The "amendment" to which Mr. Harriman referred was the so-called Hepburn Bill, which was then pending in Congress and seemed likely to pass. He had good reason to feel apprehensive with regard to the effects of this measure. According to the well-known economist and statistical expert, Joseph Nimmo, Jr., "In the six months that followed the taking effect of the Act of June 29, 1906, commonly

At a meeting of the directors held on the 19th of July, Harriman stated to the members present that when the time came for acting upon the dividend, there ought to be a dividend on the stock of the Southern Pacific and a substantial increase in the dividend of the Union Pacific. He did not then say what he thought these dividends should be, but at the regular meeting of the board on the 16th of August, he recommended that five per cent be paid on the common stock of the Southern Pacific and ten per cent on that of the Union Pacific. These dividends were declared about eleven o'clock that day, but the fact that they were not made public until about ten o'clock the next morning served as the basis for a charge that Mr. Harriman and the directors purposely withheld the announcement, in order that they might have time to buy Union Pacific stock on their advance knowledge of the great increase in the dividend rate. In commenting on this charge, five years later, Mr. Otto H. Kahn said:

Those of you who are familiar with Wall Street events will know that in August, 1906, the Union Pacific dividend was jumped from an annual rate of six per cent to ten per cent, which act unchained a storm of criticism

known as the Hepburn Act, the depreciation in the value of railroad and other corporate securities in the United States amounted to nearly $5,000,000,000, an amount in excess of the total cost of the Civil War." (*Railroad Regulation in its Political Aspects*, by Joseph Nimmo, Jr., Washington, D.C., 1909, p. 8.)

against Mr. Harriman. He was accused of having perpetrated a stock-jobbing trick, as the property, it was thought, could not possibly maintain that rate of dividend, and of having bought stock on his advance knowledge immediately preceding the declaration of the increased dividend, so as to profit, at the expense of other holders who had no knowledge of what was contemplated, from the rise in the market which was bound to follow. Both accusations were unjustified. No property for the management of which Mr. Harriman was responsible ever reduced its dividend, and the Union Pacific has maintained with ease a distribution of ten per cent per annum, derived to the extent of six per cent from the earnings of the railroad, and to the extent of four per cent from its investment holdings. Anybody who knew anything of Mr. Harriman's methods knew that his acts were not the results of sudden impulse, but of plans long prepared and determined on; that he had gone on record at every opportunity as advising owners of Union Pacific stock to retain their holdings, and that if he wanted to increase his own holdings he would do so (as, in fact, he invariably did) in times of depression and not wait to rush in a few days or weeks before the advent of some favorable consummation. At one of the hearings at which he was examined, he was asked whether it was not a fact that he had bought Union Pacific stock in anticipation of the ten per cent dividend declaration, the meaning, of course, being the accusation that he had unfairly taken advantage of his advance knowledge of the contemplated increase. To every one's surprise Mr. Harriman calmly answered "Yes." The examiner turned toward the audience with a triumphant smile and continued: "Mr. Harriman, as you have been thus frank, would you mind telling me approximately when and at what prices you bought that stock which you have just admitted you acquired in anticipation of the increased dividend?" Mr. Harriman smiled faintly in his turn as he answered slowly: "Certainly, I shall be glad to tell you. Let me think back a minute. I bought most of that stock, many thousand shares of it, in anticipation of the ten per cent dividend declared August, 1906, some eight years before, mainly in 1898, and I paid all the way from 20 to 30 for it. And I bought more of it in subsequent years, whenever prices were low, many thousand shares more; and all the time I was accumulating it I anticipated the declaration of that dividend." [1]

In telling this story I do not wish to be understood as endorsing the wisdom and propriety of the increase of the Union Pacific dividend from six to ten per cent *at one jump*. It was one of the few instances in which I ventured to differ from Mr. Harriman's judgment. A man, and especially a man at the head of a great corporation, must not only do right, but he must be very careful to avoid even appearances tending to arouse the suspicion of his not doing right; and the fact and manner of that particular act lent themselves to sinister interpretations, unjustified though, as a matter of fact, they were. [2]

The charge that Mr. Harriman and his associates concealed from the public for "two full days" the advance in the dividend rate of Union Pacific stock has been made many times since 1906. Nine years after the declaration of the ten per cent dividend Professor William Z. Ripley, an economist who

[1] Report of the Interstate Commerce Commission on the "Consolidation and Combination of Carriers." (Testimony of E. H. Harriman, p. 180.)

[2] *Edward Henry Harriman*, by Otto H. Kahn (New York, 1911), pp. 16–17.

has done a great deal of useful, if not invariably accurate, work in the railroad field, said:

It is not, however, the fact but rather the manner of increasing the Union Pacific dividend which is subject to criticism. The Southern Pacific road was the largest single outside investment of the Union Pacific. It had been gradually fattened through many years by reinvestment of all its surplus in betterments. The harvest time had now come. Directors of both roads met in the same room at practically the same time. The Southern Pacific common stock was placed upon a five per cent dividend basis. From this source and others the Union Pacific Company abruptly raised its rate from six to ten per cent, where it remained until 1914. The fact of this advance was *rigidly concealed for two days*, giving opportunity to those interested to reap large profits from the inevitable advance in price attendant upon publication of the fact. No official investigation has revealed the extent of these private operations. . . . It was a time of extraordinary speculative activity. The stock market was at the boiling point. And the opportunity afforded to insiders and their friends to make use of this information was too valuable to suppose for a moment that it failed to be utilized.[1]

Professor Ripley is mistaken in supposing that the declaration of the dividend was "rigidly concealed" for "two full days." The interval between the declaration and the public announcement was less than one day. The board of directors met at 11

[1] The italics are Professor Ripley's. In another place he says that the interval between the declaration and the announcement of the dividend was "two full days " (*Railroads: Finance and Organization,* by William Z. Ripley, pp. 209 and 508.)

A.M. August 16th, and the declaration of the dividend was announced at the opening of the Stock Exchange on the morning of August 17th.[1] The explanation of the delay is very simple. At the meeting of the board on August 16th, several prominent directors, including Marvin Hughitt and H. C. Frick, happened to be absent from the city. As a matter of courtesy to them, it was suggested that the announcement be delayed a few hours, so that they might be informed before the dividend rate was made public. The announcement, therefore, was referred to the executive committee for action. Late in the afternoon of that same day, Mr. James Stillman, president of the National City Bank, came into Mr. Harriman's office and said to him that it was rumored in the Street that the Union Pacific board had that day largely increased its dividend, but that the announcement was being withheld for speculative purposes. As a consequence there was growing and severe criticism, and he urged that the announcement be made immediately. Mr. Harriman replied that as the New York Stock Exchange had closed for the day, an announcement at that hour would throw the resulting trade to London. For that reason he thought the announcement ought to be deferred until the opening of the New York

[1] *Journal of Commerce*, New York, August 16 and 17, 1906.

Stock Exchange on the 17th. To this Mr. Stillman assented. Mr. Harriman then called in Secretary Millar and instructed him to have the notice in the hands of the secretary of the New York Exchange at the opening hour the next morning, and impressed upon him the necessity for promptness.

So far as Mr. Harriman is concerned, there never was the slightest reason to suppose that he caused the announcement of the ten per cent dividend to be delayed so that he might buy Union Pacific stock before the public had knowledge of the increased rate. It would have been an unnecessary and foolish thing to do, because it was practically certain — as certain as anything can be — that the board would declare any dividend, within the legal limit of income, that he might recommend. He was better informed than anybody else with regard to Union Pacific finances and prospects. He felt sure, as early as May, that the company could maintain a ten per cent rate, and he knew that if he advised it the directors would unhesitatingly adopt it. Assuming, therefore, that he wished to increase his holdings, he would not have waited until August, but would have bought in the spring, when the stock was temporarily depressed by the San Francisco earthquake and fire. He could have got it then much more cheaply than at any later time, because, under the

influence of large earnings and a general anticipation
of an increased rate, the stock had been steadily
rising for weeks before the board met. Mr. Harriman's invariable practice was to buy Union Pacific
stock "whenever prices were low," [1] and it would
have been a reversal of that practice if he had
waited for the high prices of August when he was
perfectly well aware that the stock was selling much
below its real value in May.

But, it may be asked, if he did not buy in the
interval between the declaration of the ten per cent
dividend and the announcement of it, why did he
refuse to answer the direct question that was asked
him by the Interstate Commerce Commission?
Simply because eminent legal counsel had advised
him that, in order to sustain his legal position while
under inquiry, he must be consistent and refuse to
answer any questions concerning his individual purchases and sales. He could not answer some without
answering all, and such questions were an invasion
of his personal rights. In taking the course he did,
therefore, he merely followed the advice of his counsel. The Commission tried to force him to answer
by resorting to the courts, but upon appeal to the
United States Supreme Court his position was
sustained.

[1] Testimony before the Interstate Commerce Commission, p. 180.

Mr. Kahn has said that "a man at the head of a great corporation must not only do right, but he must be very careful to avoid even appearances tending to arouse suspicion of his not doing right." Unquestionably true! But it is doubtful whether Mr. Harriman gave a thought to the "sinister interpretation" that might be put upon a few hours' delay in the announcement of the dividend. He was thinking of the directors, Hughitt and Frick, who were unavoidably absent from the meeting, and he seems to have been unaware of the comments that were being made in the Street until James Stillman called them to his attention late that afternoon. He then ordered the announcement to be made in the Stock Exchange at the earliest possible moment.

CHAPTER XXIII
THE IMPERIAL VALLEY OASIS

NO series of events in the history of southern California is more interesting, or more dramatic, than the creation of the beautiful and fertile oasis of the Imperial Valley in the arid desert-basin of the Salton Sink; the partial transformation of this cultivated valley into a great inland sea by the furious inpour of a runaway river; the barring-out of the flood by the courage and energy of a single man, and the final development of the valley into one of the richest agricultural areas in the world.

Twenty-one years ago, the region whose productiveness now rivals that of the lower Nile was the dried-up bottom of an ancient sea. It was seldom sprinkled by rain; it was scorched by sunshine of almost equatorial intensity, and during the summer months its mirage-haunted air was frequently heated to a temperature of one hundred and twenty degrees. The greater part of it lay far below the level of the sea; nearly all of it was destitute of water and vegetation; furious dust and sand storms swept across it, and it was regarded, by all the early explorers of the Southwest, as perhaps the dreariest and most forbidding desert on the North American continent. This ancient sea-basin, which thousands of years ago held the northern part of the Gulf of California, is now the Imperial Valley — a vast agricultural and horticultural hothouse, which produces almost everything that can be grown in lower Egypt, and which has recently been described in the San Francisco "Argonaut" as "potentially the richest unified district in the United States."

As recently as the year 1900, the Imperial Valley had not a single civilized inhabitant, and not one of its hot, arid acres had ever been cultivated. Seventeen years later it had a population of more than forty thousand, with churches, banks, ice factories, electric-light plants, and fine school buildings, in half a dozen prosperous towns, and its four hundred thousand acres of cultivated land had produced, in less than a decade, crops to the value of at least fifty million dollars. The history of this fertile oasis in the Colorado Desert will forever be connected with the name of E. H. Harriman. He did not create the Imperial Valley, nor did he develop it; but he saved it from ruinous devastation at a time when the agency that had created it threatened capriciously to destroy it, and when there was no other power in the world that could give it protection.

The story of the Imperial Valley begins with the

formation, in remote geologic times, of the great shallow depression, or basin, which modern explorers have called the Salton Sink. Tens of thousands of years ago, before the appearance of man on earth, the long arm of the Pacific Ocean which is now known as the Gulf of California extended in a north-westerly direction to a point more than a hundred miles distant from its present head. Its terminus was then near the San Gorgonio Pass, about ninety miles east of the place where Los Angeles now stands, and it extended across the Colorado Desert to the site of the present town of Yuma. If it had not been affected by external forces, it would prob-ably have retained to the present day its ancient boundary line; but into it, on its eastern side, hap-pened to empty one of the mightiest rivers of the Great West — the Colorado — and by this agency the upper part of the Gulf was gradually separated from the lower, and was finally turned into a salt-water lake, equal in extent to the Great Salt Lake in Utah. This detached body of ocean water, which had formerly been the upper part of the Gulf of Cali-fornia, completely filled the basin of the Salton Sink, and had an area of approximately twenty-one hun-dred square miles.

"But how," it may be asked, "could a river, how-ever mighty, cut the Gulf of California in two, so as to separate the upper part from the lower and leave the former isolated?" Easily enough in the long ages of geologic time. A great river like the Colorado does not consist of water only. It holds in suspension and carries down to the sea a great load of sediment, which, when deposited at its mouth, gradually builds up a delta-plain of mud, and often changes topographical conditions over a wide area. It was this deposited sediment that cut the Gulf of California in two. The drainage basin of the Colorado and its tributaries extends from the Gulf of California to the southern edge of the Yellowstone National Park, and has an area of more than 260,000 square miles. Most of this area is mountainous, and the innumerable streams that tear down through its gorges and ravines erode and gather up vast quantities of sediment, which the river carries to the Gulf and finally deposits in its waters. How great a load of silt the Colorado brought down in prehistoric times we have no means of knowing; but it transports past Yuma now about 160,000,000 tons of solid matter every year, or enough to fill a reservoir one mile square to a depth of one hundred and twenty-five feet.[1] Century after century the river poured this vast quantity of silt into the Gulf opposite its mouth, and gradually built up a delta-bar which

[1] *Report* of U.S. Geological Survey for 1916.

extended westward, year by year, until it finally reached the opposite coast. The upper part of the Gulf was then separated from the lower by a natural levee, in the shape of a delta-plain, which was perhaps ten miles in width by thirty in length, and which extended from a point near the present site of Yuma to the rampart of the Cocopah Mountains at Black Butte. When the river had thus cut the Gulf of California in two, it happened to choose a course for itself on the southeastern side of the delta-plain that it had built up, and thereafter it discharged its waters into the lower Gulf, leaving what had been the upper Gulf isolated as a salt-water lake. Under the burning sun of that region about six feet of water evaporates every year, and in course of time the lake dried up, leaving the arid basin afterward known as the Salton Sink. This depression was about one hundred miles in length by thirty-five in width. It then had a maximum depth of perhaps one thousand feet, and in the deeper parts its floor was covered with an incrustation of salt.

How long this ancient sea-bottom remained dry cannot now be determined; but many thousands of years ago, probably in Middle Tertiary times, the Colorado River, which had first cut off the basin from the ocean and thus allowed it to become waterless, proceeded to refill it. Running over a raised delta-plain of silt, which sloped both ways, the river could easily be diverted to either side, and in one of its prehistoric floods it capriciously changed its course, leaving the Gulf and pouring its waters into the dry basin of the Salton Sink. When it had refilled this basin, and transformed it into a great fresh-water lake, it broke through the silt dam, or levee, on the Cocopah Mountains side, and found a new outlet to the Gulf through what is now known as Hardy's Colorado. For many years — possibly for centuries — the Salton Sink was a fresh-water lake, into which the Colorado poured 150,000,000 tons or more of silt every year. At last, suddenly or gradually, the river again changed its course, abandoning the Sink and cutting a channel to the Gulf through the eastern part of the delta-plain. Then the Salton Sea again dried up, leaving a two-hundred-mile ellipse of fresh-water shells to mark its former level.

How many times, since the Tertiary epoch, the Salton Sink has been alternately emptied and re-filled, we have no means of knowing; but the instability of the conditions that now determine the course of the Colorado below Yuma seem to indicate that, at intervals of four or five hundred years for many millenniums, the river, like a great liquid pendulum, swung back and forth across its delta, now emptying into the Gulf on the Arizona side, and then discharging into the Sink on the California side. Every time the lake was deprived of the river water, it dried up, and every time the Sink was revisited by the river, it again became a lake. That the Colorado must have returned to this basin many times, and flowed into it for long periods, is indicated by the fact that after the Sink was separated from the Gulf of California, the river carried into it something like seventeen cubic miles of silt.[1] Artesian well borings at Holtville show that the sedimentary deposits in that part of the Imperial Valley are now more than one thousand feet in depth.

For three centuries or more — from 1540 to 1902 — the Salton Sink was a hot, arid desert. Melchior Diaz, a Spanish explorer in the service of Cortes, reached the edge of it in the fall of 1540, and the Spanish captain Juan Bautista de Anza crossed it two hundred and thirty-four years later; but neither of them saw anything like a lake. The only evidence that the Colorado River ran into the Sink, at any time between 1540 and 1905, is furnished by the so-called Rocque map, now in the British Museum, which was compiled from all the sources of

---

[1] *The Imperial Valley and Salton Sink*, by H. T. Cory, formerly Chief Engineer of the California Development Company, p. 49; San Francisco, 1915 (embodying paper read January 8, 1913, before the American Society of Civil Engineers and published in its *Transactions* as "Paper 1270").

information that were in existence in 1762. This map shows a considerable body of water in the Salton Sink, with the Colorado River flowing into it; but no written record in support of the map has ever been found, and the probability is that the water was nothing more than a comparatively small lake, or lagoon, fed by the Colorado in time of flood. Overflow water in considerable quantities often reached the basin when the river happened to be more than bank full; but the main current of the Colorado continued to flow into the Gulf, and the flood water in the Sink soon evaporated.

In the latter part of the eighteenth century and the first half of the nineteenth, many Spanish and American pathfinders crossed the Sink on their way from Yuma to the California missions, but none of them found anything like a lake. Colonel W. H. Emory, who traversed it with General Kearny in the fall of 1846, described it as a hot, arid desert, where there was a stretch of "ninety miles from water to water," and where no vegetation could be found except scattered desert shrubs and two small patches of sunburned grass. Captain A. R. Johnson, who also accompanied the Kearny expedition, was the first to notice the fact that this stretch of waterless desert was the dried-up bottom of an ancient lake; but neither he nor Colonel Emory observed the still more suggestive fact that it was below the level of the sea. In the deepest part of the basin, near the present station of Salton, they discovered a small lagoon; but its water proved to be so saturated with alkali and salt that it was "wholly unfit for man or brute." Three years later, gold-seekers from the East began to take this route to the Pacific Coast, and Bayard Taylor, in his "Eldorado," has given their impressions of the Salton Sink in the following words:

The emigrants by the Gila route gave a terrible account of the crossing of the Great Desert lying west of the Colorado. They described this region as scorching and sterile — a country of burning salt plains and shifting hills of sand, where the only signs of human habitation were the bones of animals and men scattered along the trails.

Such, seventy-five years ago, was the Salton Sink, and such it had been during the three preceding centuries of recorded history. If any one had then ventured to predict that this dried-up bed of the Gulf of California, this hot, sterile, and apparently irreclaimable desert, would eventually become a beautiful cultivated valley, producing cotton, barley, alfalfa, dates, melons and fruit, to the value of ten or fifteen million dollars every year, he would have been generally regarded as a visionary enthusiast, if not a desert-crazed monomaniac.

Although, at the beginning of the "gold rush" to California in 1849, the Salton Sink had been known to the Spániards for more than three centuries, and to American explorers for at least twenty years, no scientific examination of it had ever been made. Four years later, however, in 1853, Jefferson Davis, who was then Secretary of War, prevailed upon Congress to authorize a series of explorations for the discovery of a practicable railroad route to the Pacific Coast. Lieutenant R. S. Williamson, of the United States Topographic Engineers, was selected as leader of the southern expedition, and with him, as geologist, went Professor William P. Blake, of New York, a young graduate of the Yale Scientific School, who afterward attained great distinction as geologist, explorer, and mining engineer, in fields as widely separated as Arizona, Alaska, and Japan. Professor Blake was the first to explain the origin of the Salton Sink, to trace its ancient history, and to give a name to the great fresh-water lake that it had once held. He was also the first to suggest the possibility of irrigating it, and to predict that when it should be supplied with water it would "yield crops of almost any kind." Reclamation of desert areas is now comparatively common; but sixty years ago, only a bold and original mind could have entertained the idea of getting crops out of such a "Death Valley" as the

Salton Sink then was. Professor Blake, however, had the imagination of an investigator, tempered by the accurate knowledge of a scientist, and he could see that the sedimentary deposits in that ancient sea-basin needed only water to make them fertile.

The Kearny expedition of 1846, and the Bartlett and Williamson surveys in 1850 and 1853, demonstrated the practicability of reaching California by the southern route, and thousands of emigrants, attracted to the Pacific Coast by the discovery of gold, went that way in order to avoid the high mountains and the snow that they would have encountered farther north. This rising tide of travel soon led to improvement in the means of transportation. Early in the "gold rush," Dr. A. L. Lincoln, a relative of Abraham Lincoln, established a permanent ferry across the Colorado, near the junction of that river with the Gila; a few years later, seventy-four camels and dromedaries were imported from Africa for use on the desert part of the route; and in 1857, a private company began running bimonthly stages between San Antonio, Texas, and San Diego, California. Finally, in 1858, the Government established the "Butterfield Overland Mail," which ran a semi-weekly line of coaches from St. Louis to San Francisco, by way of El Paso, Yuma, and the Colorado Desert, on a time schedule of twenty-five days.

This line was well equipped with more than a hundred specially constructed Concord coaches, a thousand horses, seven hundred mules, and about one hundred and fifty drivers. It received from the Government a subsidy of $600,000 a year, and was the longest continuous horse-express line then in existence on the North American continent. Until the outbreak of the Civil War, this southern route was the main artery of travel from the eastern States to the Pacific Coast; and it is estimated that, between 1849 and 1860, eight thousand emigrants crossed the Colorado Desert on their way to California.

Of all these eight thousand gold-seekers or pioneers, only one seems to have been impressed by the agricultural possibilities of the Salton Sink. Dr. O. M. Wozencraft, who has been described as "a man of marked personality and far-reaching vision who lived a generation before his time," crossed the Sink on his way to San Bernardino some time in the early fifties; noticed the deposit of silt in the bed of the ancient lake; observed that the shallow basin lay so far below the level of the Colorado River that it might easily be irrigated therefrom; and reached the conclusion, previously stated by Professor Blake, that the arid waste of the Sink, if adequately supplied with water, could be made to "yield crops of

almost any kind." This idea so took possession of
his mind that, during the next five or six years, he
spent much of his time and a large part of his private
means in promoting schemes for the irrigation of this
desert area. His engineer, Ebenezer Hadley, of San
Diego, made a preliminary survey of the Sink, and
recommended a canal location practically identical
with that which forty years later was adopted. In
1859, upon the initiative of Dr. Wozencraft, the
California legislature asked Congress to cede to the
State three million acres of arid land, including the
Salton Sink, for irrigation purposes. The bill was
favorably reported by a House committee, but failed
to pass. The Congressmen of that time regarded the
reclamation of the Colorado Desert as a subject for
jocular rather than serious treatment, and most of
them were in sympathy with the California humor-
ist, J. Ross Browne, who said, "I can see no great
obstacle to success except the porous nature of the
sand. By removing the sand from the desert, success
would be insured at once."

With the failure of Dr. Wozencraft's attempt to
bring about the reclamation of the Colorado Desert,
interest in that region gradually waned. The Butterfield Overland Mail service to the Pacific Coast was
discontinued; a new "Pony Express" line to San
Francisco, by way of Salt Lake City, was estab-

lished; and before 1865, the southern route, via
Yuma and the Colorado Desert, had been practically abandoned. Dr. Wozencraft continued talking, to all who would listen, about his scheme for
the irrigation of the Salton Sink; but most people
regarded it as visionary, and nobody seemed inclined to take it up. Only in 1891, thirty-eight years
after Professor Blake first suggested irrigation, and
twenty-nine years after Dr. Wozencraft's bill failed
in Congress, was a serious attempt made to realize
the "dream" of turning water into the Salton Sink
and creating a fertile oasis in the heart of the Colorado Desert.

In 1891, John C. Beatty, of California, another
man who had imagination and foresight, became
interested in the agricultural possibilities of the
Colorado Desert, and formed a corporation under
the name of "The California Irrigation Company"
for the purpose of carrying water into the Salton Sink
from the Colorado River. He engaged as his technical adviser Mr. C. R. Rockwood, who had been in
the employ of the United States Reclamation Service, and who was regarded as "a shrewd and clever
man and engineer." [1] Mr. Rockwood made a careful
survey of the Colorado delta, and found, as Lieutenant Bergland had found in an earlier survey, that

[1] Mr. H. T. Cory.

between the river and the Sink there was a natural
obstacle in the shape of a range of sand hills, which
extended southward to the border line of Mexico.
All natural overflows of the river, in prehistoric
times, had been south of this barrier, and Mr. Rockwood thought that it would be easier and more
economical to follow the river's ancient track than
to put a conduit through these hills on the American
side of the boundary. He proposed, therefore, to
take water from the Colorado at Potholes, twelve
miles above Yuma, carry it southward into Mexico,
thence westward around the promontory of sand
hills, and finally northward, across the line again,
into southern California. This plan would involve
the digging of a curving canal, forty or fifty miles in
length, through Mexican territory; but it would
obviate the necessity of cutting through the sand
hills, and would perhaps enable the diggers to utilize,
on the Mexican side, one of the dry barrancas, or
ancient overflow channels, through which the Colorado discharged into the Sink in ages past.

Owing to the lack of public confidence in reclamation experiments, Mr. Beatty and his associates were
not able to secure as much capital as they needed
for their enterprise, and when the monetary panic
of 1893 came, they found themselves involved in
financial difficulties from which they could not ex-

tricate themselves. In the latter part of 1893 the California Irrigation Company went into bankruptcy, and its maps, records, and engineering data were turned over to Mr. Rockwood, in satisfaction of a judgment that he obtained in a suit for his unpaid salary.[1]

This seemed likely to put an end to the Salton Sink project; but Mr. Rockwood, whose observations and work in the Colorado delta had given him unbounded faith in the ultimate success of the scheme, determined to undertake the promotion of it himself. After several years of endeavor, he succeeded in forming another organization which was incorporated in New Jersey, on the 21st of April, 1896, under the title of "The California Development Company." For two years or more, this corporation tried to get permission from the Mexican Government to hold land, acquire rights, and dig an irrigating canal south of the boundary line; but the Mexican authorities refused to make any concessions, and it was finally found necessary to organize a subsidiary Mexican company. This corporation, which had a nominal capital of $62,000, was wholly owned and controlled by the California Development Company, but it operated under a Mexican charter.

As the financial resources of both companies were

[1] Mr. Cory.

largely on paper, it then became necessary to secure real capital for the prosecution of the work, and this task Mr. Rockwood found extremely difficult. The proposed reclamation of an arid desert. where the thermometer went in summer to 120 in the shade, and where only two or three inches of rain fell in the course of the whole year, did not strike Eastern capitalists as a very promising venture, and most of them were disinclined to go into it. At last, however, in 1898, Mr. Rockwood secured a promise from certain capitalists in New York that they would advance the necessary funds; but two days before the papers were to be signed, the American battleship Maine was blown up in the harbor of Havana, and this catastrophe, together with the war that followed it, put an end to the negotiations.

But the plan for the irrigation of the Salton Sink was not destined to fail. Among the men with whom Dr. Wozencraft discussed it, in the early eighties, was George Chaffey, a civil engineer and irrigation expert of Los Angeles, who had had a good deal of experience in dealing with water problems, and who had already established successful irrigation systems in other parts of California.[1] Mr. Chaffey de-

---

[1] In his *Imperial Valley and Salton Sink*, Mr. H. T. Cory, formerly chief engineer of the California Development Company, refers to Mr. Chaffey in the following words:

"The writer takes pleasure in expressing appreciation of the stand-

clined to go into it at Dr. Wozencraft's solicitation, not because he was afraid of the engineering difficulties involved, but because he thought that the torrid climate of the Sink would prevent colonization of it, even if the colonists were promised plenty of water. Most men, he reasoned, would be frightened by the prospect of having to do hard agricultural labor in shade temperatures of 110 to 120, and sun temperatures of perhaps 140 to 150. They simply would not go to a place where they would be subjected to such heat. Some years later, however, Mr. Chaffey carried through successfully an irrigation enterprise in the interior of Australia, where the temperature in the shade often reached a maximum of 125, but where, nevertheless, men were able to work without danger or serious inconvenience. This changed his view of irrigation in the Colorado Desert; and in 1900, when the California Development Company seemed unable to get money enough for its project elsewhere, Mr. Chaffey offered to finance the under-

ing of Mr. George M. Chaffey in irrigation work in the West. The Ontario Colony he founded in 1883 was selected ten years later as a model for the irrigation exhibit at the World's Exposition, and in his work at Mildura, Australia, he designed, had built in England, and installed, the first centrifugal pumps on the same shaft with a total capacity of 320 cubic feet per second lifted 20 feet. He is at present, among other things, head of the magnificent water system irrigating 10,000 acres of citrus lands near Whittier, California, including the highest priced agricultural lands in California ($5000 per acre). Furthermore he is a man of affairs, and of large means which he acquired principally in irrigation enterprises and banking."

taking and superintend the work. His proposals
were accepted, and on the 3d of April, 1900, he became president of the company, and signed a contract by which he bound himself to construct canals,
at a cost of not more than $150,000, which would
carry to the Imperial Valley 400,000 acre-feet of
water per annum.[1]

Mr. Chaffey and his associates modified the plan
of Mr. Rockwood by taking water from the Colorado
at Pilot Knob, nearly opposite Yuma, instead of at
Potholes, twelve miles above. Putting in a head-
gate there, they carried their main canal southward
across the Mexican boundary, in a course nearly
parallel with the river, until they reached the barranca, or dry overflow channel, known as the
"Alamo." As this ancient watercourse meandered
westward in the direction of the Salton Sink, they
were able to clear it out, enlarge it, and utilize most
of it as a part of their irrigation system. Then, at a
point about forty miles west of the Colorado, they
carried their canal northward, across the boundary line again, into southern California. The work
throughout was pushed with great energy, and on the
14th of May, 1901, a little more than a year after
Mr. Chaffey assumed direction of affairs, water was
turned in at the Pilot Knob head-gate, and the irri-

[1] Andrew M. Chaffey.

gation of the Salton Sink became a certainty, if not
a fully accomplished fact.

As the California Development Company was a
water-selling company only, and had no proprietary
interest in the lands to be irrigated, it was thought
best to form another organization for the promotion
of settlement; and in March, 1901, the Imperial
Land Company was incorporated for the purpose of
attracting colonists, laying out town sites, and developing the Sink by bringing its lands into cultivation. Then Mr. Chaffey and the Land Company
began an advertising campaign for the purpose of
interesting the general public in the scheme; and in
order not to frighten settlers and small investors
by using in their advertisements and circulars the
ominous words "desert" and "Sink," they changed
the name of the basin that they proposed to irrigate
and called it "The Imperial Valley." This title was
evidently alluring, because it attracted small investors in all parts of the East, and particularly in
New England. The Development Company's stock
was bought, for example, in places as far away from
the Salton Sink as Boston, Concord, Hopedale, and
Waverley, Massachusetts; Barre and Montpelier,
Vermont; Portsmouth, New Hampshire; Elgin, Illinois; Portland, Oregon; and Toronto, Canada.[1]

[1] List of stockholders in Southern Pacific office, New York.

Settlers soon began to come in; mutual water companies were organized; and before the 3d of April, 1902, when Mr. Chaffey severed his connection with the company, four hundred miles of irrigating ditches had been dug, and water was available for one hundred thousand acres or more of irrigable land.[1]

About this time, however, the future of the Valley was seriously imperiled by unfavorable reports concerning its soil. In the early part of 1902, the Bureau of Soils of the United States Agricultural Department published the results of a survey of the irrigable lands in the Colorado Desert, and reported that they were so impregnated with alkali that very few things could be successfully grown on them.

One hundred and twenty-five thousand acres of land [the report said] have already been taken up by prospective settlers, many of whom talk of planting crops which it will be absolutely impossible to grow. They must early find that it will be useless to attempt their growth. . . . No doubt the best thing to do is to raise such crops as sugar beet, sorghum, and date palm (if the climate will permit), that are suited to such alkali conditions, and abandon as worthless the lands which contain too much alkali to grow those crops.[2]

This report, which was widely quoted and commented upon, acted as a serious check to the colonization of the Valley; and if it had been made two or

[1] Andrew M. Chaffey.
[2] *Field Operations of the Bureau of Soils*, U.S. Department of Agriculture, 1901, p. 587.

three years earlier, it might have been fatal to the whole irrigation project. Fortunately, however, the crops raised by a few farmers who had already been cultivating this "alkali-impregnated" land proved conclusively that the report of the analysis of the soil made by the Government experts was unduly pessimistic, if not wholly erroneous. Almost every-thing that was tried *did* grow, in spite of expert predictions, and the practical experience of men on the ground gradually revived public confidence in the productiveness of the irrigated lands. The colonization and development of the Valley then proceeded with great rapidity. The two thousand settlers on the ground at the end of 1902 increased to seven thousand in 1903 and to more than ten thousand in 1904. A branch of the Southern Pacific Railroad was built through the Valley from Imperial Junction to Calexico and Mexicali; town sites were laid out in six or seven different places; the water system was extended by the digging of nearly four hundred additional miles of irrigating ditches and canals; and before the 1st of January, 1905, one hundred and twenty thousand acres of reclaimed land were actually under cultivation, while two hundred thousand acres more had been covered by water stock.

The observed fertility of the soil completely dis-

credited the reports of the Government experts, and
more than justified the prediction made by Professor Blake half a century before that when the Sink
should be supplied with water, it would produce
"crops of almost any kind." Grapes, melons, and
garden vegetables matured in the Valley earlier than
in any other part of California; barley was a profitable crop; alfalfa could be cut five or six times a
year; and the finest quality of long-staple Egyptian
cotton yielded more than a bale (five hundred
pounds) to the acre. Experiments proved also that
the climate and soil were well adapted to the culture
of grapes, grapefruit, oranges, lemons, olives, figs,
dates, pomegranates, apricots, peaches, and pears.

The fear that men would not be willing or able to
do hard work in the hot climate of the Valley proved
to be wholly groundless. Great heat is not necessarily weakening or prostrating unless it is accompanied with great humidity, and the air of the
Valley is at all seasons extremely dry. In a discussion of this subject, Mr. H. T. Cory, formerly chief
engineer of the California Development Company,
says:

The climate of the region, with its long, hot, dry summers, is peculiarly favorable to agricultural luxuriance.
Thus it is that here the very earliest grapes, fruits, and
vegetables are produced for the United States market,
with the consequent advantage of commanding the

highest prices. This is notably true of the Imperial Valley cantaloupe, now famous all over this country, and of the early grapes, asparagus, etc. On account of the very low humidity and gentle winds which blow most of the time in hot weather, the sensible temperature — which is indicated by the wet-bulb thermometer readings and gives the measure of heat felt by the human body — is much less than the actual temperature as measured by the dry bulb. It is conservative to say that a temperature of 110 in Imperial Valley is not more uncomfortable than 95 in Los Angeles, or 85 in the more humid sections of the Eastern States. Furthermore the nights are always cool, the low humidity resulting in rapid and large daily temperature variations.

Under these favoring conditions of soil and climate, it seemed almost certain, in 1904, that the Imperial Valley would have a great and prosperous future; but no forecast in that region is trustworthy unless it takes into account the irrigating agency, as well as the climate and the soil. The Colorado River created the Salton Sink, and made fertile the Imperial Valley; but it could destroy, as well as create; and in 1904 it showed itself in a new aspect and threatened the Valley with a terrible calamity.

The most serious problem with which engineers have to deal in the irrigation of arid land from a turbid river is the getting rid of silt, and this problem is a particularly difficult one in the Imperial Valley, owing to the immense amount of sediment that the irrigating water contains. The Colorado

River, until after it passes the Grand Cañon, is almost everywhere a swift, turbulent stream, with great eroding capacity. As Mr. E. C. LaRue has said, in a brief but graphic description of it:

When the snows melt in the Rocky and Wind River Mountains, a million cascade brooks unite to form a thousand torrent creeks; a thousand torrent creeks unite to form half a hundred rivers beset with cataracts; half a hundred roaring rivers unite to form the Colorado, which flows, a mad, turbid stream, into the Gulf of California.[1]

Such a river, naturally, dissolves the earth and gnaws the rocks over which it tears its way, and takes up millions of tons of solid matter, in the shape of gravel, sand, and finely pulverized soil. This great volume of sediment, when finally dropped, not only tends to change the river's course by creating bars at or near its mouth, but gradually fills up the irrigating ditches and canals and thus lessens their carrying capacity. A single day's supply of water for the Imperial Valley contains silt enough to make a levee twenty feet high, twenty feet wide, and one mile long.[2] If this silt is not dredged out, sluiced out, or collected in a settling basin, it eventually raises the beds of the canals, fills the ditches, and chokes up the whole irrigation system.

[1] *Colorado River and its Utilization*, a Geological Survey report, Government Printing Office, Washington, 1916.
[2] *Imperial Valley Press*, July 25, 1916.

The managers of the California Development Company had difficulty, almost from the first, in keeping their waterways open. As more and more land was brought into cultivation, more and more water was required, while the silting-up of the canals lessened the ability of the company to meet the constantly increasing demand. There was a shortage as early as the winter of 1902–03; but the situation did not become serious until the following year, when the main canal, for a distance of four miles below the intake, became so silted-up that it could not possibly carry the volume of water that was imperatively needed. An attempt was made to remedy this state of affairs by putting in a waste-gate, eight miles below the intake, for the purpose of sluicing out the channel in time of high water.

The idea [as stated by Mr. Cory] was to divert a large quantity of water during the flood season, waste it through the Best waste-gate, and in this way scour out the upper portion of the canal. At first, the action was as expected, and some two feet in the bottom were carried away. When, however, the river reached its maximum height, . . . and carried an excessive silt content, especially of the heavier and sandy type, this scouring action was entirely overcome, and the bottom of this stretch was raised approximately one foot higher than during the previous year.

This silting-up of the main canal, and the consequent reduction of its carrying capacity, caused great injury to the agricultural interests of the Valley. Crops in many places perished for lack of water, and hundreds of farmers put in damage claims, which amounted in the aggregate to half a million dollars. In the late summer of 1904, it became evident that radical measures would have to be taken at once to increase the water supply. As the managers of the company had neither the financial means nor the requisite machinery for quickly dredging out the silted part of the canal, they decided, in September of that year, to cut a new intake from the river at a point about four miles south of the international boundary. This would eliminate the choked-up part of the canal, and let water directly into the part that was unobstructed.

If President Heber and Chief Engineer Rockwood had been aware of the fact that the Colorado was even then preparing to pour its waters into the Salton Sink, by making one of its semi-millennial changes of course, they might perhaps have fortified the western bank instead of cutting through it; but there was little or nothing to show the extreme instability of the conditions that were then determining the trend of the river across its delta, and the idea that it might burst through this intake and again turn the Valley into a fresh-water lake does not seem to have occurred to any one. The cutting was therefore made and the water shortage relieved; but at the cost of imminent peril to the whole Valley and its twelve thousand inhabitants.

In view of the tremendous and disastrous consequences of this measure, it is only fair that Chief Engineer Rockwood should be allowed to state, with some fullness, his reasons for adopting it, and for failing to put in a head-gate to control the flow of water through the channel and thus prevent its enlargement. In an article entitled "Born of the Desert," published in the second annual magazine number of the "Calexico Chronicle," in May, 1909, he sets forth his reasons in the following words:

As soon as the summer flood (1904) dropped, I discovered that instead of the bottom [of the canal] being lower, it was approximately one foot above that of the year previous. . . . We knew that with the dredging tools which we had it would be impossible to dredge out this four miles of canal in sufficient time for the uses of the Valley, providing the water in the river should drop as low as it had the previous year. . . . We were then confronted with the proposition of doing one of two things, either cutting a new heading from the canal to the river below the silted four-mile section of the canal, or else allowing the Valley to pass through another winter with an insufficient water supply. The latter proposition we could not face, for the reason that the people of the Valley had an absolute right to demand that water should be furnished them, and it was questionable in our minds as to whether we would be able to keep out of bankruptcy if we were to be confronted by another period of shortage in the coming season of 1904–05.

The cutting of the lower intake, after mature deliberation, and upon the insistence of several of the leading men of the Valley, was decided upon. We hesitated about making this cut, not so much because we believed we were incurring danger of the river's breaking through, as from the fact that we had been unable to obtain the consent of the Government of Mexico to make it, and we believed that we were jeopardizing our Mexican rights should the cut be made without the consent of the Government. On a telegraphic communication, however, from our attorney in the City of Mexico, to go ahead and make the cut, we did so, under the presumption that he had obtained the necessary permit from the Mexican authorities. It was some time after this, in fact after the cut was made in the river, before we discovered that he had been unable to obtain the formal permit, but had simply obtained the promise of certain officials that we would not be interfered with, providing that plans were at once submitted for the necessary controlling structures to be placed in this heading.

. . . In cutting from the main canal to the river at this point, we had to dredge a distance of 3300 feet only, through easy material to remove, while an attempt to dredge out the main canal above would have meant the dredging of four miles of very difficult material. We began the cut the latter end of September and completed it in about three weeks. As soon as the cut was decided upon, elaborate plans for a controlling gate were immediately started, and when completed, early in November, were immediately forwarded to the City of Mexico for the approval of the engineers of the Mexican Government, without whose approval we had no authority or right to construct the gate. Notwithstanding the insistence of our attorney in the City of Mexico, and various telegraphic communications insisting upon this approval being hurried, we were unable to obtain it until twelve months afterward, namely, the month of December, 1905.

In the meantime, serious trouble had begun. We have since been accused of gross negligence and criminal carelessness in making this cut; but I doubt as to whether any one should be accused of negligence, or carelessness, in failing to foresee what had never happened before. We had before us at the time the history of the river as shown by the rod-readings kept at Yuma for a period of twenty-seven years. In the twenty-seven years there had been but three winter floods. In no winter of the twenty-seven had there been two winter floods. It was not probable, then, that there would be any winter flood to enlarge the cut made by us, and without doubt, as it seemed to us, we would be able to close the cut, before the approach of the summer flood, by the same means that we had used in closing the cut for three successive years around the Chaffey gate at the head of the canal.[1] During this winter of 1905, however, we had more than one winter flood. The first flood came, I believe, about the first of February, but did not enlarge the lower intake. On the contrary, it caused such a silt deposit in the lower intake that I found it necessary, after the flood had passed, to put the dredge through in order to deepen the channel sufficiently to allow water to come into the valley for the use of the people. This was followed shortly by another heavy flood that did not erode the banks of the intake, but, on the contrary, the same as the first, caused a

[1] The sill of the Chaffey gate proved to be too high for low stages of water, and a canal, at a lower level, was cut around the structure and closed every year with a brush-and-earth dam before the approach of the summer flood.

deposit of silt and a necessary dredging. We were not alarmed by these floods, as it was still very early in the season. No damage had been done by them, and we still believed that there would be no difficulty in closing the intake before the approach of the summer flood, which was the only one we feared. However, the first two floods were followed by a third, coming sometime in March, and this was sufficient notice to us that we were up against a very unusual season, something unknown in the history of the river as far back as we were able to reach; and as it was now approaching the season of the year when we might reasonably expect the river surface to remain at an elevation that would allow sufficient water for the uses of the Valley to be gotten through the upper intake, we decided to close the lower.[1]

At the time when the first attempt to close the intake was made, the cutting was about sixty feet wide. A dam of piles, brush, and sandbags was thrown across it in March, 1905, but it had hardly been completed when another flood came down the Colorado and swept it away. A second dam of the same kind, built a few weeks later, shared the same fate. By the middle of June, the river was discharging ninety thousand cubic feet of water per second; the width of the lower intake had increased from sixty feet to one hundred and sixty; water was overflowing the banks of the main canal and accumulating in the deepest part of the Sink; and a new Salton Sea was in process of formation.

[1] " Born of the Desert," by C. R. Rockwood, *Calexico Chronicle*, May, 1909.

Such was the state of affairs when Mr. Harriman
and the Southern Pacific Railroad Company first
became directly interested in the problem of river
control. Early in 1905, the California Development
Company, finding itself in pecuniary difficulties,
applied to Mr. Julius Kruttschnitt, general manager
of the Southern Pacific, for a loan, on the alleged
ground that the Imperial Valley was furnishing a
great deal of traffic to the railroad, and the irrigation
company was therefore warranted in asking for
financial assistance. Mr. Kruttschnitt, however, declined to consider the application. The petitioners
then addressed the president of the railroad company, Mr. E. H. Harriman, who, it was thought,
might be induced to give the necessary aid, even
though he had no personal interest in the Valley and
no connection whatever with the California Development Company. Mr. Harriman, as a man of imagination and far-seeing vision, was naturally in sympathy with the bold attempt to irrigate and reclaim
the arid lands of the Colorado Desert, and when the
matter of the loan was presented to him, he not only
gave it immediate consideration, but ordered an
investigation and a report. He finally consented,
against the advice of Mr. Kruttschnitt and other
counselors, to loan the Development Company
$200,000, "to be used in paying off certain of its

floating indebtedness and in completing and perfecting its canal system." Inasmuch, however, as the financial management of the irrigation company had not always been judicious, Mr. Harriman and the Southern Pacific stipulated that they should have the right to select three of its directors, one of whom should be president, and that fifty-one per cent of its stock (6300 shares) should be placed in the hands of a trustee as collateral security for the loan. This stipulation was agreed to, and on the 20th of June, 1905, the Southern Pacific Company, as chief creditor, took temporary control of the California Development Company by selecting three of its directors, and by appointing as its president Mr. Epes Randolph, of Tucson, who was then acting also as president of the Harriman lines in Arizona and Mexico.[1]

When Mr. Harriman and the Southern Pacific

[1] Mr. Randolph was a distinguished civil engineer and railroad manager, who had been, at one time, superintendent of the Tucson division of the Southern Pacific under Mr. C. P. Huntington. After the latter's death, he went to Los Angeles, where he built and managed Mr. H. E. Huntington's interurban system of electric railways and where he made the acquaintance of Mr. Harriman. Finding that his health would not permit him to live in the climate of Los Angeles, he returned in 1904 to Arizona, where he was appointed president of the Arizona Eastern Railroad Company and the Southern Pacific Railroad Company of Mexico — Harriman lines. Mr. Randolph, at that time, was regarded as one of the ablest civil engineers in the United States, and he had already had much experience in dealing with river-control problems in the South. He was also one of Mr. Harriman's most trusted counselors, and it was upon his recommendation that the Southern Pacific Company's lines were extended into Mexico.

thus took over the management of the California Development Company, they had no intention of assuming its responsibilities, directing its engineering work, or deriving revenue from its operations. All they aimed to do was to see that the money loaned was honestly and judiciously spent. The financial management of the company had not previously been above criticism, .to say the least; and Mr. Harriman was fully justified in taking such control as might be necessary to ensure proper expenditure of the funds that the Southern Pacific Company furnished. From the representations made by the Development Company at that time, it was thought that the lower Mexican intake might be closed at a cost of not more than $20,000, and the Company proposed to use the remainder of the $200,000 loan in "completing and perfecting its canal system," under the direction of its own technical experts. When, however, President Randolph made a personal investigation of the state of affairs, shortly after his appointment, he found the situation much more serious than the Development Company had represented it to be, and telegraphed Mr. Harriman that the Imperial Valley could not be saved by the expenditure of $200,000. To control the river, he said, under the conditions then existing, would be extremely difficult. Nobody could foresee what

would be the ultimate cost of the engineering operations, but it "might easily run into three quarters
of a million dollars."

Mr. Harriman could have insisted, even then,
upon a return of the unspent loan, and could have
withdrawn from the financially hazardous undertaking; but instead of doing this, he telegraphed
President Randolph: "Are you certain you can put
the river back into the old channel?" Mr. Randolph
replied: "I am certain that it can be done." "Then,"
wired Mr. Harriman, "go ahead and do it."

As Chief Engineer Rockwood was thought to be
familiar with the problem of river control, and quite
competent to deal with it, he was allowed, at first,
to take such measures for closing the intake as
seemed to him best. He had made the cutting long
before the Southern Pacific had anything to do with
the irrigation of the Valley, and upon him, primarily,
devolved the responsibility of averting consequences
that might be disastrous.

Although the Mexican cutting, at that time, had
virtually become a crevasse, the flow through it
was not great enough to endanger the cultivated
lands of the Valley. The excess of water overflowed
the banks of the canal — the old Alamo barranca —
but it ran into the deepest part of the Sink, where it
slowly accumulated without flooding anything ex-

cept the works of the New Liverpool Salt Company.
Civil Engineer C. E. Grunsky, of the United States
Reclamation Service, who made an inspection of the
intake three days after the loan to the California
Development Company, described the situation as
"not serious, but sufficiently alarming to require
some attention." The most disquieting feature of it
was the steepness of the incline toward the Imperial
Valley as compared with that toward the Gulf of
California. The fall of the Colorado from the intake
to the Gulf was only one hundred feet, while that
from the intake to the bottom of the Valley was
nearly four hundred feet. As the distance was about
the same, either way, the Valley incline was approximately four times as steep as the river-bed incline,
and if the whole stream should break through the
intake and go down the steeper slope, the velocity
of the current would make the stopping of it extremely difficult, if not absolutely impossible. When
a turbulent river, in flood, discharges at the rate of
one hundred thousand cubic feet per second down
an easily eroded and comparatively steep declivity
into an immense basin four hundred feet deep, it
soon gets beyond control.

The difficulty of dealing with these conditions was
greatly increased by the impossibility of predicting
or anticipating floods. The annual rise of the Colo-

rado, above its junction with the Gila, begins in the spring, reaches its maximum in July, and subsides to normal about the middle of August. This period of high water is fairly regular and may be counted upon. Floods in the drainage basin of the Gila, however, are capricious, occur at all seasons of the year, and are particularly violent in the fall and winter months. "These floods," as Mr. Cory says, "are far more to be feared and reckoned with, in preparing and conducting engineering work along the lower Colorado River, than anything coming down the Colorado River proper," partly because they come suddenly and unexpectedly, and partly because they carry immense quantities of driftwood. During the Gila flood of November 29–30, 1905, the water at Yuma rose ten feet in ten hours, with a maximum discharge of 102,000 cubic feet per second, while driftwood almost completely covered the water surface. Such floods, coming with little or no warning, are almost irresistible.

When, in July, 1905, the summer flood in the Colorado began to subside, Chief Engineer Rockwood determined to fend off the main current, and lessen the pressure on the crevasse, by means of a jetty. Just opposite the intake was a bush-overgrown island, five eighths of a mile long by a quarter of a mile wide, which split the river into two channels. Across the western channel, from the head of the island to the bank, a semi-barrier was built, of piling, barbed wire, and brush. This obstruction, it was thought, might check the flow into the western channel, cause a deposit of heavy silt, and eventually create a bar which would deflect the main current around the northern end of the island and thus carry it away from the mouth of the crevasse. The attempt was only partly successful. A bar was formed, but it did not completely close the channel, nor deflect the main current. There was still an opening, about one hundred and twenty-five feet in width, through which the rush of water was so great that it could not be controlled. The attempt to deflect the main current into the eastern channel, by means of a jetty, was then abandoned.

Up to this time, the Southern Pacific Company had not taken part directly in the work of river control. After the failure of the jetty, however, in August, 1905, President Randolph sent his assistant, Mr. H. T. Cory,[1] to the scene of operations, with instructions to confer with Chief Engineer Rockwood and ascertain what his views and intentions were.

[1] Mr. Cory was a talented civil engineer who had left his professorial chair in the engineering department of the University of Cincinnati to enter the service of the Southern Pacific Railroad system. Just prior to this time — in May, 1905 — he had been appointed assistant to President Randolph, with headquarters at Tucson.

Mr. Rockwood, at that time, did not regard the situation as at all alarming. The flow through the crevasse, he said, was doing useful work in scouring out and deepening the main canal (the old Alamo barranca) and there was little danger that the whole river would go that way. He was not in favor of closing the enlarged intake altogether, because that would shut off the water supply of the Imperial Valley and cause more damage than was then being done by the river. The deeper part of the Salton Sink, he said, was a natural drainage basin, and as it was much below the zone of cultivation in the Valley as a whole, the accumulation of water in it was not likely to do a great amount of damage.

"I told him," Mr. Cory says, "that I thought the situation was serious, even granting all he said were true; that he would better shut the break right away, for while the water might be doing good work in enlarging the canal of the California Development Company, the situation was dangerous; that it was playing with fire."

Throughout the month of August, 1905, the intake continued to widen, with the caving away of its banks, and in September Mr. Harriman and President Randolph decided that another effort must be made either to close the break, or to regulate and control the flow of water through it. About the first

of October, at the suggestion and under the supervision of Mr. E. S. Edinger, a Southern Pacific
engineer, an attempt was made to close the channel
west of the island by means of a six-hundred-foot
barrier-dam of piling, brush-mattresses, and sandbags. This dam, which was built in October and
November at a cost of about $60,000, might perhaps
have checked or lessened the flow through the crevasse if nothing unforeseen had happened; but on
the 29th–30th of November a tremendous flood,
carrying great masses of driftwood, came down the
Gila and increased the discharge of the Colorado
from 12,000 to 115,000 cubic feet per second. The
dam could not withstand such pressure, and even
before the peak of the flood was reached, it went out
altogether, leaving hardly a vestige behind. As a
large part of the island was eroded and carried away
at the same time, further operations in this locality
were regarded as impracticable. The crevasse had
then widened to six hundred feet, and nearly the
whole of the river poured through it into the deepest
part of the Sink, where there was already a lake with
a surface area of one hundred and fifty square miles.
The main line of the Southern Pacific, in many
places, was almost awash, and the whole population
of the Valley was alarmed by the prospect of being
drowned out. If the break could not be closed and

the river brought under control before the period of high water in the spring and summer of 1906, it seemed more than probable that sixty miles of the Southern Pacific track would be submerged; that the irrigation system of the California Development Company would be destroyed; and that the whole basin of the Imperial Valley would ultimately become a fresh-water lake.

The difficulty of dealing with this menacing situation was greatly increased by the necessity of furnishing an uninterrupted supply of water to the farmers of the Valley while engineering operations were in progress. It would not do to shut the river out altogether, because that would leave without irrigation nearly two hundred square miles of cultivated land. The Colorado must be controlled, but not wholly excluded. Several methods of solving this problem were suggested, but the only two that seemed likely to succeed were advocated by Consulting Engineer Schuyler and Chief Engineer Rockwood. Mr. Schuyler proposed that a new steel-and-concrete head-gate be put in near Pilot Knob, where a solid rock foundation could be secured; that the four miles of silted channel be reëxcavated and enlarged by a powerful steam dredge specially built for the purpose; and that the whole low-water flow of the river be then turned through this head-gate into the enlarged canal and thence into the Alamo barranca west of the break. By this means the settlers would be continuously supplied with water, while the crevasse-opening would be left dry enough, to close with a permanent levee or dam. The whole work, it was thought, could be finished in three months, or at least before the coming of the next summer flood.

Chief Engineer Rockwood's plan also involved the building of a new head-gate, but he proposed to locate it on the northern side of the intake, and to carry the whole low-water flow of the river through it by means of an excavated by-pass. This, too, would keep the settlers supplied with water and leave the crevasse-opening dry while it was being closed. The chief objection to the latter plan was that the head-gate would necessarily be of wood, and would have to stand on a treacherous founda-tion of easily eroded silt which might possibly be undermined. Late in November, after full considera-tion, President Randolph decided to try both plans and to work on them simultaneously. Contracts for the structural steel and iron work for the con-crete head-gate were let in Los Angeles; the ma-chinery for the 850-ton floating dredge Delta was ordered in San Francisco; materials for the Rock-wood head-gate were collected on the northern side of the intake, and work was pushed on all of these

structures with the greatest possible energy throughout the winter. In spite, however, of all efforts, none
of them could be finished in the allotted time. The
steel-and-concrete head-gate was not completed
until the 28th of June; the dredge Delta, owing to
the partial destruction of San Francisco, was not
ready until the following November, and even the
Rockwood gate, on which alternate shifts of men had
worked night and day, was not in working order
until the 18th of April. Meanwhile, the summer flood
of 1906 had begun, with a discharge of 32,200 cubic
feet per second through the crevasse. This flow
would have exceeded the capacity of the Rockwood
gate, even if it had been possible to turn the river
through the by-pass that led to it, and the attempt
to bring the Colorado under control was again temporarily abandoned.

Then a long series of misfortunes and catastrophes followed, one after another. On the 18th of
April, 1906, San Francisco was partially destroyed
by earthquake and fire, and Mr. Harriman hurried
to the scene of the disaster for the purpose of affording help. President Randolph soon joined him there,
and, at the first opportunity, described to him the
almost desperate state of affairs in the Colorado
delta. The California Development Company had
used up the $200,000 loaned to it by the Southern

Pacific the previous year; the river was still uncontrolled, and the impending flood threatened to inundate the Valley and deprive twelve thousand people of their property and homes. Mr. Harriman was not a man to be daunted or "rattled" by a sudden and menacing emergency. "There, in the bustle and confusion of temporary offices, with the ruins of San Francisco still smoking, with the facilities of his roads taxed to the utmost in carrying people away from the stricken city, with the wonderful railway system which constituted his life-work crippled to an unknown extent, and with the financial demands resulting from the disaster impossible to determine," he consented to advance an additional sum of $250,000 for controlling the Colorado River and protecting the Imperial Valley. "It has always seemed to me," writes Mr. Cory, "that this was really the most remarkable thing in the whole series of extraordinary happenings."

With the promise of this additional sum of $250,-000, President Randolph returned to the Imperial Valley to take up again the fight with the runaway river. The flood, at that time, was steadily rising; the width of the crevasse had increased to a quarter of a mile, and the Colorado was pouring into the Salton basin more than four billion cubic feet of water every twenty-four hours.

On the 19th of April, 1906, the day after the San
Francisco earthquake, Mr. C. R. Rockwood, who
had been the chief engineer of the California Development Company for about four years, tendered his
resignation, and Mr. H. T. Cory, President Randolph's assistant, was appointed in his place. The
Southern Pacific Company then assumed full control and direction of defensive operations, and all
subsequent work was planned and executed by its
engineers, with the powerful support of Mr. Harriman and his great railway system.

The task set before Messrs. Randolph, Cory,
Hind, and Clarke was one that might well have
daunted even engineers of their great ability and
experience. As the summer flood approached its
maximum, in the latter part of June, the crevasse
widened to more than half a mile, and the whole
river, rushing through the break, spread out over
an area eight or ten miles in width, and then, col-
lecting in separate streams as it ran down the slope
of the basin, discharged at last into the Salton Sea
through the flooded channel of the New River
barranca. Thousands of acres of land, covered with
growing crops, were inundated, and thousands of
acres more were so eroded and furrowed by the
torrential streams that they never could be cultivated again. The works of the New Liverpool Salt

Company were buried under sixty feet of water; the towns of Calexico and Mexicali were partially destroyed, and in many places the tracks of the Inter-California Railroad (a branch of the Southern Pacific) and the Holtville Interurban were deeply submerged or wholly carried away. The wooden flumes which carried the irrigating water over the New River barranca were swept down into the Salton Sea, and thirty thousand acres of cultivated land in the western part of the Valley became dry, barren, and uninhabitable. At the height of the flood, the Colorado discharged through the crevasse more than seventy-five thousand cubic feet of water per second, or six billion cubic feet every twenty-four hours, while the Salton Sea, into which this immense volume of water was poured, rose at the rate of seven inches per day over an area of four hundred square miles. The main line of the Southern Pacific was soon inundated, and five times in the course of the summer the company had to move its track to higher ground.

The most dangerous and alarming feature of the situation was the "cutting-back" of the torrents into which the flood-water collected as it rushed down the delta slope toward the Salton Sea. The fine silt of which the soil was composed washed out like powdered sugar, and wherever there happened to be a strong current, the flow soon produced a miniature rapid. The rapid then became a cascade, the cascade grew into a fall, and the fall finally developed into a roaring cataract, which "cut back," up-stream, at the rate sometimes of four thousand feet a day, widening as it receded, and leaving below it a deep gorge with almost perpendicular walls. Some of the gorges eroded in the light friable silt by these receding waterfalls were fifty to eighty feet deep and more than a thousand feet across. It was estimated that the channels thus formed during the floods of 1906 had an aggregate length of more than forty miles, and that the solid matter scoured out of them and carried down into the Salton Sea was nearly four times as great as the whole amount excavated in the digging of the Panama Canal. But the damage actually done by these receding waterfalls was unimportant in comparison with the damage that they threatened to do. If one of them should "cut back" far enough to break into the irrigation system of the California Development Company, all the water in the latter's canals and ditches would instantly flow down into the deep gorge below the cataract, and bring about a disaster almost unprecedented in history. The twelve thousand settlers in the desert oasis were wholly dependent upon the irrigation system for their supply of drinking water, and if that supply should be cut off, they would be compelled by thirst either to camp around the margin of the Salton Sea, which was ten or fifteen miles away from most of them, or else get out of the valley within forty-eight hours in a wild precipitate stampede. Paradoxical as it may seem, the danger of being driven out by lack of water was even greater and more immediate than the danger of being drowned out by the rising flood.

The changes in the topography of the Colorado delta brought about by the crevasse and the floods of 1906 were greater than any that had occurred there in the three preceding centuries of recorded history. In referring to them Mr. Cory says:

The effect of this flood, in a geological way, was of extraordinary interest and very spectacular. In nine months, the runaway waters of the Colorado had eroded from the New and Alamo River channels and carried down into the Salton Sea a yardage almost four times as great as that of the entire Panama Canal. The combined length of the channels cut out was almost forty-three miles, the average width being one thousand feet and the depth fifty feet. To this total of 400,000,000 to 450,000,000 cubic yards must be added almost ten per cent for side cañons, surface erosions, etc. Very rarely, if ever before, has it been possible to see a geological agency effect in a few months a change which usually requires centuries.

CHAPTER XXIV

THE FIGHT WITH A RUNAWAY RIVER

WHEN the Southern Pacific engineers undertook to avert the peril that menaced the Imperial Valley in the summer of 1906, they found little in recorded history to help or guide them. Inundations, of course, had often occurred before, on the Mississippi River and its tributaries, in the valley of "China's Sorrow," and in many other parts of the world; but these floods were merely overflows on a relatively flat surface. The cosmical plunge of a great river into the dried-up basin of an ancient sea was an unprecedented phenomenon, and one which raised engineering problems that were wholly new. Nobody had ever before tried to control a rush of 360,000,000 cubic feet of water per hour, down a four-hundred-foot slope of easily eroded silt, into a basin big enough to hold Long Island Sound. There was nothing in the past experience of the world that could suggest a practicable method of dealing with such conditions. Neither was much help to be obtained from the advice of hydraulic experts. Of the forty or fifty eminent engineers who visited the Colorado delta in 1905 and 1906, hardly any two

AT HIS PRIME

agreed upon a definite plan of defensive work, while almost every one found something objectionable in the measures suggested by others. All admitted, however, that "the situation was a desperate one"; that it was "without engineering parallel"; and that "there seemed to be only a fighting chance of controlling the river."

Mr. Harriman, who believed and who once said that "nothing is impossible," never doubted that the control of the Colorado River was within human power and human resources. In building the Lucin cut-off across the Great Salt Lake of Utah he had successfully carried through one "impossible" enterprise, and he did not hesitate to undertake another. Inspired by his invincible courage, President Randolph and his engineers set about their herculean task.

In preparing for a fifth attempt to bring the Colorado under control, they determined to modify the plan of operations previously followed by substituting rock for the materials that had before been used in the construction of dams. Practical experience had shown that piling, brush, sandbags, and earth could not be made to support the pressure of the river in full flood, while a series of rock-fill barrier dams, of sufficient width and height, might be strong enough to stand even a flood discharge of 115,000 cubic feet of water per second. In making this change of plan, Mr. Randolph acted on his own judgment and in direct opposition to the views and advice of experts who were acquainted with the situation. Almost all of the engineers who had visited the break, including many of national and international reputation, regarded a rock-fill barrier dam as wholly unworthy of consideration, for at least two reasons. First, the rock would probably sink into the soft silt bottom, and keep on going down indefinitely. It might, perhaps, be supported by a strong brush-mattress foundation, but even then, the mattress would be likely to break under the weight of the load and thus fail to answer its purpose. Second, the water going over a rock-fill dam, while it was in course of construction, would almost certainly wash away some one rock at the top. This, by increasing the overflow at that point, would dislodge more rocks, and finally create a breach that could not be closed. President Randolph who had used brush-mattresses and rock-fill dams on the Tombigbee River in Alabama many years before, fully considered these objections, but did not find them convincing and steadfastly adhered to his own plan.

The preparations made for the summer's work were far more thorough and comprehensive than any that had ever been made before. Realizing the importance of adequate transportation, President Randolph and his engineers immediately began the construction of a branch railroad from the main line of the Southern Pacific to the scene of operations at the crevasse, with ample sidings and terminal facilities at both ends. Then they borrowed from the Union Pacific three hundred of the mammoth side-dump cars known as "battleships," which had been used in the construction of the Lucin cut-off, and which had a carrying capacity of fifty or sixty tons each. The California Development Company had three light-draught steamers and a number of barges that could be used on the river, and the Southern Pacific Company furnished complete work-trains, from time to time, until a maximum of ten was reached. The next requisite was material for levees and dams, and this they secured by drawing upon all the rock quarries within a radius of four hundred miles, and by opening a new one, with a face of six hundred feet and a height of forty feet, on the granite ledge at Andrade near the concrete head-gate. Clay they obtained from a deposit just north of the Mexican boundary, and gravel they hauled from the Southern Pacific Company's "Mammoth Gravel Pit," which was situated on the main line about forty miles west of the crevasse spur.

From Los Angeles they brought eleven hundred ninety-foot piles, nineteen thousand feet of heavy timbers for railway trestles, and forty miles of steel cable to be used in the weaving of brush-mattresses. The Southern Pacific Company furnished pile-drivers, steam shovels for the granite quarry and gravel pit, several carloads of repair parts, and a large quantity of stores and materials of various kinds. It also detailed for service on the spur railroad and at the crevasse as many engineers, mechanics, and skilled workmen as were needed. The chief reason, Mr. Cory says, "for having the railroad company supply so great a quantity of labor, equipment, and supplies, was that it afforded an opportunity to assemble quickly a thoroughly organized and efficient force of men; the advantage of obtaining material and supplies through the purchasing department of the Harriman systems; immediate shipment of repair parts not kept on hand; and the ability to increase or decrease rapidly the force and equipment without confusion."

The requisite most difficult to obtain, in sufficient amount, was unskilled labor. An attempt was made to get five hundred peons from central Mexico; but it did not succeed, and Mr. Cory was finally compelled to mobilize all the Indian tribes in that part of the Southwest — Pimas, Papagoes, Maricopas,

and Yumas from Arizona and Cocopahs and Die-
gueños from Mexico. These Indians fraternized and
got along together amicably, and constituted with
their families a separate camp of about two thousand
people. The rest of the laborers were Mexicans from
the vicinity, and drifting adventurers from all parts
of the United States who were attracted to the place
by the novelty of the work and the publicity given
to it in the newspapers. Arrangements were made
with the Mexican authorities to put the whole region
under martial law and to send a force of rurales
with a military commandant to police the camps.

Active work began on the 6th of August, 1906,
when the summer flood had fallen enough to reduce
the flow through the crevasse to about twenty four
thousand cubic feet per second. By that time the
receding water had left exposed extensive sand-bars
on both sides of the river, which narrowed the
channel to six hundred or seven hundred feet, and
President Randolph's plan was to dam this channel
sufficiently to throw all or most of the water through
the by-pass and the Rockwood head-gate, and then
permanently to close the break. As it was deemed
essential to blanket the bed of the river with a
woven brush-mattress, to prevent bottom erosion
and to make a foundation for the rock, two shifts
of men were set at this work. In twenty days and

nights, they constructed, with baling-wire, steel cable, and two thousand cords of brush, about thirteen thousand square feet of mattress, which was enough to cover the bed of the river from shore to shore with a double thickness of blanketing about one hundred feet in width. When this covering had been completed and sunk, a railway trestle ten feet wide was built across the crevasse, and on the 14th of September work-trains of "battleships" began running across it and dumping rock on to the mattress at the bottom of the stream. Meanwhile, the by-pass to the Rockwood head-gate was completed and enlarged, and in less than two weeks the dam was high enough to close the crevasse in part and thus divert water through the by-pass and gate. On the 10th of October, nearly thirteen thousand cubic feet of water per second was passing through the gate, while only one tenth of that amount was flowing over the dam. The gate, however, under the pressure to which it was subjected, both by the water and by great masses of accumulated drift-wood, began to show signs of weakness, and at two o'clock on the following day two thirds of it gave way, went out, and floated down-stream. The by-pass then became the main river, while the top of the diversion dam was left practically dry. Thus ended, in almost complete failure, the fifth attempt to control the Colorado. The river had been barred in one channel, but it burst through another, carrying with it a two-hundred-foot head-gate which represented four months of labor and an expenditure of $122,000.

Mr. Harriman and the Southern Pacific engineers were disappointed, but not disheartened. The steel-and-concrete head-gate at Andrade had been ready for use since June, and powerful dredges were set at work clearing out and enlarging the four miles of silted-up canal south of it, so that water might be furnished to the Imperial Valley by that route while another attempt was being made to close completely both the Rockwood by-pass and the original intake.

An inspection of the rock-fill dam, which had been left exposed by the diversion of the river, showed that the objections made to a structure of this kind were not well founded. The brush-mattress had not been broken by the weight of the rocks; the rocks themselves had not sunk out of sight in the soft silt of the bottom, and the dam had not been breached or seriously injured. It leaked a little, but its good condition in other respects suggested the possibility of quickly closing the by-pass and the intake with rock-barriers of this type. Additional trestles were built across both waterways; ten trains of flatcars and "battleships" were set at work bringing rock from three or four different quarries, and the laboring force was increased to about a thousand men with seven hundred horses and mules. Operations were pushed night and day, and in a little more than three weeks, high rock-fill dams were built across both intake and by-pass, and were connected by massive levees so as to make a continuous barrier about half a mile in length. Leakage through the dams was stopped by facing them with gravel and clay, forced into the interstices and puddled with streams of water from powerful pumps, and the levees at both ends were connected with those that had previously been built up and down the river by the California Development Company. In the course of the work there were used, first and last, about three thousand carloads of rock, gravel, and clay, while four hundred thousand cubic yards of earth were moved by dredges and teams.

On the 4th of November, a little more than two years after the cutting of the lower Mexican intake, the crevasse into which it had grown was closed, and the river was forced back into its ancient bed. The danger had apparently been averted and the Imperial Valley was safe; but where a treacherous river like the Colorado is concerned, danger is never over and safety can be secured only by incessant watchfulness and continual labor. On the 7th of December, another sudden flood came down the Gila and increased the discharge of the Colorado from nine thousand to about forty-five thousand cubic feet per second. The rock-fill dam of the Southern Pacific engineers stood fast; but, about midnight, a reconstructed earthen levee of the California Development Company, twelve or fifteen hundred feet farther south, was undermined, began to leak, and finally gave way. The breach at first was small; but it was so rapidly deepened and widened by erosion and caving that it soon became a crevasse, and in less than three days the whole river was pouring through a break a thousand feet wide and again rushing down the slope of the basin to the Salton Sea.

This new crevasse, taken in connection with the history and the experience of the two preceding years, showed conclusively: (1) that the tendency of the Colorado to flow into the Salton Sink was increasing rather than diminishing; (2) that floods of from 180,000,000 to 360,000,000 cubic feet of water per hour were liable to occur at almost any season of the year; (3) that the defensive dikes of the California Development Company were everywhere inadequate or untrustworthy; and (4) that in order to afford certain protection to the Imperial Valley, it would be necessary not only to close the new break, but to build a stronger, higher, and more massive levee along the west bank of the river for a distance of at least twenty miles.

These considerations raised, of course, the question whether it was worth while for the Southern Pacific Company to continue this work, upon which it had already spent about $1,500,000. The interests chiefly imperiled were those of the National Government. It owned all the irrigable land along the lower Colorado, including even that upon which the Imperial Valley settlers had filed.[1] It was then constructing an immense dam at Potholes, twelve miles above Yuma, upon which it had already expended about one million dollars (the Laguna dam) and with the water to be impounded thereby it expected to irrigate and reclaim about ninety thousand acres of fertile land in Arizona and southern California. If the uncontrolled river should continue to "cut back," by means of its receding waterfalls, it not only would destroy the Laguna dam, and the irrigation works upon which the Imperial Valley depended for its very existence, but would eventually

[1] The settlers had made desert or homestead entries on the land, were actually in possession of it, and had an equitable right to it; but the original survey of this part of California had been found inaccurate and defective, and the Government would not — possibly could not — issue patents until boundaries had been more clearly defined by a resurvey. The settlers, therefore, could not raise money on their farms by mortgaging them, because the legal title was still vested in the Government. This became a very serious matter when they wished to help the Southern Pacific in its fight with the river.

turn the whole bed of the lower Colorado into a gorge, out of which water for irrigation purposes could never be taken. This would make valueless more than two thousand square miles of potentially fertile land, which, if intensively cultivated, would support a quarter of a million people.

The interests of the Southern Pacific Company, on the other hand, were comparatively unimportant. The traffic of the Imperial Valley, at that time, amounted to perhaps $1,200,000 a year, from which the railroad derived a revenue of only $20,000 or $30,000 for freight transportation.[1] This, in its relation to the whole business of the company, was so insignificant as hardly to be worth consideration. The flooding of the Valley, moreover, could not injure the road much more than it had already been injured. A section of new line, about sixty miles in length, had been surveyed and graded, and the ties and rails for it were on the ground. At an additional cost therefore of only $50,000 or $60,000, the imperiled part of the track could be moved to a higher location where the rising waters of the Salton Sea could not reach it.

President Randolph, after full investigation, reported the existing state of affairs to Mr. Harriman by telegraph, and informed him that while the

Maxwell Evarts.

original break might be closed at a cost of from $300,000 to $350,000, permanent control of the river would require about twenty miles of muck-ditching [1] and levee reconstruction, and that if he (Mr. Harriman) decided to proceed with the work, he might have to spend $1,500,000 more. In view of this possibility, Mr. Randolph suggested that the Government, or the State of California, be called upon to render aid.

Mr. Harriman, who had implicit confidence in the sound business judgment as well as the engineering ability of Mr. Epes Randolph, accepted the latter's view of the situation. He did not doubt that the Colorado River might ultimately be controlled; but as the expense would be very great, and as the chief interests imperiled were those of the Nation, he did not think that the Southern Pacific Company, of which he was president, was equitably or morally bound to do the work alone and at its own expense. In a long telegram to President Roosevelt, dated New York, December 13th, he fully set forth the state of affairs, but did not comment upon it further than by saying: "In view of the above, it does not seem fair that we should be called to do more than join in to help the settlers."

[1] Where the soil, on the site of a proposed levee, is loose and porous, so that water percolates rapidly through it, a "muck-ditch" is dug, to a depth of six or eight feet; material of more solid consistency is packed into it, and the levee is then built on the impervious foundation.

The following telegraphic correspondence then ensued:

Washington, December 15, 1906

MR. E. H. HARRIMAN, New York

Referring to your telegram of December 13, I assume you are planning to continue work immediately on closing break in Colorado River. I should be fully informed as to how far you intend to proceed in the matter.

THEODORE ROOSEVELT

New York, December 19, 1906

THE PRESIDENT, Washington

Further referring to your telegram of the 15th inst. our engineers advise that closing the break and restoring the levees can be most quickly and cheaply done, if the work is undertaken immediately, at a cost of $300,000 to $350,000. The Southern Pacific Company, having been at an expense of about $2,000,000 already, does not feel warranted in assuming this responsibility and the additional expenditure which is likely to follow to make the work permanent, besides the expenditure which the company is already undergoing to put its tracks above danger line. We are willing to coöperate with the Government, contributing train service, use of tracks and switches, use of rock quarries, train crews, etc., and the California Development Company will contribute its engineers and organization, the whole work to be done under the Reclamation Service. Can you bring this about?

E. H. HARRIMAN

Washington, December 20, 1906

E. H. HARRIMAN, New York

Replying to yours of 19th, Reclamation Service cannot enter upon work without authority of Congress and suitable convention with Mexico. Congress adjourns to-day for holidays. Impossible to secure action at present. It is incumbent upon you to close break again. Question of future permanent maintenance can then be taken up. Reclamation engineers available for consultation. That is all the aid that there is in the power of the Government to render, and it seems to me clear that it is the imperative duty of the California Development Company to close this break at once.

The danger is ultimately due only to the action of that company in the past in making heading completed in October, 1904, in Mexican territory. The present crisis can at this moment only be met by the action of the company which is ultimately responsible for it, and that action should be taken without an hour's delay. Through the Department of State I am endeavoring to secure such action by the Mexican Government as will enable Congress in its turn to act. But at present Congress can do nothing without such action by the Mexican Government.

This is a matter of such vital importance that I wish to repeat that there is not the slightest excuse for the California Development Company waiting an hour for the action of the Government. It is its duty to meet the present danger immediately, and then this Government will take up with it, as it has already taken up with Mexico, the question of providing in permanent shape against the recurrence of the danger.

THEODORE ROOSEVELT

Seldom, if ever before, in our country, had material and financial interests of such tremendous importance been dependent upon the decision of a single man. If Mr. Harriman should order a continuance of the work, he would put at hazard a million and a half dollars of his own money, or the money of the Southern Pacific stockholders, in addition to the million and a half or two millions already spent. He would have to do this, moreover, mainly for the benefit of the Imperial Valley and the Nation, without any assurance of reimbursement or compensation, and without any certainty of success. If, on the other hand, he should decline to sink any more capital in the effort to retrieve a disaster for which neither he nor the Southern Pacific Company was in the slightest degree responsible, the Laguna dam and the Imperial Valley would both be destroyed; twelve thousand ruined and impoverished people would be driven out into the desert, and 1,600,000 acres of Government land would be lost to the Nation forever.

Mr. Harriman, at that time, was being prosecuted by the Interstate Commerce Commission as presumably a malefactor, and President Roosevelt, only a few weeks before, had characterized him as an "undesirable citizen"; but in the supreme test of character to which he was subjected, he showed magnanimity, courage, and public spirit. On the same day that he received the President's telegram of December 20th, he replied in the following words:

You seem to be under the impression that the California Development Company is a Southern Pacific enterprise. This is erroneous. It had nothing to do with its work, or the opening of the canal. We are not interested in its stock and in no way control it. We have loaned it some money to assist in dealing with the situation. What the Southern Pacific has done was for the protection of the settlers as well as of its own tracks, but we have determined to remove the tracks onto high ground anyway. However, in view of your message, I am giving authority to the Southern Pacific officers in the West to proceed at once with efforts to repair the break, trusting that the Government, as soon as you can procure the necessary Congressional action, will assist us with the burden.

The contention of the Government was that inasmuch as the Southern Pacific Company loaned $200,000 to the California Development Company in June, 1905, and assumed temporary control of the latter's affairs for the purpose of safeguarding its loan, the lending company thereby made itself responsible for all the unforeseen consequences of a ditch dug by the borrowing company almost a year earlier. This contention will not bear a moment's scrutiny. The Southern Pacific Company did not, at any time, own any of the Development Company's stock. The shares pledged as collateral for the loan were in the hands of a trustee. The Southern Pacific Company did not even elect the president and three directors of the Development Company. They were elected by the latter's stockholders under

the terms of the loan agreement.[1] The Southern
Pacific was a creditor of the Development Company, but in no sense a "successor in interest" by
virtue of ownership.

The lower Mexican intake, which admitted the
river to the Valley and caused the disaster, was dug
long before the Southern Pacific Company had any
control whatever over the Development Company,
and it would be a violation of the most elementary
principles of equity if a lender were held responsible
for all previous transactions of a borrower, merely
because the latter had voluntarily agreed to share
control of his business in order to obtain the loan.
If a farmer goes to a bank, gives a mortgage on his
farm as security for a loan, and agrees that a representative of the bank shall supervise his agricultural operations until the loan is repaid, the bank
does not become reponsible for a dam across a stream
on the farmer's property built by the farmer himself
a year before he had any relations with the bank.
The bank might be responsible for a dam built under
the direction of its representative, but not for a dam
built by the farmer a year before such representative
was appointed.

When President Roosevelt received Mr. Harri-

---

[1] The text of the agreement may be found in Report 1936, House
of Representatives, 61st Congress, 3d Session, January 18, 1911.

man's telegram of December 20th, saying that orders had been given to proceed with the work, he replied in the following words:

Am delighted to receive your telegram. Have at once directed the Reclamation Service to get into touch with you, so that as soon as Congress reassembles I can recommend legislation which will provide against a repetition of the disaster and make provision for the equitable distribution of the burden.

While the negotiations between President Roosevelt and Mr. Harriman were in progress, the river-fighting organization on the lower Colorado was kept intact. The rock quarry at Andrade was further developed; sidings just across the Mexican boundary were lengthened to seven thousand feet, and material and equipment of all possible kinds which might be needed were gathered and held in readiness. When, therefore, on the 20th of December, an order was received from Mr. Harriman to go ahead and close the break, President Randolph, backed by all the resources of the Southern Pacific, began a last supreme effort to control the river and save the Imperial Valley. The crevasse, at that time, was eleven hundred feet wide, with a maximum depth of forty feet, and the whole current of the Colorado was rushing through it and discharging into the basin of the Sink about 160,000,000 cubic feet of water every hour. There was not time enough for the construction of another brush-mattress, so the Southern Pacific engineers determined to build two railway trestles of ninety-foot piles across the break, and then, with a thousand flatcars and "battleships," bring rocks and dump them into the river faster than they could possibly be swallowed up by the silt or carried down-stream. Three times, within a month, the ninety-foot piles were ripped out and swept away and the trestles partly or wholly destroyed; but the pile-drivers kept at work, and on the 27th of January the first trestle was finished for the fourth time and the dumping of rock from it began.

Mr. F. H. Newell, Director of the United States Reclamation Service, in a description of the final closure of the crevasse, says:

The stones used were as large as could be handled or pushed from the flatcars by a gang of men, or by as many men as could get around a stone. In some cases the pieces were so large that it was necessary to break them by what are called "pop-shots" of dynamite laid upon the stone while it rested on the cars. In this way the stones were broken and then could be readily thrown overboard by hand. The scene at the closure of the break was exciting. Train after train with heavy locomotives came to the place and the stones, large and small, were pushed off by hundreds of workmen as rapidly as the cars could be placed. While waiting to get out upon the trestle the larger stones were broken by "pop-shots," and the noise sounded like artillery in action. Added to the roar of the waters were the whistle signals, the orders to the men, and the bustle of an army working day and night to keep ahead of the rapid cutting of the stream.

As the rock-heap rose gradually, it checked the river, causing it also to rise higher and higher and to cascade over the pile of stone. Riffles were caused, and an undercutting of the lower slope of the rock-heap allowed it to settle and the stones to roll down-stream. All of this undercutting and settling had to be made up and overcome by the rapid dumping of other large stones.

It was necessary to raise the river bodily about eleven feet. As the water rose and became ponded on the upper side of the rock-heap, train-load after train-load of small stone and gravel from the near-by hills was dumped to fill the spaces between the large rocks. Finally, after days and nights of struggle, the water was raised to a point where it began to flow down its former channel and less and less to pass over the rock-heap. Then finer material was added and rapidly piled up on the accumulated rock-mass. At first, a large amount of water passed through, and steps were taken as rapidly as possible to close the openings by dumping sand and gravel, finishing this work by hydraulicking silt or mud over the area and washing this in with a hose. By thus piling up finer and finer material and distributing it, the seepage or percolation through the mass was quickly checked and the barrier became effective. [1]

The crevasse was closed and the river forced into its old bed on the 10th of February, 1907, fifty-two days after President Roosevelt appealed to Mr.

[1] "The Salton Sea," by F. H. Newell, Director of the U.S. Reclamation Service; *Annual Report* of the Smithsonian Institution for 1907, p. 331.

Harriman, and fifteen days after the first "battle-ship" load of rock was dumped from the first completed trestle. In order, however, that this gigantic work might be accomplished, the transportation of commercial freight on the western part of the transcontinental railroad had to be temporarily abandoned. In testifying before a House committee, about a year later, Chief Engineer Cory said:

For three weeks, two divisions of the Southern Pacific system, embracing about twelve hundred miles of main line, were practically tied up because of our demands for equipment and facilities. We had a thousand flatcars exclusively in our service, and shipping from Los Angeles' seaport — San Pedro — was practically abandoned for two weeks until we returned a considerable portion of the equipment. It was simply a case of putting rock into that break faster than the river could take it away. . . . In fifteen days after we got the trestle across and dumped the first carload of rock we had the river stopped. In that time I suppose we handled rock faster than it was ever handled before. . . . We hauled it from Patagonia, Arizona, four hundred and eighty-five miles, over two mountain passes; from Tacna, sixty miles to the east; from three other quarries — one on the Santa Fé, one on the Salt Lake road, and one on the Southern Pacific — all near Colton, two hundred miles to the west, and over the San Gorgonio Pass. . . . We brought in about three thousand flatcars loaded with rock from these immense distances, and we put in, all together, about eighty thousand cubic yards of rock in fifteen days.

But the work of the Southern Pacific engineers

was not confined solely to the closing of the crevasse. In order to prevent a future break in some other part of the irrigation company's defensive system, they were compelled to extend their branch railway, and to build or reinforce levees all up and down the river. Describing this work soon after its completion in 1907, the Director of the United States Reclamation Service said:

There now extends from the head works in the United States along the river, between it and the canal, a double row of dikes, the outer one being occupied by a railroad. These extend in an unbroken line for a dozen miles near the river and shut it off from the lowlands to the west. The river side of this dike is protected by a thick layer of gravel, and the railroad affords immediate access to all parts, so that if menaced by the cutting of the banks it will be possible to bring men and materials to check the floods from encroachment upon the dike itself. Secondary dikes or cross levees run from the main structure to certain subsidiary works, so that if the outer main dike is broken or water flows through, this will be ponded, for a while at least, against the inner line of defense, thus affording time to assemble the necessary equipment to fight another intrusion.

In closing the second crevasse and completing the so-called "Hind-Clarke" dam[1] there were used 1200 ninety-foot piles; 16,000 feet of eight-by-seven-

[1] The northern part of this dam, across the by-pass and intake, was built under the immediate supervision of Superintendent Thomas J. Hind, and the southern part, across the second crevasse, under that of Superintendent C. K. Clarke. Both were Southern Pacific engineers.

teen-inch pine stringers, and 5765 carloads of rock, gravel and clay. In reconstructing and extending the levee system nearly 900,000 cubic yards of earth were excavated or placed in embankments, while 5285 carloads of gravel for blanketing were brought from the Mammoth Gravel Pit, forty miles west of the river on the main line. The total cost of the defensive work done after President Roosevelt made his appeal to Mr. Harriman was about $1,600,000, and this added to the cost of previous operations made a total of approximately $3,100,000 expended in the effort to control the Colorado and keep it out of the Imperial Valley. But the work was thoroughly and effectively done. The river has never broken through the Southern Pacific defenses, although since the final closing of the second crevasse in 1907 there have been two floods in which the discharge of water has exceeded 140,000 cubic feet per second, or twelve billion cubic feet every twenty-four hours.

The great service thus rendered by Mr. Harriman to the people of the Imperial Valley and to the Nation has never been set forth more clearly, perhaps, than it was in the message sent by President Roosevelt to the Congress on the 12th of January, 1907, while the work of closing the second crevasse was in progress. In that historic paper he said:

The Governor of the State of California and individuals and communities in southern California have made urgent appeals to me to take steps to save the lands and settlements in the sink, or depression, known as the Imperial Valley, or Salton Sink region, from threatened destruction by the overflow of Colorado River. The situation appears so serious and urgent that I now refer the matter to the Congress for its consideration. . . .

By means of the facilities available to the Southern Pacific Company, the break in the west bank of the Colorado River was closed on November 4, 1906. A month later, however, a sudden rise in the river undermined the poorly constructed levees immediately south of the former break, and the water again resumed its course into the Salton Sea.

The results have been highly alarming, as it appears that if the water is not checked it will cut a very deep channel which, progressing upstream in a series of cataracts, will result in conditions such that the water cannot be diverted by gravity into the canals already built in the Imperial Valley. If the break is not closed before the coming spring flood of 1907, it appears highly probable that all of the property values created in this valley will be wiped out, including farms and towns, as well as the revenues derived by the Southern Pacific Company. Ultimately the channel will be deepened in the main stream itself, up to and beyond the town of Yuma, destroying the homes and farms there, the great railroad bridge, and the Government works at Laguna dam above Yuma. . . .

If the river is not put back and permanently maintained in its natural bed, the progressive back-cutting, in the course of one or two years, will extend upstream to Yuma, as before stated, and finally to the Laguna dam, now being built by the Government, thus wiping out millions of dollars of property belonging to the Government and to citizens. Continuing farther, it will deprive all the valley lands along the Colorado River of the possibility of obtaining necessary supply of water by gravity canals.

The great Yuma bridge will go out, and approximately 700,000 acres of land as fertile as the Nile Valley will be left in a desert condition. What this means may be understood when we remember that the entire producing area of southern California is about 250,000 acres. A most conservative estimate, after full development, must place the gross product from this land at not less than one hundred dollars per acre per year, every ten acres of which will support a family when under intense cultivation. If the break in the Colorado is not permanently controlled, the financial loss to the United States will be great. The entire irrigable area which will be either submerged or deprived of water, in the Imperial Valley and along the Colorado River, is capable of adding to the permanent population of Arizona and California at least 350,000 people, and probably 500,000. Much of the land will be worth from $500 to $1500 per acre to individual owners, or a total of from $350,000,000 to $700,000,000. . . .

The point to be especially emphasized is that prompt action must be taken, if any; otherwise the conditions may become so extreme as to be impracticable of remedy. . . . It is probable now that with an expenditure of $2,000,000 the river can be restored to its former channel and held there indefinitely; but if this action is not taken immediately, several times this sum may be required to restore it, and possibly it cannot be restored unless enormous sums are expended.[1]

[1] House Report No. 1936, 61st Congress, 3d Session, pp. 153–57.

One might naturally suppose that when a private citizen, at the head of a great railroad company, averted a national calamity, and saved for the country public property that was actually worth $25,000,000 and that had a potential value of "from $350,000,000 to $700,000,000," he would be entitled, at least, to the thanks of the national legislature. If, even in Russia, a railroad president, at the request of the Czar, controlled a great flood in the Volga, barred that river out of the city of Astrakhan, and saved from total destruction "700,000 acres" of fertile land potentially worth "from $350,000,000 to $700,000,000," he would certainly receive the thanks of the nation, expressed in a suitably worded resolution of the Duma and the Council of the Empire. It is more than probable that, even in China, something of this kind would have been done for a railroad president who had controlled a disastrous flood in the valley of the Hoang-ho. But no such acknowledgment of valuable service was ever made by the Congress of the United States.

Perhaps, however, Mr. Harriman was not entitled to credit, for the reason that the work in the field was done by the Southern Pacific Company and its engineers. This was not the view taken by the company and the engineers themselves. If Mr. Harriman, personally, had been asked who finally controlled the Colorado River and saved the Imperial Valley, he undoubtedly would have replied: "Epes Randolph, H. T. Cory, Thomas J. Hind, C. K. Clarke, and their associates." But these gentlemen have publicly said that the driving power behind their work — the one thing that made it successful — was the invincible determination of their chief. In a written discussion of the operations on the lower Colorado, which was conducted by the American Society of Civil Engineers, Mr. C. K. Clarke said:

The writer desires to put on record the fact that the accomplishment of the work was due primarily and exclusively to the independent judgment and courage of Mr. Harriman, who persisted in his belief that the breaks could be closed, and his determination to close them, in the face of opposition, and regardless of the positive assertions of a host of eminent engineers that the closure was a physical impossibility.[1]

In the course of the same discussion, Mr. Elwood Mead, Chief of the Irrigation and Drainage Division of the United States Department of Agriculture, said:

It was the duty of the State or Nation to take charge, and provide the money and men needed to restore the river to its former channel. Apparently no one in authority was interested; the State Government only

[1] *Transactions* of the American Society of Civil Engineers, Paper 1270, pp. 1551-52.

considered the matter long enough to write a letter to
the President, and the President, having Congress on
his hands, shifted the responsibility to the head of a
railroad company; and it was not until the railroad company took charge that we have the first refreshing example of generosity and public spirit. Nothing could
have been finer than the action of Mr. Harriman. The
loan of $250,000, when his time and resources were
overtaxed by the earthquake at San Francisco, and the
providing more than $1,000,000 for the last hazardous
attempt to save the valley, furnish an inspiring contrast
to the supine indifference and irresponsibility shown by
both the State and Federal authorities.[1]

Mr. Epes Randolph, who as President of the
California Development Company directed and
controlled the engineering operations in the lower
Colorado from 1905 to 1907, said, in a private letter
to a student of the subject:

It was a great work, and I do not believe that any
man whom I have ever known, except Mr. Harriman,
would have undertaken it. All of those of us who actually handled the work were merely instruments in the
hands of the Master Builder.

From these expressions of opinion it clearly appears that, in the judgment of the men "on the firing
line," the fight with the Colorado was inspired, directed and won by E. H. Harriman; but no acknowl-
edgment of indebtedness to him personally was ever
made by the Congress of the United States. The

[1] *Transactions* of the American Society of Civil Engineers, Paper
1270, p. 1510.

service that he personally rendered was recognized and publicly acknowledged only by the people of the Imperial Valley. In testifying before the House Claims Committee, in March, 1910, Mr. J. B. Parazette, speaking for the farmers of the Valley, said:

We do feel rather differently in that Valley toward Mr. Harriman from the way others seem to feel elsewhere over the United States. We believe that Mr. Harriman felt a very human interest in our troubles there. . . . We volunteered to furnish about five hundred horses, and to bed and board them, and to furnish men to work during the time that the break was being closed; but we heard that Mr. Harriman said that the farmers down there, he supposed, had a great deal to do (it was seeding time with them) and they had about all the work to attend to that they could handle, and the Southern Pacific would fix the break anyway. What we could have done would not have amounted to much to the railroad company, but it would have amounted to considerable to the farmers there, taking their teams out at that time of the year when they wanted to put in crops.

This expression of gratitude to Mr. Harriman for "showing a human interest" in the farmers' "troubles," and for declining to increase their hardships by shifting a part of the burden of work from his own shoulders to theirs, must have pleased him more than any formal vote of thanks from Congress could have done.

When Mr. Harriman, on the 20th of December,

1906, telegraphed the President that, "in view of" his "message," he would resume efforts to control the Colorado, he ventured to express the modest hope that the Government, as soon as the necessary Congressional action could be secured, would "assist with the burden." Mr. Roosevelt replied that he would recommend legislation to "provide against a repetition of the disaster and make provision for an equitable distribution of the burden." [1] Three weeks later, however, when the work was actually in progress, he merely said, in his message to Congress, that "the question as to what sum, *if any*, should be paid to the Southern Pacific Company for work done since the break of November 4th, 1906, is one for future consideration. For work done prior to that date no claim can be admitted." [2] This may have seemed to Mr. Roosevelt a proper recommendation, and one likely to secure "an equitable distribution of the burden"; but it would not have made that impression upon an irrigation expert, say, from the planet Mars, because it suggested a doubt whether "*any*" of the burden should be borne by the chief beneficiary, namely the Government. However, when a bill to reimburse the Southern Pacific Company was introduced in the House of Repre-

[1] House Report No. 1936, 61st Congress, 3d Session, p. 163.
[2] Ibid., p. 157.

sentatives in 1908, the President did give it cordial support by saying, in a letter to the chairman of the Claims Committee:

... I accordingly wrote an earnest appeal to the officials of the road [the Southern Pacific] asking them to act. They did act, and thereby saved from ruin many people in southern California, and saved to the Government the Laguna dam. ... I feel that it is an act of justice to act generously in this matter, for the railroad, by the prompt and effective work that it did, rendered a notable service to the threatened community. In no other way could this result have been accomplished. [1]

Mr. Roosevelt's "earnest appeal" had been addressed, as a matter of fact, to E. H. Harriman, not to "the officials of the road"; but the President, apparently, could not bring himself, either in this letter or in his previous message, to mention the name of the man who, at the very time when he was struggling with the Colorado River at the request of the Government, was being prosecuted by that same Government as a malefactor. Names are often embarrassing, and the name in this case might have suggested to the public mind the obnoxious idea that Mr. Harriman, after all, might not be a wholly "undesirable citizen." Then, too, there would have been a certain incongruity in denouncing "Harriman," by name as a public enemy, while asking the same

[1] House Report No. 1936, 61st Congress, 3d Session.

"Harriman," by name, to render a great public service; so it was apparently thought safer to mention the name in one case and drop it out of sight in the other.

The President's appeal to Congress to "act generously" was not so successful as had been his appeal to Mr. Harriman to stop the Colorado River and save the Imperial Valley. Congress seldom acts "generously" except on measures likely to influence votes, such as pension bills, public building bills, and bills for the improvement of rivers and harbors. Mr. Harriman and the Southern Pacific Company had "improved" a national river, at a cost to themselves of about $3,000,000; but inasmuch as they were then under a cloud of unpopularity, created by official and unofficial misrepresentation, their influence on Congressional elections was negligible, and Senators and Representatives might safely — perhaps judiciously — ignore their claim, regardless of its merits. The reimbursement bill, therefore, dragged along without action for about three years. Hearings were held, witnesses from California and Arizona were examined, expert engineers were consulted, and the whole subject was thoroughly threshed out. Memorials in support of the bill were received from towns, communities, and chambers of commerce in the Imperial Valley; and the entire

Congressional delegation from California, as well as almost all the newspapers of the State, urged reimbursement as a matter of simple justice. But Congress could not make up its mind to do justice, either to Mr. Harriman or to a railroad company. In 1909, when William H. Taft became President, he at once took up the matter, and in his first message to Congress referred to it in the following words:

This leads me to invite the attention of Congress to the claim made by the Southern Pacific Company for an amount expended in a similar work of relief called for by a flood and great emergency. This work, as I am informed, was undertaken at the request of my predecessor, and under promise to reimburse the railroad company. It seems to me the equity of this claim is manifest, and the only question involved is the reasonable value of the work done. I recommend the payment of the claim, in a sum found to be just.[1]

Two years later, when nothing had been done, President Taft sent to the Chairman of the House Committee on Claims the following letter:

White House
Washington, Jan. 16, 1911

HON. GEORGE W. PRINCE
    Chairman of Committee on Claims
MY DEAR MR. PRINCE:
    As I recommended in my message, I sincerely hope that Congress, at this time, will compensate the South-

[1] House Report No. 1956, 61st Congress, 3d Session.

ern Pacific Railway for work which it did in the Imperial Valley under stress of great emergency. I do not know what amount is just, but I do know that that company came to the rescue of the Government at the instance of President Roosevelt, and that there was an implied arrangement under which they were to be compensated, and I think that Congress should take up the matter and do justice to that corporation in this instance.

Sincerely yours

W. H. TAFT

Under this pressure from the White House, the Committee on Claims finally acted. On the 28th of January, 1911, after having reduced the proposed appropriation from $1,663,000 to $773,000, the committee, by a divided vote, reported the bill to the House with the recommendation that it pass. Five members, however, namely, Representatives Goldfogle, Kitchin, Candler, Shackleford, and Adair, presented a minority report in which they described the bill as "an attempted raid on the Federal Treasury"; denied that there was "any legal, equitable, or moral obligation on the part of the Government" to pay this sum, "or any amount, for closing the break in the Colorado River"; referred to the proposed appropriation as "purely a gratuity," "a gift of the people's money," and declared that they were opposed to this "gift to the Southern Pacific Company, as well as all other gratuities to private enterprise."[1]

[1] House Report No. 1936, part 2, 61st Congress, 3d Session.   2

This minority report seems to have given the *coup de grace* to the reimbursement bill. Whether the members of the House were lacking in a sense of justice; whether they were indifferent to the bill because there was "nothing in it for them"; or whether they were afraid, in an election campaign, to face the charge that they had "given the people's money," as "a pure gratuity" to one of Mr. Harriman's railroad corporations, it is impossible to say. Certain it is that no action was ever taken on the bill, although it had been favorably reported by the Committee on Claims; had been repeatedly recommended by two Presidents, and had been unanimously supported, regardless of party lines, by the people of the Imperial Valley and by the whole State of California. There are certain events which may seem inexplicable, but upon which it is not necessary to comment. The barest recital of facts is eloquent enough.

Shortly before his death, Mr. Harriman made a trip through the Imperial Valley and over the reconstructed levee which kept the Colorado River within bounds. Upon his return to Imperial Junction, he was met by a representative of the "Los Angeles Examiner," who, in conversation about the work, said:

Mr. Harriman, the Government hasn't paid you that money, and your work here does not seem to be duly appreciated; do you not, under the circumstances, regret having made this large expenditure?"

"No," replied Mr. Harriman. "This valley was worth saving, was n't it?"

"Yes," said the reporter.

"Then we have the satisfaction of knowing that we saved it, have n't we?"

It is unfortunate that so fine an achievement as the controlling of the Colorado River and the saving of the Imperial Valley should have been clouded by national ingratitude or indifference; but if Mr. Harriman were living to-day, he would doubtless find compensation and satisfaction enough in the results of his work as they now appear. The Salton Sea, which once threatened to submerge and destroy the artificially created oasis in the desert, ceased to rise in 1907 and is now slowly drying up. The great Laguna dam above Yuma is done, and is furnishing water to tens of thousands of acres in southern California and Arizona. The territory along the Colorado River below the Grand Cañon, whose prospective value President Roosevelt estimated at "from $350,000,000 to $700,000,000," is safe. The Imperial Valley, which was yielding only $1,200,000 to its cultivators fifteen years ago, is now producing cotton, barley, alfalfa, cantaloupes, grapes, vegetables, and live stock worth more than ten times that amount. According to an editorial in the "Imperial Valley Press" in June, 1916, the farmers of the Valley expected to earn that year a sum equivalent to the interest on $500,000,000. And all of this actual and potential wealth, as well as the land that has produced or will produce it, was threatened with total destruction in 1906, and was saved for the Nation by the constructive genius and the invincible resolution of the "Master Builder."

CHAPTER XXV

THE BREAK WITH PRESIDENT ROOSEVELT

T HE crisis in Mr. Harriman's career," says Mr.
Kahn, "came early in the year 1907. A few
of his bitterest enemies had set out the year before
on a carefully planned, astutely prepared, campaign
of destruction against him. To their banners flocked
a number of those whom in his conquering course he
had met and vanquished; some whom by his rough,
domineering ways he had unknowingly offended;
others who were simply envious and jealous; certain
politicians whose ill-will he had incurred; many who,
in perfect honesty and without any axes to grind,
but basing their opinion mainly on hearsay, saw in
his personality, his methods, his ambition, and his
growing power a real menace and danger to the
public good; and, lastly, a few who had reason to
throw public opinion off the scent and to divert
vigilance and search from themselves by concen-
trating it on another. . . . The Harriman Extermination League — if I may so call it — played its
trump card by poisoning President Roosevelt's mind
against Mr. Harriman, with whom he used to be on
friendly terms, by gross misrepresentations, which

caused him to see in Mr. Harriman the embodiment of everything which his own moral sense most abhorred and the archetype of a class whose exposure and destruction he looked upon as a solemn patriotic duty. With Mr. Roosevelt leading the attack, the League felt so certain of their ability to hurl Mr. Harriman into outer darkness, defeat, and disgrace, that they actually sent considerate warning to his close associates to draw away from him whilst there was yet time to do so, lest they be struck by fragments of the bomb which would soon explode under Mr. Harriman, and which was certain to hurl him to destruction. Mr. Harriman, of course, was fully aware of all this. He braced himself against the coming blow, but did nothing to avert it, let alone run away from it." [1]

He did try, however, to protect his associates, who, he feared, might be injured by attacks made primarily upon him. He was ready to meet anything that might come, so far as he, personally, was concerned, but he did not wish to have discredit reflected upon those with whom he happened to be connected. In the late summer of 1906, soon after the "Extermination League" began its campaign of misrepresentation, he thought he had reason to be-

[1] *Edward Henry Harriman*, by Otto H. Kahn (New York, 1911), pp. 37-38.

lieve that the hostile criticisms aimed at him in the newspapers were affecting injuriously the National City Bank, of which he was then a director. He therefore wrote a note to James Stillman, president of the bank, in which he expressed this belief and tendered his resignation. Mr. Stillman replied in the following letter:

New York, August 21, 1906

DEAR MR. HARRIMAN:

The impression you gathered from our informal conversation last Sunday evening, as expressed in your note of to-day, is entirely erroneous. I do not believe that the criticisms leveled against all of us by the press are provoked, by any means, by you alone. It is because we are prominent, and because this or that newspaper, as the case may be, is hostile to the large interests with which we are identified that gives reason for the onslaughts against us.

It is quite immaterial which one of us is singled out at any particular time; the rest of us get the same treatment at other times. If newspaper attacks on prominent men governed their qualifications as directors, corporations would be weakly organized. You are too valuable a director and too much esteemed by your co-directors to permit of the course proposed by your letter. Accordingly I return your resignation and beg you to tear it up and not think any more about the matter.

Sincerely yours

JAMES STILLMAN

The rupture of friendly relations between Roosevelt and Harriman, which gave to the "Extermina-

tion League" its most effective weapon, had its
origin in a misunderstanding as to what was said, or
meant, in an interview that Roosevelt had with
Harriman in the White House just before the Presidential election of 1904.

Between September 14, 1901, when Roosevelt
became President of the United States, and November 4, 1904, when he was elected for a second
term, his relations with Mr. Harriman were cordial and harmonious, if not intimate. He often invited the latter to the White House; addressed him
always as "My dear Mr. Harriman," said that it
was "a real pleasure to see him," and expressed a
desire to consult him about his "letter of acceptance," about his "message to Congress," and about
other "Government matters not connected with the
campaign."

In the fall of 1906, these friendly relations were
suddenly broken off, as the result of a disagreement,
or misunderstanding, with regard to the purport of
a conversation which the President had with Mr.
Harriman at an interview in the White House about
two weeks before the Presidential election of 1904.
The circumstances that brought about that interview were these. In the early summer of 1904, while
Mr. Harriman was in Europe, President Roosevelt
wrote him the following letter:

White House
Personal   *Washington, June 29, 1904*
MY DEAR MR. HARRIMAN:

I thank you for your letter. As soon as you come home I shall want to see you. The fight will doubtless be hot then. It has been a real pleasure to see you this year.

Very truly yours
THEODORE ROOSEVELT

In reply to this, Mr. Harriman, after his return from Europe, wrote the President:

New York, September 20, 1904
DEAR MR. PRESIDENT:

I was very glad to receive your note of June 29 last while I was in Europe. I am now getting matters that accumulated during my absence cleared up and, if you think it desirable, will go to see you at any time, either now or later. It seems to me that the situation could not be in better shape.

Yours sincerely
E. H. HARRIMAN

From these letters it clearly appears that it was the President who sought an interview with Mr. Harriman, not Mr. Harriman who sought an interview with the President. The matter is of no consequence except in so far as it shows who it was that wanted something. In the correspondence furnished by the President to the press for publication, in April, 1907, the first of the above letters was omitted, and also the opening sentence of the second. The effect of these omissions was to give the impression that Mr. Harriman, in the fall of 1904, voluntarily proposed to call on the President, presumably for purposes of his own. Such was not the case. The initiative was the President's, and Mr. Harriman expressed a readiness to call simply because the President had asked him to do so.

On the 23d of September, 1904, the President, reassured perhaps by Mr. Harriman's statement that the political situation "could not be in better shape," decided that it would not be necessary to see Mr. Harriman. He therefore wrote him another letter in which he said:

At present there is nothing to see you about, though there were one or two points in my letter of acceptance which I should have liked to discuss with you before putting it out.

Upon receipt of this letter, Mr. Harriman, of course, gave up the idea of going to Washington. He had offered to go only because the President had written him, in June, 1904, "I shall want to see you as soon as you come home." If, between June and September, the situation had so changed, and political prospects had so improved, that there was "nothing to see him about," Mr. Harriman, of course, had no reason for making the visit. The correspondence, up to this point, may be briefly summarized thus:

The President to Mr. Harriman in June: "As soon as
you get home I shall want to see you."
Mr. Harriman to the President in September: "All
right. I am home. I will come to see you at any time,
either now or later."
The President to Mr. Harriman in September: "At
present there is nothing to see you about."

This ended the first stage of the correspondence.
The interview was off simply because the President
no longer desired it.

In order to make clear the reasons for the renewal
of this correspondence two weeks later, and for Mr.
Roosevelt's second request that Mr. Harriman come
to Washington, it seems necessary to review briefly
the political state of affairs in New York at that
time. Early in the election campaign of 1904 (some
time in July) Governor Odell, who was the chairman
of the Republican State Committee, had a more or
less definite understanding with Chairman Cortelyou and Treasurer Bliss of the Republican National
Committee that the latter should collect the funds
for all political purposes, both State and National,
and should make disbursements to the State Committee from time to time as money was needed.
In pursuance of this agreement, or understanding,
the National Committee, during the summer and
early fall, gave the State Committee about $300,000
for campaign expenses. This sum proved to be in-

sufficient, and some time in October, the State Committee found itself in need of about $200,000 more. The National Committee declined to furnish any more, and this refusal placed the State Committee in an embarrassing position. Failure to obtain this sum, it was thought, might imperil the election of Mr. Higgins, the Republican candidate for Governor, or even endanger the election of Mr. Roosevelt, the Republican candidate for President. This state of affairs was apparently brought to the attention of Mr. Roosevelt, and early in October, from the White House, he telephoned the National Republican Headquarters in New York and asked for Mr. Cortelyou (the chairman) or Mr. Bliss (the treasurer). Neither of these gentlemen happened to be in the building, and the President was therefore put into communication with Senator Nathan B. Scott, a member of the executive committee, who was there. When examined afterward by the Senate Committee on Privileges and Elections, Senator Scott testified that in the telephonic conversation with President Roosevelt which then ensued, the following questions were asked and answered:

The President: "What is this trouble I hear about Higgins? I hear there is some danger of his being defeated."

Senator Scott: "Well, if the election was now, I fear he would be defeated."

The President: "What is the trouble?"

Senator Scott: "The committee claim they have no funds sufficient to carry out the plan of their campaign."

The President: "Well, can't Mr. Bliss settle that?"

Senator Scott: "I understand that Mr. Bliss says that he has not any additional funds that he can give the State Committee."

The President: "Can't the State Committee raise the funds?"

Senator Scott: "Well, the understanding was, when the campaign started, that the National Committee would do the soliciting and turn over a certain amount to the State Committee for their campaign."

The President: "I would rather lose the election in the country than be defeated in my own State."

Senator Scott: "There is no danger, Mr. President, of your being defeated in New York State. While there is danger of Higgins, there is no danger whatever of your not carrying the State. If the funds were provided the State Committee to carry out their plan, I have no doubt that we could elect Higgins."

The President: "I will send for Mr. Harriman."

Senator Scott explained to the committee that he could not remember precisely whether the President said he would "send for Mr. Harriman," or whether he said, "Mr. Harriman is coming to see me and I will see if we can't arrange to raise the funds for the election of Mr. Higgins." "I cannot," said Senator Scott, "give the exact language. It was that he [Mr. Harriman] 'was coming,' or he 'would have him come.'" [1]

[1] Testimony given before the sub-committee of the Senate Com-

On the 10th of October, 1904, presumably just after this talk with Senator Scott, the President wrote to Mr. Harriman a letter in which he said:

In view of the trouble over the State ticket in New York, I would like to have a few words with you. Do you think you can get down here within a few days and take either luncheon or dinner with me?

To this Mr. Harriman replied by return mail:

I am giving a very large part of my time to correcting the trouble here and intend to do so if any effort on my part can accomplish it. . . . I will take occasion the first of next week to run down to see you and think by that time the conditions will be very much improved.

With this letter the second stage of the correspondence might naturally have ended. The President had again invited Mr. Harriman to Washington; Mr. Harriman had again accepted the invitation, and the first of the following week had been fixed as the date for the proposed visit. What need was there for further parley? And yet, within forty-eight hours, the President wrote to Mr. Harriman a very curious letter in which he seemed to assume that the invitation had not been accepted; that

mittee on Privileges and Elections, which investigated in 1912 the matter of campaign contributions (pp. 685–87 of the collected testimony). Mr. Scott, at that time, was Senator from West Virginia, and was a member of the executive committee of the Republican National Committee.

Mr. Harriman was still in doubt as to the wisdom of accepting it, and that if he could overcome his reluctance to refuse a direct request from the President of the United States, he might finally decide to remain in New York. The letter follows:

Personal   *White House*
                                                  October 14, 1904
MY DEAR MR. HARRIMAN.

A suggestion has come to me in a roundabout way that you do not think it wise to come on to see me in the closing weeks of the campaign, but that you are reluctant to refuse, inasmuch as I have asked you. Now, my dear sir, you and I are practical men, and you are on the ground and know the conditions better than I do. If you think there is any danger of your visit to me causing trouble, or if you think there is nothing special I should be informed about, or no matter in which I could give aid, of course give up the visit for the time being, and then, a few weeks hence, before I write my message, I shall get you to come down to discuss certain government matters not connected with the campaign.

With great regard
                        Sincerely yours
                            THEODORE ROOSEVELT

If the above letter had been written before the President received any reply to his invitation, it would be perfectly natural and understandable; but it is hard to see why, with Mr. Harriman's unqualified acceptance in hand, and with the date for the visit approximately fixed, Mr. Roosevelt should suddenly assume that the matter was still in doubt.

Perhaps, between October 10th and October 14th, somebody suggested to the President — or upon reflection he himself thought — that in view of Mr. Harriman's prominence as a railroad man and capitalist, it would not be prudent to seem to seek his help in the closing weeks of a "hot" political campaign; that such action might be politically prejudicial, and that, in order to guard against the possibility of future trouble, it would be advisable to write a second and more cautious letter and send it on the heels of the first. If this were the case, it would explain why Mr. Roosevelt, in his second letter, made the proposed visit subject to certain conditions. Mr. Harriman was not to come unless he had "special" information to impart, or unless he thought that *the President's "aid"* would be desirable. This put Mr. Harriman in the attitude of taking the initiative; threw upon him the responsibility for the interview, and suggested the idea that he himself was seeking aid.

Cases have been known in which a letter has been written not to produce an immediate effect, but to serve as a record for future reference. When, for example, Mr. Roosevelt, in October, 1906, wrote a long letter about Harriman to James S. Sherman, his object was not to inform Sherman, but, as Maxwell Evarts has shrewdly remarked, "to have the letter on hand if anything happened." [1] The President's second letter to Mr. Harriman seems to have been a letter of this kind. Mr. Roosevelt, apparently, did not want to prevent Mr. Harriman from coming to Washington; his object merely was to write a letter that could subsequently be used to prove: (1) that Mr. Harriman made the visit on his own initiative, and (2) that he was seeking the President's aid in carrying out his own political purposes. As a matter of fact, the letter afterward *was* used to bolster up both of these suppositions.

On account of the death of his wife's brother in Rochester, Mr. Harriman was not able to go to Washington as soon as he expected, and on the 15th of October, 1904, he had his secretary write to the President's secretary an explanation of the delay. Upon his return from the funeral in Rochester, Mr. Harriman telegraphed Mr. Loeb, the President's private secretary, asking the latter to call him up on the long-distance telephone. Mr. Loeb did so, and another appointment was made for the proposed visit. In his testimony before the Senate investigating committee, Mr. Roosevelt attempted to

---

[1] The President's letter to Mr. Sherman was made up, in large part, of information that Sherman himself had given to Mr. Roosevelt orally that same day. The only conceivable object that the President could have had in re-transmitting the information to its author was to make a written record of it for future use in case of need.

maintain that by his letter of October 14th he "expressly released Mr. Harriman from coming down," and that when he did come, a few days later, he came on his own initiative and because he himself wanted help. In the course of the examination the following questions were asked and answered:

> *Senator Paynter:* "As I understand it the substance of your testimony was that Mr. Harriman visited you on his own initiative?"
> *Mr. Roosevelt:* "He did. . . . That letter of October 14 expressly released him from coming down."
> *Senator Paynter:* "After you having given him, in the letter of October 14th, the right to exercise his judgment as to the propriety of coming down, is it quite just to Mr. Harriman to say that he sought the interview because he called up Mr. Loeb?"
> *The President:* "It is, sir; it is exactly just and scientifically accurate to do so."

With regard to the object of the visit Mr. Roosevelt testified:

> I call your attention to the letter of October 14th, 1904. . . . [Reads letter.] I call your attention to the fact that there is not a hint or a suggestion of my getting aid, but it was as to whether I could give aid. You will see that that letter is absolutely incompatible with any theory that I was asking Mr. Harriman to come down in my own interest, or that I intended to make any kind of request for aid from him.

From the above testimony, and from the President's letter to James S. Sherman in October, 1906, it is perfectly evident that the Roosevelt-Harriman note of October 14, 1904, served, eventually, a very useful purpose. It did not prevent Mr. Harriman from coming to Washington, and probably was not intended to do so; but it was so framed that it could be used, and subsequently was used, to show that Mr. Harriman made the visit on his own initiative, and that he sought the interview not because the President wanted his help, but because he wanted the President's help.

The sequence of events, up to the time of the visit, may be briefly summarized thus:

June 29, 1904, the President to Mr. Harriman: "As soon as you come home [from Europe] I shall want to see you."

September 20, 1904, Mr. Harriman to the President: "I am home. I will go to see you at any time, either now or later. It seems to me that the [political] situation could not be in better shape."

September 23, 1904, the President to Mr. Harriman: "At present there is nothing to see you about."

About October 8, 1904: A conversation takes place between Senator Scott and the President in which the latter learns of the shortage of funds in New York; expresses fear of his own defeat in that State, and says he will send for Mr. Harriman.

October 10, 1904, the President to Mr. Harriman: "I would like to have a few words with you. Do you think you can get down here within a few days and take either luncheon or dinner with me?"

October 12, 1904, Mr. Harriman to the President:

"I will take occasion the first part of next week to run down to see you."

October 14, 1904, the President to Mr. Harriman (after receiving his note of the 12th): "If you think there is nothing special I should be informed about, or no matter in which I could give aid, why, of course, give up the visit for the time being."

October 15, 1904, Mr. Harriman's secretary to Mr. Loeb, the President's private secretary: "Kindly say to the President that owing to the death of Mrs. Harriman's brother, William H. Averell, at Rochester, Mr. Harriman will not return to the city until after the funeral. . . . On his return he will go down to Washington to meet the President."

October 20, 1904, Mr. Harriman to Mr. Loeb (by telegraph): "Please call me up by long-distance telephone."

October 20, 1904: conversation between Mr. Harriman and Mr. Loeb by telephone. (In this conversation another appointment was apparently made for the interview and Mr. Harriman went to Washington to keep it.)

It would not be necessary to give these events again in chronological sequence if Mr. Roosevelt had not subsequently declared under oath that the visit was made upon Mr. Harriman's own initiative, and for the purpose of getting the President's help in carrying out his (Mr. Harriman's) political plans. The facts speak for themselves and it is not necessary further to comment upon them.

The "trouble over the State ticket in New York," to which both the President and Mr. Harriman referred, had a threefold aspect. There was a factional fight between the supporters and the opponents of Senator Depew (which was apparently the chief "trouble" that Mr. Harriman had in mind); there was an extensive "bolt against Mr. Higgins," the Republican candidate for Governor (which seems to have been the trouble that the President had in mind), and there was a lack of funds for the State campaign (which, undoubtedly, was a "trouble" that both correspondents had in mind). All of these "troubles," therefore, were likely to be taken up in the course of the interview.

Mr. Harriman had been particularly requested by Governor Odell to bring the Depew matter to the President's attention, because the contest between the supporters of Depew and the supporters of Governor Black for the United States Senatorship was weakening the party. In his testimony before the Senate investigating committee, Governor Odell said:

I requested Mr. Harriman, on his visit to President Roosevelt, to bring to his attention the condition of affairs in the State of New York with reference to the coming senatorial situation, and state to him that the organization was in favor of the election of Governor Black to succeed Senator Depew. At the same time they had a very kindly feeling for Senator Depew and they would like to have him taken care of. I suggested

to Mr. Harriman that he state to the President that, if
he could consistently do so, it would be a very happy
solution of the problem if he would send Senator Depew
as Ambassador to France.[1]

That Mr. Harriman would call the attention of
the President to this "trouble" was, therefore, antecedently probable, if not certain. The President,
on the other hand, was most concerned, (1) over the
"extensive bolt against Mr. Higgins"; and (2)
(after his talk with Senator Scott) over the lack of
funds for the New York campaign. Mr. Harriman
also had the latter "trouble" in mind, because
Governor Odell, prior to the Washington visit, had
forewarned him that the President would probably
"consult him with reference to New York and the
financial condition of the National Committee,
which, at that time, was at rather a low ebb."[2]

With all these subjects for discussion in mind, the
President and Mr. Harriman began their conference
in the White House soon after the 20th of October,
1904. With regard to the nature of the conversation
that ensued, we have no information except the subsequent statements of the two principals and a
fragment of testimony from Mr. Loeb, the President's private secretary, who heard a part of the

---

[1] Governor Odell's testimony before the Senate investigating committee.
[2] *Ibid.*

talk. The interview seems to have been perfectly harmonious and to have satisfied both the President and Mr. Harriman. When the latter returned to New York, he told his intimate friend and legal adviser, Judge Lovett, that the National Committee was very short of funds, and that they owed the State Committee $200,000. "They are in a hole," said Harriman to Lovett, "and the President wants me to help them out. I've got to do it and I'm going to raise the money." [1]

Mr. Harriman made substantially the same statement to Charles A. Peabody (now president of the Mutual Life Insurance Company), and in Mr. Peabody's presence telephoned to Hamilton Twombly, an intimate friend of Senator Depew, asking his help in raising the money. [2]

Mr. Wayne MacVeagh (Attorney-General in the Cabinet of President Garfield) happened to be present in Twombly's office when the request was made, and he understood from Twombly that the money was being raised "because the President was anxious for it." [3]

Mr. Harriman also reported the result of the inter-

[1] Judge Lovett's testimony before the Senate investigating committee, p. 693.
[2] Mr. Peabody's testimony before the Senate investigating committee, p. 251.
[3] Mr. MacVeagh's testimony before the Senate investigating committee, pp. 611–12.

view to Governor Odell, chairman of the State
Republican Committee. "He told me," said Odell,
"that I was correct; that the President was anxious
about the financial condition in New York, and that
he would be glad to have Mr. Harriman help. I
asked him about the conference with reference to
the solution of the senatorial matter [the appointment of Depew as Ambassador to France] and he
said that the President had said to him that if it
were necessary he would do as requested. He [Har-
riman] told me he was ready to help the National
Committee." [1]

As the practical net result of the conference in the
White House (whatever may have been said in that
conference), Mr. Harriman raised $250,000, of which
amount he, personally, contributed $50,000. Judge
Lovett, as Mr. Harriman's representative, turned
over this whole sum of $250,000 to Cornelius N.
Bliss, treasurer of the National Republican Committee.[2] Mr. Bliss subsequently gave $200,000 of
this sum to Governor Odell, chairman of the State
Republican Committee, and the latter receipted
for it.[3]

[1] Governor Odell's testimony before the Senate investigating
committee.

[2] Judge Lovett's testimony before the Senate investigating committee, p. 693.

[3] Governor Odell's testimony before the Senate investigating committee, pp. 112–13.

It is difficult, if not impossible, to imagine any reason, at that time, for untruthfulness or misrepresentation on the part of Mr. Harriman. He was not hostile to the President, he was friendly to him. The White House interview had not separated the two men, it had apparently drawn them more closely together. Why, then, should Mr. Harriman, upon returning to New York, raise a quarter of a million dollars for campaign expenses, and then make an untruthful statement to Judge Lovett, Mr. Peabody, Mr. Twombly, and Governor Odell with regard to his reasons for raising this fund? Such misrepresentation would be in the highest degree foolish and irrational and no adequate motive for it can be suggested.

The same may be said of Mr. Harriman's statement to Governor Odell with regard to "taking care" of Senator Depew. If the President had not given some sort of assurance that he would appoint Mr. Depew as Ambassador to France, why did Mr. Harriman, in his effort to raise money, go first of all to Hamilton Twombly, one of Senator Depew's most intimate friends?

During the entire campaign of 1904, and for more than a month afterward, Mr. Harriman's relations with the President continued to be friendly.[1] There

[1] In November, 1904, two or three weeks after Mr. Roosevelt's

was no shadow of disagreement until December, 1904, when, on his way back to New York from Virginia, Mr. Harriman stopped in Washington and had a short talk with the President. The latter then told him that he did not think it necessary to appoint Depew as Ambassador to France, but rather favored his reëlection to the Senate. This virtual withdrawal from the agreement entered into at the White House in October seems to have made upon Mr. Harriman an unfavorable impression. He said nothing, but, as subsequent events proved, he felt that by the President's change of attitude, he (Harriman) had been placed in a false position in his relation to Senator Depew's friends. All that he could do, after the President refused to appoint Depew as Ambassador to France, was to promote Depew's candidacy for the United States Senate, which he did.

Mr. Harriman's first impression with regard to this disagreement with the President seems to have been that it was the result of a misunderstanding.

election as President, he had some correspondence with Mr. Harriman about railroad matters and the Interstate Commerce Commission, but it had no relation to the subjects discussed at the White House interview in October, except in so far as Mr. Roosevelt, two years later, tried to twist it into such a relation, for the purpose of suggesting that railroad matters were probably in Mr. Harriman's mind when, "on his own initiative," he went to Washington in October, 1904.

In a conversation with his friend, Charles A. Peabody, a week or two later, he called it a "misunderstanding," and said that, as a result of it, he had been unable to carry out his intentions. When Mr. Peabody was examined before the Senate investigating committee, he testified that in Christmas week, 1904, he had a talk with Mr. Harriman at Arden.

The conversation [said Mr. Peabody] related to the reëlection of Senator Depew. He told me on that occasion that there had been a misunderstanding. . . . At the time he raised this fund [the $250,000 given to Treasurer Bliss] he supposed ne had an understanding as to the appointment of Senator Depew to a foreign mission; but it could not be carried out. . . . Some of the friends of Senator Depew thought that there was an implied understanding that he should be taken care of in some way, and as he could not be taken care of with a foreign mission, it had become necessary to arrange for his reëlection.

Question (by Senator Paynter): "Did you understand from him [Mr. Harriman] that the up-State politicians were opposing the election of Senator Depew to the Senate, and that Mr. Harriman thought it important to remove that element of discord by securing a promise from the President to send him to France in the event of his [Mr. Roosevelt's] success in the election?"

Mr. Peabody: "That was my understanding. I do not know how much he said to me on that occasion, or how much I have since acquired in reading these letters. I have no doubt of the fact myself." [1]

[1] Charles A. Peabody's testimony before the Senate investigating committee, pp. 252–54.

Some time in 1905, Mr. Harriman, as the result, perhaps, of getting later information, made up his mind apparently that the President had not treated him fairly; and when, in December of that year, he received a letter from his old and trusted friend, Sidney Webster,[1] warning him against being drawn into politics and expressing doubt as to his capacity for political activity, he replied in the following words:

As to my political instincts, to which you refer in your letter of December 13th, I am quite sure that I have none, and my being made at all prominent in the political situation is entirely due to President Roosevelt, and because of my taking an active part in the autumn of 1904, at his urgent request, and his taking advantage of conditions thus created to further his own interests. If it had been a premeditated plot, it could not have been better started or carried out.

After narrating his experience with the President in the matter of the Depew appointment, Mr. Harriman added:

This is the way I was brought to the surface in political matters; as I had never before taken any active part and had only done what I could, as any other citizen might. So you see I was brought forward by Roosevelt in an attempt to help him at his own request.

[1] Sidney Webster was a well-known lawyer of New York who had been associated with Mr. Harriman in the directorate of the Illinois Central Railroad Company. The two friends had carried on a confidential correspondence for many years.

What reply Mr. Webster made to this letter — if any — is not known. The letter was confidential and was not intended, of course, to influence public opinion in any way. It did not come to the knowledge of the world until a year and a half later, when it was published, as the result of a breach of trust on the part of one of Mr. Harriman's stenographers. This man, who had been dismissed, sold an imperfect copy of it to a New York newspaper, for the purpose of getting revenge, or money, or both.

About the end of 1905, the correspondence between President Roosevelt and Mr. Harriman, which had been carried on intermittently for a number of years, entirely ceased.

In the fall of 1906, shortly before the Congressional elections, the leaders of the Republican Party found themselves again in need of money for campaign expenses, and Mr. James S. Sherman, chairman of the Republican Congressional Committee, remembering Mr. Harriman's generosity in 1904, decided to make another appeal to him for funds. Mr. Maxwell Evarts, counsel at that time for the Union Pacific Railroad System,[1] happened to be a

[1] Maxwell Evarts was a son of William M. Evarts, Secretary of State under President Hayes. He was a distinguished member of the New York Bar, and acted as counsel for the Southern Pacific Railroad when that corporation tried to get reimbursement from Congress for expenses incurred, at the request of President Roosevelt, in stopping the great crevasse in the Colorado River.

friend of Sherman, and when the latter proposed to call on Harriman, for the purpose of soliciting a subscription, Evarts agreed to go with him. The interview took place in the office of the Union Pacific Railroad Company. Mr. Harriman flatly refused to contribute, and told Sherman that he could use his money to better advantage himself. Then, for the purpose perhaps of explaining his refusal, he got out and read to Sherman the Sidney Webster letter.

A few days later, Mr. Sherman went to President Roosevelt and made a report to him of the Harriman interview. Exactly what the nature of that report was we do not know, as Mr. Sherman himself never published anything on the subject. Mr. Roosevelt, however, for the purpose of making a record to which, if necessary, he could refer, sat down that same day and wrote a letter to Sherman in which he re-transmitted to the latter the information that he had just obtained from him orally. The letter, in part, follows:

October 8, 1906

MY DEAR SHERMAN:

Since you left this morning I succeeded in getting hold of the letters to which you referred, and I send you a copy of Governor Odell's letter to me of December 10, 1904.

As I am entirely willing that you should show this letter to Mr. E. H. Harriman, I shall begin by repeating what you told me he said to you on the occasion last

week when you went to ask him for a contribution to
the campaign. You informed me that he then expressed
great dissatisfaction with me and said, in effect, that as
long as I was at the head of the Republican Party he
would not support it and was quite indifferent whether
Hearst beat Hughes or not, whether the Democrats
carried Congress or not. He gave, as a reason for his
personal dislike of me, partly my determination to have
the railroads supervised, and partly the alleged fact
that after promising him to appoint Depew Ambassador
to France, I failed to do it; and I understood you to say
that he alleged that I made this promise at a time when
he had come down to see me in Washington, when I
requested him to raise $250,000 for the Republican
Presidential campaign which was then on. Any such
statement is a deliberate and wilful untruth — by rights
it should be characterized by an even shorter and more
ugly word. I never requested Mr. Harriman to raise a
dollar for the Presidential campaign of 1904. On the
contrary, our communications, as regards the campaign,
related exclusively to the fight being made against Mr.
Higgins for Governor of New York, Mr. Harriman
being immensely interested in the success of Mr. Higgins
because he regarded the attack on Higgins as being
really an attack on him, Mr. Harriman, and on his
friend Governor Odell; and he was concerned only in
getting me to tell Mr. Cortelyou to aid Mr. Higgins as
far as he could, which I gladly did. He also (I think
more than once) urged me to promise to make Senator
Depew Ambassador to France, giving me in detail the
reasons why this would help Governor Odell, by pleasing
certain big financial interests. I informed him that I
did not believe it would be possible for me to appoint
Mr. Depew. . . .

So much for what Mr. Harriman said about me personally. Far more important are the additional remarks

he made to you, as you inform me, when you asked him if he thought it was well to see Hearstism and the like triumphant over the Republican Party. You inform me that he told you that he did not care in the least; because those people were crooks and he could buy them; that whenever he wanted legislation from a State legislature he could buy it; that he "could buy Congress," and that, if necessary, "he could buy the judiciary." This was doubtless said partly in boastful cynicism and partly in a mere burst of bad temper because of his objection to the Interstate Commerce Law and to my actions as President. But it shows a cynicism and deep-seated corruption which make the man uttering such sentiments, and boasting, no matter how falsely, of his power to perform such crimes, at least as undesirable a citizen as Debs, or Moyer, or Haywood. The wealthy corruptionist, and the demagogue who excites, in the press or on the stump, in office or out of office, class against class, and appeals to the basest passions of the human soul, are fundamentally alike and are equally enemies of the Republic. I was horrified, as was Root, when you told us to-day what Harriman said to you. As I say, if you meet him, you are entirely welcome to show him this letter, although, of course, it must not be made public unless required by some reason of public policy, and then only after my consent has first been obtained.

Sincerely yours
THEODORE ROOSEVELT

HON. J. S. SHERMAN
  St. James Building
    No. 1133 Broadway, New York

That Mr. Harriman would make such statements as those attributed to him by Sherman was antecedently improbable, and the assertion that he ac-

tually *did* make them, in the presence of Maxwell
Evarts, his friend and legal counsel, is absolutely
incredible. He was not a man who lost his temper
easily, nor a man given to bragging of what he would
or could do. The supposition, therefore, that merely
because Sherman asked him for a campaign contribution he became so angry and irrational as to
boast, in the presence of a third person, of his
ability to buy legislatures, Congress, and the judiciary, is a supposition too violent and improbable for
belief.[1]

[1] Mr. F. D. Underwood, president of the Erie Railroad, who was
closely associated with Mr. Harriman for many years in the management of the Erie and the Baltimore & Ohio, says: "In an intimate acquaintance of ten years, I never saw Mr. Harriman angry but once.
He seldom judged others harshly, and the strongest term I ever heard
him apply to any one was 'nincompoop.'"

CHAPTER XXVI

THE BREAK WITH PRESIDENT ROOSEVELT
(*Continued*)

FORTUNATELY, in this case, we do not have to depend wholly for our information upon what Roosevelt said that Sherman said that Harriman said. Maxwell Evarts, who was a friend of Sherman as well as of Harriman, made, after the latter's death, a statement of the case based upon first-hand knowledge of the facts. This statement, which has not before been published, follows:

During the Congressional campaign of 1906, a move-ment was started trying to get everybody to give a dollar toward the Republican campaign fund. Sherman and I had always been good friends, and he tried to get me to get Harriman to assist the Republicans in running the Congressional campaign. I saw Harriman several times about it, and he always said that he would not do it; that there was no use in asking him, as he could use his money to better advantage himself. I told Sherman that, and he became somewhat discouraged with the outlook.

I made an appointment for Sherman to see Harriman, and he came to my office one day and we went down-stairs and saw Harriman. That was in September, 1906. Harriman always went right to the point, and this time there was no beating about the bush. He hauled out the Sidney Webster letter and read it to Sherman. Harri-

man told Sherman just about what he told me, viz.,
that he would not contribute a dollar. I remember that
after that Sherman came upstairs and we went to lunch
together, and the whole thing went out of my mind.

The following December I was up in Vermont at the
Legislature and got a telegram from Harriman asking
me to meet him on a train bound for Washington. I did
not know anything about what was wanted, and went
with what I had on. I met Harriman on the train and
he asked me if I remembered the conversation that
he had with Sherman in my presence the September
previous, and I said I did. He asked me to repeat it to
him, which I did. He asked me if I was willing to see
Roosevelt. I said that I was, and he said, "Well, we are
going to Washington to the Gridiron dinner and I want
you to come along." I protested that I had no evening
clothes; that they had no use for such things in Vermont.
He insisted, and some fellows hired me a suit down
in Washington and I went to the Gridiron dinner with
Harriman. In the course of the dinner Harriman said
that he had arranged for me to see President Roosevelt
the next day at the White House and would let me know
the hour.

The next day, about noon, I was in bed when Loeb
called me up and said that I could see the President late
in the afternoon, about five o'clock I think it was.
When I went to the White House I saw the President
in his riding-boots and he asked me to wait a few minutes, as he was polishing off the Bellamy-Story letter.
When we got together he said, "I suppose you know
what Harriman wanted you to come to see me about?"
I replied that I did. I said, "I suppose you would like
to have me tell you this thing from the beginning."
Roosevelt said, "I would." I told him the story about
Sherman and prefaced it by saying that Sherman and I
were good friends, and that I had tried to help him out;

but that Harriman insistently said he could not do anything, and afterwards I made the appointment between
Sherman and Harriman. I told him that we went to
Harriman's office, that Harriman had a very brusque
way of going at things, and that in this case, instead of
talking about the weather, he went straight for Sherman
and pulled out the Sidney Webster letter and read it,
and told Sherman that he was not going to let him have
any money, because he thought it was no use, and he had
a great deal better use for his money anyway. He told
Sherman he could help the cause out generally, and he
would do that, but that was as far as he would go.

At this point Roosevelt interrupted me and asked
what Harriman said about him, and I told him he said
nothing about him, and that there was nothing in the
whole conversation that could not have been repeated
to him, or anybody else. Then he told me that Sherman
had told him that Harriman said he could get anything
he wanted, anyhow, and that he could buy the courts
and buy the legislatures, etc. I said that nothing of the
kind was ever talked about, and that Mr. Sherman must
have misunderstood the conversation. I told him that
they had discussed campaign funds pretty thoroughly,
and Harriman insisted that he could not see any use
in making contributions, and that he could use his
money more effectively in other ways, and I told Roosevelt that after Harriman read the Webster letter, he
remarked that it proved that there was no advantage in
making general subscriptions for party purposes, that
if there was any desire to spend money it had better be
spent in some other way, and that so far as he was concerned he never even got any thanks for campaign
contributions. I told Roosevelt that I did not know
just why Harriman read the letter, and that I was surprised at the time, because it did not seem to have any
bearing on the matter. I told him that they afterward

talked about the question of the tariff, and Harriman came out strongly to Sherman for a general revision of the tariff. Mr. Sherman opposed that promptly, and we finally left.

Roosevelt then said to me, "Why, my conversation with Mr. Sherman would show Harriman to be the most wicked, cynical man in the world. It was so bad that I had Sherman repeat it to Root, and then I had Sherman write out the whole conversation in a letter to me. Now why did Sherman tell me all this?" I replied that I could not understand it. He asked me if I thought it was vindictiveness, and I said, "Probably not; there must have been a misunderstanding." Then Roosevelt said, "I want party harmony in New York, and I want to know if you will do something for me. I believe you are the only man who can do it. I want you to see Sherman and get him to write me that his conversation was all a misunderstanding." I replied that there was a short session of Congress and asked if it would not do after Congress adjourned. He told me to take my time about it.

(I had planned to take care of the matter immediately after the adjournment of Congress. In the meanwhile Roosevelt went to Panama and before he came back all the correspondence was made public and the whole thing was off. I presume the truth of the matter is that when Sherman told Roosevelt this story, Roosevelt sat right down and wrote his letter to Sherman, so as to have it on hand if anything happened. What he wrote in his letter to Sherman was his version of what Sherman told him, and not what Sherman had written out for him. I do not believe Sherman wrote anything out for him, because if he had done so, Roosevelt would not have hesitated to make use of it when he gave his letter out for publication afterward.)

The outstanding feature of the above statement is

the fact that, as early as December, 1906, President Roosevelt was informed, and apparently believed, that there was no truth in the representations made to him by Sherman with regard to the latter's talk with Harriman. In view of the use that Mr. Roosevelt afterward made of these untruthful representations, the fact is important, because it shows that when he finally employed them as a weapon against Harriman, he knew, or had every reason to believe, that they were false.

Another salient feature of Mr. Evarts's statement is the fact that as soon as Mr. Harriman became aware of these misrepresentations, he made an attempt to correct them, by sending Evarts to the White House to tell the President what was really said, and what was not said, when Sherman (in the presence of Evarts) asked Harriman for a campaign contribution.

The situation, therefore, at the beginning of 1907, was this: Mr. Harriman was dissatisfied with the outcome of the White House interview of October, 1904, and had expressed that dissatisfaction in a private and confidential letter to his friend, Sidney Webster. The Sidney Webster letter, however, had not been made public, and the President, apparently, had no knowledge of it prior to his talk with Mr. Evarts. All that he knew of Harriman's dissatisfaction was what Sherman told him, and Sherman's statements had been flatly contradicted by his own friend, Evarts. As a result of this contradiction, Roosevelt had asked Evarts to see Sherman and get from him an admission that his report of his interview with Harriman was due to a "misunderstanding."

Such was the state of affairs in April, 1907, when a discharged stenographer of Mr. Harriman sold an imperfect transcript of the Sidney Webster letter to Hearst's newspaper, the "American." The latter, for reasons of its own, did not publish the letter at once, and the stenographer, seeing that it did not appear, sold it a second time to the "New York World." Mr. Harriman made an attempt to prevent the publication of it, but did not succeed, and it was "featured" in the "World" of April 2, 1907. The President at once denied the truth of the statements contained in it, and in order to support his denial and strike Mr. Harriman a counter-blow, gave to the press for publication his letter to James S. Sherman of October 8, 1906 — a letter based largely upon information that Sherman had given him orally.

Mr. Roosevelt had known, for more than three months, that Sherman's statements were untruthful — Evarts had told him so — and yet he did not hesitate to use them as evidence of Harriman's

RODIN'S BUST OF E. H. HARRIMAN

"deep-seated corruption," and as a proof that he was an "undesirable citizen" and an "enemy of the Republic." These are not the methods of fair controversy. No conscientious man, even in anger, uses against his opponent hearsay statements that he has every reason to believe are untruthful; but Mr. Roosevelt never admitted that he did Mr. Harriman injustice, nor did he ever refer to the interview in which Maxwell Evarts assured him that he (Evarts) was present when Sherman asked Harriman for a campaign contribution; that no reference whatever was made to the President; and that not only did Harriman not boast of being able to "buy legislatures, Congress, and the judiciary," but he "did not say a word that could not be reported to him [Roosevelt] or anybody else," and yet Roosevelt, many years later, in a letter to Professor William Z. Ripley, of Harvard University, quoted again the discredited statements of Sherman with regard to the buying of legislatures, Congress, and the judiciary, and never intimated that the truthfulness of the statements was — at least — in doubt.[1]

Many years later also, Mr. Roosevelt, regardless of the sworn testimony of Senator Scott, Governor Odell, Mr. Peabody, Wayne MacVeagh, Judge Lovett, and others, continued to reassert that Mr.

[1] *North American Review*, January, 1916, p. 549.

Harriman visited the White House in October, 1904, "on his own initiative"; that his object was to get the President's help; that he was not asked to aid either the National Committee or the New York State Committee; that there was "no possibility of a misunderstanding," and that there was "not a shred of truth" in his (Harriman's) statements. It would certainly be a curious thing if Mr. Harriman went to Washington "on his own initiative" to get the President to help *him*, and then immediately returned to New York and, without solicitation from anybody, raised a quarter of a million dollars to help *the President*. That is virtually what he did. The money thus raised was not turned over to the New York State Committee, it was given by Judge Lovett to Treasurer Bliss, of the National Committee, who was managing the financial side of Mr. Roosevelt's campaign.[1] That a part of it was intended for the State Committee is doubtless true; but the State Committee's work was of such a nature as to help the President almost as much as it helped Mr. Higgins, the candidate for Governor.

Mr. Roosevelt afterward said that Mr. Harriman sought his aid in behalf of the State ticket for the reason that he (Harriman) and his friend Governor

[1] Judge Lovett's testimony before the Senate investigating committee, p. 693.

Odell were especially interested in the election of Higgins. Judge Lovett, however, who was in a position to know the facts, testified before the Senate investigating committee that this was not the case. Odell's first choice for Governor of New York was Joseph H. Choate (at that time Ambassador to Great Britain) and in July, 1904, he (Odell) cabled Mr. Harriman, who was then in Europe, asking him to see Choate and ascertain whether he would accept the nomination. Some time later this plan was abandoned — for what reason does not appear — and Higgins was nominated. There is no reason, however, to suppose that Harriman was particularly interested in Higgins' election. Upon this point Judge Lovett testified: "Mr. Harriman had no interest whatever, so far as I ever knew, in the election of Mr. Higgins, except such interest as he might have in the election of the nominee of the Republican Party, as he was a consistent Republican." [1]

This testimony throws further doubt upon two, at least, of Mr. Roosevelt's assertions. In his letter to Sherman the President declared, (1) that Harriman was "immensely interested in the election of Mr. Higgins, because he regarded the attack on Higgins as an attack on him, Mr. Harriman, and his

[1] Judge Lovett's testimony before the Senate investigating committee, p. 720.

friend Governor Odell"; and (2) that when Harriman, "on his own initiative," made his visit to Washington in October, 1904, his only object was to get the President's help in a fight against his (Harriman's) enemies. These assertions do not seem to be supported by anything except perhaps Mr. Roosevelt's own belief.

Mr. Roosevelt and his former secretary, Mr. Loeb, both testified before the Senate investigating committee that in the course of the White House interview of October, 1904, they telephoned the National Republican Committee in New York to give all possible aid to the State Committee, and that this telephoning was done in Mr. Harriman's presence and at his request. This is doubtless true; but without some knowledge of the previous talk it is impossible to tell what significance the fact had. If Mr. Harriman already contemplated raising a fund for campaign expenses in New York and turning it over to the National Committee, it was natural enough that he should ask the President to use his influence in getting the National Committee to help the State Committee. This agrees perfectly with what Harriman subsequently said to Judge Lovett, namely, that the National Committee was "in a hole," because it owed $200,000 to the State Committee which it could not pay, and that the

President wanted him (Harriman) to "help them out."

In a personal controversy of this kind, where each participant flatly contradicts the other with regard to matters of fact, due weight should always be given to personal character and general reputation for truthfulness. In testifying before the Senate investigating committee, Judge Lovett said: "I have never heard Mr. Harriman's word called in question except in this single controversy. He was a man who was regarded as of the strictest integrity in speaking the truth. I have never heard his word questioned in any other matter, and I think it is fair to state that, and to say, further, that I cannot believe that he would have accomplished the things he did achieve if he had not been a strictly truthful man." It is doubtful whether as much could be said of Mr. Roosevelt. The members of the so-called "Ananias Club" can testify that the trustworthiness of his memory, at least, with regard to matters that affected his political interests, was called in question many times.

The rupture of friendly relations between Mr. Harriman and President Roosevelt was not, in itself, a matter of great importance; but it was followed by consequences which affected injuriously not only Mr. Harriman himself, but the great railroad sys-

tems that he controlled. In November, 1906, after
the President, in a letter to James S. Sherman,
characterized Harriman as a man of "deep-seated
corruption," an "undesirable citizen," and an
"enemy of the Republic," the Interstate Commerce
Commission, acting either upon its own initiative or
upon suggestion, went back seven years into railroad
history, and began an investigation of the "undesirable citizen's" past activities — particularly his
reconstruction of the Union Pacific and Chicago &
Alton Railroads in 1899–1901. These transactions
had been known to the Commission, as well as to
the general public, for many years; but it was apparently thought, in 1906, that by raking them over
carefully some reason might be found for subjecting
Mr. Harriman to a criminal prosecution. Mr. Roosevelt afterward denied indignantly that he had anything to do with this investigation, and characterized as a mean "innuendo" the suggestion that
between the quarrel with Mr. Harriman and the beginning of the investigation there might possibly
be some other relation than that of mere chronological sequence. "The suggestion," he said, that
the Interstate Commerce Commissioners "would
listen to, or that I would make, a request that they
proceed against a railroad president because of
my personal disagreement with him, is monstrous

in its iniquity and equally monstrous in its absurdity." [1]

But when action in a particular direction is desired, it is not always necessary to make a request,
or issue an order. The Interstate Commerce Commission, it is true, reported to Congress and was
nominally independent of the Executive; but if it
was not largely controlled by the President, why did
so many railroad and business men go directly to
him when they wanted the Commission to do something, or refrain from doing something? They
evidently thought that the Commission was controlled, or at least largely influenced, by Mr. Roosevelt's dominating personality.

In 1915, when the directors of the New York &
New Haven Railroad were tried for alleged conspiracy to violate the provisions of the Sherman
Anti-Trust Law, Mr. Charles S. Mellen, formerly
president of the road, testified that he went to
Washington in 1907 (the year when the investigation of Mr. Harriman's activities was made) for the
purpose of finding out whether, under the provisions
of the Sherman Law, his road would be allowed to
keep its Long Island Sound steamers. He went first
not to the Commission, but to President Roosevelt.

[1] Letter to Professor William Z. Ripley, *North American Review*,
April, 1916.

216 E. H. HARRIMAN

The latter sent for Commissioners Knapp and Prouty, and presumably consulted them; but he seems to have taken the final determination of the question into his own hands when he said to Mr. Mellen: "I cannot promise you any kind of protection if you break the law; but so far as I and my Administration are concerned, if you do not sell, you will have no trouble about those steamship lines."[1]

A little later, that same year, Mr. Mellen again went to President Roosevelt, to ascertain whether the Interstate Commerce Commission would interfere if the New York & New Haven Railroad Company should buy the Boston & Maine. Again the President seems to have taken the decision of the question into his own hands by saying: "I would buy it, if I were you."[2]

Mr. Henry M. Whitney, of Boston, who evidently thought that in railroad matters the President was more to be feared than the Interstate Commerce Commission, wrote to Mr. Mellen, on the 21st of May, 1907:

I have also thought it possible that the Little Father in Washington might like to get his finger into the pie [the purchase of the Boston & Maine] in which case, if it should happen before the public had become reconciled to the change, it might result in infinite harm to all your interests.[3]

[1] *New York Times*, Nov. 11, 1915, [2] *Ibid*, Nov. 23, 1915. [3] *Ibid*.

In March, 1907, it was currently reported in New York that the Government intended to follow up the attack on the Harriman lines by making a "general raid" on other great railroad systems. So much was public confidence unsettled by these reports that, on the 11th of March, a delegation of New York men of affairs, headed by Mr. J. Pierpont Morgan, went to Washington to make inquiries. Apparently, however, they did not go to the Interstate Commerce Commission; they went directly to President Roosevelt. Upon laying the situation before him, they were given to understand that "no raid was contemplated by the Commission; that nothing would be done in a spirit of resentment, or that would have a tendency to add to, or even continue, the existence of the prevailing public distrust." [1]

From the fact that the Morgan delegation went directly to President Roosevelt to ascertain the intentions of the Interstate Commerce Commission, it would seem to be a fair inference that, in the opinion of business men, the Commission was greatly influenced, if not largely controlled, by the President's views of public policy. Why Mr. Roosevelt decided that it would not be necessary to extend the investigation to other great railroad systems does not appear. Perhaps he thought that the object-

[1] *Commercial & Financial Chronicle*, March 16, 1907

lesson afforded by the attack on the Harriman lines
would serve as a sufficient warning to other railroad
managers, should they feel inclined, at any future
time, to disregard the menace of the "big stick."

In December, 1906, when Maxwell Evarts told
the President about Sherman's misrepresentations,
and when he (the President) began to doubt whether,
after all, Harriman was a man of "deep-seated corruption," an "undesirable citizen," and an "enemy
of the Republic," he asked Mr. Evarts the question:

"You represent Mr. Harriman, don't you?" I replied,
"Yes." He said, "I wish you would talk with me about
this investigation of the Interstate Commerce Commission." I complied. He had a memorandum of Kellogg's
with reference to taking up the investigation of the
Union Pacific and Southern Pacific.[1] Roosevelt asked
me if I had any suggestions to make about this. I said
that I had, and he told me to go ahead and I talked to
him substantially as follows:

"Why do you start a public investigation of the Harriman lines without first ascertaining whether there
ought to be any investigation at all? I do not know
what you think about it, but it seems to me it may be
well to find out first, in a quiet and private investigation, whether the Government ought to bring any proceedings. Suppose, after you get through with the
investigation, you find there is no cause for any proceeding. Then you will have done a great deal of harm to
everybody. It seems to me it is to the general interest
that you look into the matter quietly at first. We will

---

[1] The reference is to Mr. Frank A. Kellogg, then counsel for the
Interstate Commerce Commission.

furnish you with everything you want. Then, if you want to have a public investigation and are sure that there is ground for an investigation and a proceeding, there ought to be time enough to go ahead. But to rush into the matter now, without knowing what you are going to find, seems to me to be a mistake." [1]

This, unquestionably, was judicious advice, and it was fully justified by the outcome of the investigation; but the machinery of the Interstate Commerce Commission had already been set in motion and it was too late, perhaps, to stop it. The fact that the President, when Evarts called on him, had in his possession a "memorandum" concerning the Harriman investigation, which the Commission's attorney had drawn up, throws some light on what Mr. Roosevelt afterward called the "monstrous iniquity and absurdity" of supposing that he had anything to do with it.

Whether the President directly instigated the prosecution of Mr. Harriman, or not, may be regarded as uncertain; but that his view of the "undesirable citizen's" moral character influenced the Interstate Commerce Commission, and turned its investigation of certain railroad transactions into what has since been called "a one-man hunt," seems fairly established.

[1] MS. statement of Maxwell Evarts with regard to the Roosevelt-Harriman controversy.

The bitterness of Mr. Roosevelt's hostility to certain men was largely due to the fact that he often allowed his judgment to be controlled by his emotions. He was easily swayed by passion, and when he was angry — righteously angry, as it seemed to him — his judgment and his memory were so clouded by personal feeling that he could neither see with perfect clearness, nor remember with perfect accuracy. He passionately believed, nevertheless, that his judgment was fair and his memory infallible; and in reviewing his past controversies, he was firmly convinced that he had always been right, or nearly right, and that those whom he regarded as his enemies had always been "monstrously" wrong.

It was this dominating influence of personal feeling that made Mr. Roosevelt see the characters of other men not objectively, as they were in themselves, but subjectively, as they appeared to him in the light of personal relationship. If a man sympathized with him, agreed with him, and supported him, such a man was a good and honorable citizen; but if, on the other hand, a man opposed him, or questioned the fairness, wisdom, or propriety of his actions, such a man became an "undesirable citizen" with a more or less defective moral character. The Taft whom Mr. Roosevelt eulogized in the early part of 1908, while he and Taft were still friends, differed widely

from the "deceitful" and "hypocritical" Taft whom
he saw in his mind's eye during the election campaign
of 1912. The eminent railroad president whom he
always addressed, between 1901 and 1905, as "My
dear Mr. Harriman"; whom he invited again and
again to the White House as an honored guest; whom
he said it was "a real pleasure to see," and whom he
desired to consult about his letter of acceptance, his
message to Congress, and "other Government matters not connected with the campaign," became a
totally different Harriman when the quarrel occurred
in 1906, and when Mr. Roosevelt looked at his
former friend through the distorting medium of a
changed personal relation. This disposition to judge
men narrowly, by their relation to him, rather than
broadly, by the sum total of their activities, was a
marked trait of Mr. Roosevelt's character.

He thought it "monstrously iniquitous" to suppose that he would ask the Interstate Commerce
Commission to proceed against a railroad president
merely because he, Mr. Roosevelt, had had a personal disagreement with him. But that was not the
supposition, nor is that the way in which he looked
at it. His attacks on Mr. Taft and Mr. Harriman
were not, in his own mind, the outcome of personal
disagreements; they were duties imposed upon him
by considerations of public welfare. As Mr. Taft, in

1912, seemed to him an unworthy candidate for the
Presidency, whom it was his duty to oppose, so
Mr. Harriman, in 1906, seemed to him the leading
exponent of a pernicious railroad policy, whom it
was his duty to check. In each case, the quarrel first
changed Mr. Roosevelt's view of the man, and then,
in each case, the changed view resulted in antagonis-
tic action, based on a sense of duty. If he instigated,
inspired, or influenced the proceeding against Mr.
Harriman, it was not, primarily, because he had had
a personal disagreement with him, but because he
thought he was under a moral obligation to make an
example of a man whom he had come to regard as a
dangerous railroad speculator and monopolist. But
he did not take anything like this view of the railroad
president until after he had quarreled with him, although all of Mr. Harriman's more important operations, including the reorganization of the Union
Pacific, the Chicago & Alton transaction, the purchase of control in the Southern Pacific, the Northern Pacific "corner," and the Northern Securities
merger, had been fully set forth in the newspapers,
or litigated in the courts, and had been well known,
not only to students but to the general public, for
years. It cannot reasonably be supposed that the
President, throughout the period of his friendly association with Mr. Harriman, was wholly ignorant

of them; and yet, neither he, nor the Interstate Commerce Commission, took action upon them until after the quarrel in 1906.

Four months later, when the investigation had begun, Mr. Harriman made an effort to see the President, for the purpose of discussing with him railroad affairs and policies in their relation to the public welfare.[1] Maxwell Evarts, who acted as Mr. Harriman's representative in the matter, says:

In March, 1907, Harriman went down to Washington and asked me to go along. This was after he had been examined by the Interstate Commerce Commission. Among other things he suggested that we call on the Interstate Commerce Commission, which we did. The entire body were in Commissioner Knapp's room when Harriman walked in. At first it was somewhat awkward; but somebody asked him a question as to the most important engineering feat he had anything to do with, and he told them about the Salton Sea matter, which was then a fresh incident. We had a pleasant interview and Harriman made a great impression on the Commission.

After we left, he said he wished that I would arrange a meeting between him and Roosevelt to discuss railroad questions. I asked him how I was going to do it, and he told me to do it any way I wanted to. I telephoned to the White House, asked to see the President, and they told me to come around. I went over and met the President. Whenever he saw me in the corridor, he used to bawl out, in the presence of everybody, "Here

[1] This was before the publication of the Webster and Sherman letters which led to the final break.

comes Harriman's ambassador!" or, "Here is the ambassador of plutocracy!" and he seemed to take a great deal of pleasure in shoving out that phrase and introducing me in that way.

I told him I wanted him to meet Harriman and sit down and discuss with him the railroad situation. He threw up his hands and said: "How can I do it? What will the newspapers say?" I asked him what the newspapers could do about it and what he cared for the newspapers anyway. I suggested that the most important question of the day was the regulation and control of the railroads.

He acquiesced, and I said: "Mr. President, Harriman is nothing but an incident in the history of the railroads of this country. He is not a pioneer railroad-builder — the day of pioneer railroad-builders has gone by — but he has a wonderful power of comprehension of the whole situation that confronts the railroads at the present time. No man has the knowledge of this subject that he has, and no man knows better what ought to be done. Personalities ought to be buried and this whole thing treated as a condition."

He said: "Well, you don't know what Morgan and some of these other people say about Harriman." I said: "Mr. President, I know one thing: you never heard Harriman say one word about Morgan, or any of the rest of them." He said: "I never heard him say such things about them as they say about him"; and I insisted that he had never heard Harriman say a word of any kind about them. I told him Morgan was not a railroad man, but a banker, and that all I wanted him to do was to sit down with Harriman as a railroad man knowing more about railroads than anybody else in the country.

I told him it might interest him to know that only yesterday the chairman of the Interstate Commerce

Commission said: "The Union Pacific and Southern Pacific are way ahead of all the other railroads in the country, in their road-bed and equipment and in their application of safety appliances to prevent injuries and loss of life."

I reminded him that way back in 1906, Harriman had sent me down to Washington to urge that Congress include in the Hepburn Law a section providing for the giving of no passes whatsoever, to employees or anybody else. I told him there was not another railroad man in the whole country who would do that. Harriman wanted to abolish passes absolutely, but Congress would not go that far. I told him that the man who took such views as these in matters of the day, and who played such a conspicuous part in the upbuilding and making over of the Pacific roads, was a great railroad man and knew his business, and that nothing could be lost by a discussion of practical railroad matters between such a man and the President of the United States, and that if the President of the United States wanted to get information about the railroads, he ought to see the man who knew more about the railroads than anybody else living.

After a while I made an impression, and he said: "Do you want me to see him with my Cabinet?" I replied that that had never occurred to me, but that I had no objection. All that I wanted him to do was to sit down and talk with Harriman, and the Cabinet and everybody else could do as they pleased. He said he would have to talk the matter over with his Cabinet, as to whether he should see Harriman, and promised to take it up and let me know.

For some unknown reason, he told the newspaper men afterward that Harriman wanted to make an appointment with him, and the news got out. I think that was on a Thursday, and Morgan was going to Europe on the following Monday, or something of that sort. Morgan started for Washington, lickety-split, as soon as the news got out, and arranged for four or five railroad presidents to meet Roosevelt with reference to the railroad question. The appointment was made for him to see these presidents, I think, the following Monday. Harriman asked what we were going to do about it, and I said: "We won't do anything. We will wait until after these fellows get through, and then, when the matter quiets down, we will go down on our trip." . . .

Harriman got busy preparing maps of the whole railroad situation and figures and everything else. Roosevelt wrote me, March 6th, that he would be glad to see Harriman, and he insisted in his letter that a stenographer would have to be present, so that there could be no misunderstanding afterward. Before we got down there, the "New York World" came out with the Roosevelt correspondence and everything was off.[1]

Mr. Harriman did not afterward see Mr. Roosevelt, nor have any communication with him. The only reply he ever made to the personally abusive attack made on him by the President in the Sherman letter was contained in a dignified and temperately worded statement which he gave to the press for publication April 3, 1907. At the end of that statement he said: "I am not responsible for what Mr. Sherman may have said to the President with reference to the conversation he had with me. All that I have to say is that I did not meet his urgent

[1] MS. statement of Maxwell Evarts with regard to the Roosevelt-Harriman controversy.

requests that I contribute to his campaign fund, and that the statements alleged to have been attributed to me by him were false. The President was assured of this fact by a mutual friend who was present at the interview."

CHAPTER XXVII

INVESTIGATION OF THE HARRIMAN LINES

THE investigation of railroad affairs undertaken by the Interstate Commerce Commission in 1906 was, ostensibly, an inquiry into "The Consolidation and Combination of Carriers";[1] but it did not include all carriers, nor did it cover the consolidations and combinations of all railroad corporations. It was restricted, geographically, to Western roads, and specifically, to roads that were controlled, or had at some time been managed, by E. H. Harriman, namely, the Union Pacific, the Southern Pacific, the Chicago & Alton, and the Illinois Central. The inquiry, therefore, ought by rights to have been entitled: "An Investigation of the so-called Harriman Lines." The Commission, of course, was well aware that practically all of the great railway systems in the East had been built up by combinations and consolidations, and that many of them had been repeatedly reorganized; but, for reasons of its

[1] "The Consolidation and Combination of Carriers; Relation between such Carriers and Community of Interest Therein, their Rates, Facilities and Practices." See *Reports* of Interstate Commerce Commission (Government Printing Office, Washington, D.C., 1908), vol. XII, p. 277.

own, it decided to limit its inquiries to combinations, consolidations, and reorganizations for which Mr. Harriman and his associates were responsible. It devoted most of its time and attention to the reorganization of the Chicago & Alton Railroad Company in 1899; not, apparently, because that transaction was particularly important, but because the financing of it was most open to attack. In that case, if any, the Commission seemed to think, Mr. Harriman could be found guilty of improper conduct, if not of actual dishonesty and fraud. The reorganization, at the time when it occurred, excited little comment or criticism; but when, seven years later, the Government began its campaign against Mr. Harriman, through the Interstate Commerce Commission, the transaction was characterized as "indefensible financing"; and was described as the "crippling," "looting," and "scuttling" of a well-managed and prosperous railroad by a syndicate of unscrupulous financiers, in which Mr. Harriman was the "main conspirator." [1] In view of these criticisms, it seems necessary to subject the reorganization to a fuller and more careful examination than it has hitherto had.

[1] *Reports* of Interstate Commerce Commission, vol. XII, pp. 301–03; statement of Senator Cullum, New York *Independent*, vol. LXII, p. 692; *Railroads: Finance and Organization*, by Professor W. Z. Ripley (New York, 1915), pp. 262–67.

The Chicago & Alton Railroad, when Mr. Harriman became connected with it, was an apparently prosperous and well-managed road. It had paid dividends of eight per cent on its invested capital for thirty years or more; its credit was good, and its shares of common and preferred stock were selling at from seventy-five to one hundred points above their par value. From a financial point of view, it seemed to be as strong as any railroad of its class in the Middle West. Unfortunately, however, its managers had pursued an ultra-conservative policy in the matter of expenditures, and had neglected, for a long time, to make necessary appropriations to cover depreciation, and to provide for extensions, betterments, replacements, and additional equipment. The road had grown old without improving in physical condition; and had become more or less incapable of rendering the service demanded by a rapidly growing and developing territory. Speaking of this state of affairs, the well-known economist, Professor E. S. Mead, says:

The condition of the Alton was far below that of its competitors. The standards of construction were those of fifteen years before. The track was laid with steel rails, but these were only seventy pounds to the yard. The bridges were in good condition, but were too light for heavy engines. The capacity of the sidings and second track was inadequate to handle large increase of traffic. In short, the company had not maintained a sufficient depreciation account, and its property had not been kept up to standard.[1]

According to J. H. McClement, expert accountant, who had occasion to investigate the affairs of the company:

It had not added one mile of road in seventeen years. It had little or no reserve capacity to conduct a larger business. Its cost of operation, per unit of traffic, was very high in comparison with similar roads. Its grades were uneconomical. Its shops and equipment were uneconomical and old. Its settled policy against the expansion of its facilities, because of declining rates, was an absolute bar to the development of the tributary country. While for twenty-five years it had paid an average dividend of 8.3 per cent on its capital stock, the gross earnings for the year 1898 [the year before Mr. Harriman became interested in it] amounting to $6,286,000, were the lowest since 1880, and had been gradually falling since 1887, when they amounted to $8,941,000. In many respects the company was being conducted like a commercial enterprise having in view ultimate liquidation, instead of like a public carrier.[2]

The ultra-conservative — not to say parsimonious — policy of the management, the progressive deterioration in the physical condition of the road,

[1] *Corporation Finance*, by Edward Sherwood Mead, Ph.D., Wharton School of Finance and Commerce, University of Pennsylvania (New York, 1914), pp. 252–53.
[2] *Statement of the Recapitalization of the Chicago & Alton Railroad Company*, by J. H. McClement, Expert Accountant. (New York, 1907.)

and the decline of $2,655,000 in annual earnings in a period of eleven years, naturally created dissatisfaction and excited a feeling of uneasiness among the owners of the company's securities; and in the fall of 1898 a number of the large stockholders, actuated by a feeling of apprehension as to the future of the road, requested John J. Mitchell, president of the Illinois Trust Company, to open negotiations with Mr. Harriman, with a view to the sale of the property and a financial reorganization of the company.[1]

Mr. Mitchell had an interview with Mr. Harriman in New York, and represented to him that "many of the Alton stockholders were dissatisfied with the existing management; that the stock might be bought for less than the real value of the property; that if betterments and improvements were made and modern methods introduced, the earnings might be largely increased, and that if control of the road were purchased, if funds for such betterments were provided, and if the road were developed, there would be an opportunity for a substantial profit."

[1] Among the prominent stockholders of the Chicago & Alton at this time were Morris K. Jessup of New York, Marshall Field of Chicago, John A. Stewart of New York (president of the United States Trust Company and formerly Assistant Treasurer of the United States), Albert A. Sprague (of Sprague, Warner & Co., Chicago), A. C. Bartlett (vice-president of Hibbard, Spencer, Bartlett & Co., Chicago), and John J. Mitchell (president of the Illinois Trust Company). These were not men likely to be hoodwinked or deceived by "unscrupulous financiers" bent on wrecking the Alton road.

Mr. Harriman, who had never before thought of purchasing the Chicago & Alton, told Mr. Mitchell that he would take the matter into consideration, and ascertain as soon as possible the condition of the road. Shortly after this interview Mr. Harriman requested Mr. S. M. Felton, a well-known expert and railroad manager,[1] to make a thorough examination of the property and submit a detailed report on its condition, requirements, and earning capacity. Mr. Felton's report was favorable. He estimated that better management, and the expenditure of $5,200-000 for improvements and additional equipment would enable the road to increase its earnings by at least $1,000,000 a year on the traffic then existing, to say nothing of the increased traffic that might be expected when the road should be able to afford adequate facilities to the then rapidly developing territory that it served.

Becoming satisfied that the road could be bought for less than its potential value, Mr. Harriman invited Jacob H. Schiff (of Kuhn, Loeb & Co.), James Stillman (president of the National City Bank), and

[1] Mr. Felton had had long and varied railroad experience as chief engineer of the Chester & Delaware River Railroad; general superintendent of the P.C. & St. L.; general manager of the N.Y. & N.E.; vice-president of the Erie, of the East Tenn., Va. & Ga. system, of the Memphis & Charleston, and of the Mobile & Birmingham; and president of the Alabama Great Southern, and of the N.O. & Texas Pacific.

George Gould to join him in making the purchase
on the terms suggested, and in providing the necessary funds for betterments and additional equipment, as well as for the refunding or retirement of
the company's maturing bonds. Upon the representations made by Mr. Harriman, Messrs. Schiff, Stillman, and Gould agreed to coöperate with him, and
the four men formed a syndicate for the purchase,
reorganization, and recapitalization of the Chicago
& Alton road.

This syndicate was ultimately made to include
Morris K. Jessup, John A. Stewart (ex-Assistant
Treasurer of the United States), John J. Mitchell
(president of the Illinois Trust Company), and other
individuals of like character, as well as some of
the leading financial houses and institutions of the
country. The supposition that men and firms of
such standing would join a band of "pirates" and
"looters" for the purpose of "wrecking" and "gut-
ting" the Alton is, to say the least, highly improbable. The public assumed, or was led to believe, that
Messrs. Harriman, Stillman, Schiff, and Gould were
the sole managers and beneficiaries of the reorganization; but this was not the case. The four gentlemen named organized the syndicate, but it included
about one hundred members.

In January, 1899, the syndicate purchased ninety-seven per cent of the capital stock of the Chicago & Alton Company (about 218,000 shares) and paid therefore the sum of $38,815,000 in cash. They then proceeded to readjust the accounts of the company by crediting to surplus the sum of $12,444,000, which the old managers of the road, in previous years, had taken out of current income and invested in permanent betterments. In the opinion of the new owners and their legal counsel, permanent improvements and additions to the property ought to have been charged to capital account, and not taken out of surplus earnings, which belonged to the stockholders and might properly have been distributed in dividends. The newly elected directors, therefore, charged to capital the sum of $12,444,000 previously spent in betterments, and credited it to surplus, with a view to distributing a part of it ($6,669,000) in the shape of a thirty per cent dividend on the old stock, and so lessening the cost of the road to its purchasers.

Having thus acquired the property, and transferred the cost of previous betterments to capital account, the syndicate, which included ninety-seven per cent of the stockholders, reorganized the corporation and elected as president Mr. S. M. Felton, upon whose report the road had been bought. They then recapitalized the company by issuing securities in the following amounts:

50-year 3 per cent bonds.....................	$31,988,000 [1]
50-year 3½ per cent bonds..................	22,000,000
4 per cent preferred stock..................	19,544,000
Common stock............................	19,542,000
Total................................	$93,074,000

The $31,988,000 of three per cent bonds actually
issued were offered to all the stockholders and taken
by them pro rata, at 65, which was believed at the
time and in the circumstances to be a fair rate. The
purchase of these securities at a cost of $20,792,200
and the acquirement of ninety-seven per cent of the
stock of the old company at a cost of $38,815,000,
made the investment of the syndicate in the reorganized road $59,607,200. This sum was soon after-
ward increased by the purchase of the Peoria Northern Line at $3,000,000 and the payment of $500,000
for commissions, charges, legal expenses, etc., in
connection with the reorganization. This made the
total investment of the new owners of the road
$63,107,200, as shown below.

Purchase of 97 per cent of the old company's stock.................................	$38,815,000
Purchase of $31,988,000 3 per cent bonds at 65.	20,792,200
Purchase of Peoria Northern Line...........	3,000,000
Commissions, legal expenses, etc	500,000
Total................................	$63,107,200 [2]

[1] Forty millions in three per cent bonds were authorized, but
$8,012,000 were held in reserve for future requirements. These eight
millions were subsequently sold at market rates, and the proceeds
were spent on the property.

[2] It is quite possible that the syndicate did not have this whole

As soon as the sale of the bonds put sufficient money into the treasury and made available the $12,444,000 of surplus created by capitalizing the sums previously spent in betterments, the new directors declared a cash dividend of thirty per cent on the old company's stock, for the purpose of lessening the cost of the road to its buyers. This reduced the sum of their investment as follows:

Total cost of the road to its purchasers (as shown above)..	$63,107,200
Less dividend of 30 per cent on the old stock...	6,669,180
Reduced cost.........................	$56,438,020

To represent this investment, the new stockholders had in hand, for sale at the best prices they could get:

3 per cent bonds, par value................	$31,988,000
3½ per cent bonds, par value...............	22,000,000
4 per cent preferred stock, par value........	19,544,000
Common stock par value..................	19,542,000
Total..............................	$93,074,000 [1]

In order to get back the amount that they had actually put into the property ($56,438,020 as above shown) the stockholders would have to sell the

amount invested at any one time, because some of the securities may have been sold before the transaction was completed. The figures are given in this way only for the purpose of showing how much money the stockholders put into the venture from first to last.

[1] This capitalization was increased to $101,086,000 when the reserved bonds ($8,012,000) were issued. The total of three per cent bonds was then $40,000,000 instead of $31,988,000, as here stated.

bonds and preferred stock at approximately the following figures:

$31,988,000 3 per cent bonds at 80	$25,590,400
22,000,000 3½ per cent bonds at 74	16,280,000
19,544,000 preferred stock at 75	14,658,000
Total	$56,528,400
Money invested	56,438,020

They would then have the common stock as clear profit, and if they sold it at, say, 25, they would make about $5,000,000 on the purchase and recapitalization of the road. This would be equivalent to about nine per cent on their total investment. They perhaps made more than this, but how much more it is impossible to determine. After the securities were distributed among the members of the syndicate, they were sold by the individual owners at various prices, and at various times between 1900 and 1907. The profit realized depended, in every case, upon market conditions at the date of sale. Professor Ripley states, as a fact, that the profits of the syndicate — that is, of the one hundred or more stockholders — were $23,600,000;[1] but as he does not give his method of computation there is no possibility of testing his results. The Attorney-General of Illinois figured that the syndicate made a profit of $24,648,600; but his calculations were

[1] *Railroads: Finance and Organization*, by Professor W. Z. Ripley (New York, 1915), p. 266.

soon discredited. Expert Accountant J. H. Mc-
Clement showed that, even accepting the inordi-
nately high prices at which the Attorney-General
assumed the stockholders sold, their profit was only
$11,124,300. In other words, the figuring did not
work out.[1]

As a matter of fact, the computations of both
Ripley and the Attorney-General were mere guesses,
made under the influence of a strong anti-Harriman
bias. If the stockholders sold their securities at the
average prices that prevailed between 1901 and
1907, they made $7,624,000. If they sold in the
summer of 1903, when the control of the road was
acquired by the Rock Island, they made $2,800,000.
If they held on until 1907, and sold then, they lost
$1,400,000.[2] The probability is that most of the
stockholders sold at the most favorable time —
that is, in the first year, or the first two years, after
the securities were distributed. By an Act of the
New York Legislature, approved February 26, 1900,
the three per cent bonds of the Alton road were made
a legal investment for the savings banks of that
State, and this immediately created a good demand
for them at prices which ranged from 82½ to 94.
As there is no means, however, of ascertaining when

[1] *Statement of the Recapitalization of the Chicago & Alton Railroad Company* (New York, 1907), pp. 13–14.
[2] McClement, pp. 13–14 *et seq.*

the hundred or more stockholders disposed of their holdings, nor what prices they obtained for them, it is impossible to know what their profits were; and for that reason all estimates are more or less conjectural. The most that can be said with certainty is that owing to favorable market conditions, those who happened to sell at top prices realized more than they had anticipated.

A prominent New York banking house which had no connection with the Chicago & Alton transaction, except that it participated to the extent of $250,000 in the investment, was asked recently to look up its records and find out what its profits were. The value of its participation, and of the securities represented thereby, varied from time to time according to the market value of the securities. There were times when the transaction showed little or no profit. The maximum profit that it showed at any one time was about 8.2 per cent. The impression of these bankers is that if a participant got out at the most favorable time, he made a profit of about nine per cent. The result of the reorganization, so far as the stockholders are concerned, may be summarized in the statement that they invested $56,000,000 or $57,000,000 in the property (including the purchase of the three per cent bonds), expanded the capitalization by issuing new securities to the par value of

$93,074,000 (excluding the $8,012,000 held in reserve for betterments), and finally sold these securities at prices which gave them a net profit of probably eight per cent, and possibly twelve or fifteen per cent, upon their total cash investment.

At the time when the road changed ownership, the series of transactions above outlined excited little if any adverse criticism. Every detail of the reorganization, including the thirty per cent dividend and the sale of the three per cent bonds to the new stockholders at 65, had the widest possible publicity; but nobody complained of injury or injustice. The former owners of the road were satisfied with the price that they received; the three per cent of the old stockholders who declined to sell their shares enjoyed precisely the same rights and privileges that were given to the new stockholders; the purchasers of the new securities bought with full knowledge of the syndicate's operations, and did not complain that they had been either misinformed or misled; the governors of the New York Stock Exchange considered all the details of the recapitalization and then listed the new securities without objection or question; and, finally, the patrons of the road — the farmers, manufacturers, and shippers — were more than satisfied with the lower rates and greatly increased facilities that they enjoyed under the new management.

Serious and hostile criticism of the Chicago &
Alton reorganization did not begin until 1906, when
President Roosevelt broke off friendly relations with
Mr. Harriman, and when the Interstate Commerce
Commission, at the President's suggestion or upon
its own initiative, began an investigation of Mr.
Harriman's past activities.[1] This investigation was
largely devoted to the Chicago & Alton case, and the
report thereon described the reorganization as "indefensible financing." The features of the transaction most severely criticised were the dividend of
thirty per cent on the stock of the old company, the
selling of the three per cent bonds to the new stockholders at 65, and the alleged "watering" of the
original stock by increasing the number of shares
without adding to the physical assets of the road
a sum equal to the increase of capitalization. It
will be most convenient, perhaps, to take up these
transactions in the order in which they have been
mentioned.

1. *The thirty per cent dividend.*

That the new stockholders had a legal right to
charge to capital the cost of permanent betterments
which had previously been charged to income is

[1] "Consolidation and Combination of Carriers." Investigation be-
gun November 15, 1906; case submitted April 5, 1907; case decided
July 11, 1907. *Reports* of the Commission (Washington, 1908), vol.
XII, p. 277.

unquestionable. The practice had not only the approval of expert accountants, but the sanction of the courts. In a precisely similar case in England the High Court of Appeal said:

The circumstance that they had been paying what ought to be charged to capital out of revenue does not prevent their right, or their duty to the persons who are looking for their payment out of revenue, to credit back to revenue those things which have been carried, for the time being, to capital account.[1]

The new stockholders also had a legal right to transform the book surplus thus obtained into an actual cash surplus, by selling bonds to the necessary amount, and then to declare a cash dividend from the surplus so obtained. W. W. Cook, the standard authority on corporation law, says:

When the company has used profits for improvements, it may lawfully borrow an equivalent sum of money for the purpose of a dividend. And it may properly borrow money for a dividend, if upon a fair estimate of its assets and liabilities it has assets in excess of its liabilities, and capital stock equal to the amount of the proposed dividend.[2]

In paying a dividend of thirty per cent out of a surplus created by capitalizing the cost of previous betterments, the new management was only doing what the old management had intended to do. In a

[1] Mills vs. Northern Railway & Co., 5 Chancery Appeals, 621.
[2] Cook on "Corporations" (5th edition), section 546.

circular letter to the old stockholders, written in
February, 1899, T. B. Blackstone, then president of
the Chicago & Alton Railroad, said:

In case a majority of the shares of the company are not
sold to the syndicate, I shall advise that you authorize
the refunding of the outstanding bonds of the company,
and the issue of a stock dividend to represent earnings
heretofore invested in permanent improvements.

His reasons for making this recommendation were
not only that large sums had previously been expended in permanent improvements, which ought to
have been charged to capital, but that, as a result
of this policy, the existing capitalization (bonds and
stock together) represented less than sixty per cent
of the actual cost of the property.[1]

Inasmuch as this undistributed surplus from past
earnings was mainly responsible for the high price
that the purchasers had to pay for the old stock
($175 and $200 per share), they naturally thought
that they were justified in taking out of such surplus
a part of the purchase money. That it belonged to
them there can be no question. W. M. Ackworth,
the leading European authority on railway administration, says, in a recent review of William E.
Hooper's "Railway Accounting"

Here in England no one has yet doubted that undi-
vided profits, put back into the business, belong to the

[1] Report of President Blackstone for 1894.

shareholders just as much as the property purchased
with the capital originally subscribed.[1]

Halford Erickson, a member of the Railroad Commission of Wisconsin, an authority not likely to
have a pro-railroad bias, seems to think that it
might be expedient even to capitalize past losses and
discounts.[2] Under recent rulings, moreover, of the
Interstate Commerce Commission, permanent betterments must be charged to capital account, or at
least kept separate from maintenance expenses in the
books.[3]

In view of these considerations, it is hard to see
why it was not proper, as it unquestionably was
legal, to charge past betterments to capital account
and declare a dividend of thirty per cent on the old
stock for the purpose of lessening the cost of the road
to its buyers. The only reasonable objections to
such a course are stated, very fairly, by Professor
Mead and President Fink. The former is of opinion
that capitalization of sums previously spent for betterments is justifiable only when the betterments
have actually increased earnings, which in the
Chicago & Alton case they had not done. "Its

[1] *Railway Age Gazette*, August 23, 1915.
[2] *Government Regulation of Security Issues of Public Utility Corporations* (Madison, Wis., January, 1909), p. 54.
[3] W. M. Ackworth, in *Railway Age Gazette*, July 23, 1915. The
subject is also discussed by Beale and Wyman in their *Railroad Rate
Regulation*, secs. 355–62.

earnings for many years," Professor Mead says, "had been stationary," and "its property had not been kept up to standard." If the company had maintained a proper depreciation account, there would have been no such surplus. For these reasons he disapproves of the capitalization of past betterments and the issue of bonds to pay a dividend thereon; but he admits that, in the absence of state legislation expressly forbidding it, "the legality of the proceeding is not to be questioned." [1] This judgment, however, does not change the facts that the money *was* expended, the betterments *were* made, and the cost might properly have been charged, at the time, to capital account. The proceeding involves a question of financial expediency, but not, in any sense, of illegality.

President Fink objects to the capitalization of the cost of past betterments for the reason that it may afford an opportunity for manipulation of accounts.[2] In the Chicago & Alton case, however, no one ever asserted that the accounts had been tampered with, or that the sum of $12,444,000 had not actually been spent for permanent betterments. Both the old management and the new recognized the past expenditures for improvement as real and legitimate.

[1] *Corporation Finance*, pp. 246–53.
[2] *Federal Regulation of Railroad Securities*, pp. 4–5.

2. *The issue of $31,988,000 of three per cent bonds to the new stockholders at 65.*

It was perfectly proper, and in accordance with general practice, to offer the new bonds to the stockholders before offering them to the public. The stockholders had taken the risk of putting $38,815,-000 into the property, and it was only just that they should have the first chance to buy the securities issued by the company upon reorganization. "But," it may be said, "the price at which the bonds were offered was too low; it enabled the buyers to resell them at a great advance, and thus to realize a profit which ought to have gone into the treasury of the company." That the stockholders did make a large profit when they resold the bonds is unquestionable; but that the price at which they acquired them was too low, measured by the standards and conditions of the time, is not so certain. A three per cent bond was then an untried experiment. The bonds of the old company, which were about to mature, bore interest at six and seven per cent, and nobody could tell in advance what the market value of a low-rate security would prove to be. That the price at which the three per cent bonds were offered to the stockholders was low enough to give them a chance of profit is true; but there was no intention of giving them an exorbitant profit. A market for bonds bearing as low an interest rate as three per cent had to be created. Such securities would naturally be taken by savings banks; but the bill making the three per cent bonds of the Chicago & Alton Company a legal investment for the savings banks of New York had not then passed the legislature, and it was uncertain whether it would pass. If it did not, the demand for such bonds would be comparatively limited and they might not bring more than 70, at which price they would yield 4.28 per cent. The bill which authorized savings banks to invest in them did not become law until February 26, 1900, more than a year after the syndicate bought the road. It was then signed by Theodore Roosevelt, Governor of the State, who apparently thought that the bonds of the "looted," "wrecked," and "gutted" corporation were a safe investment for savings banks.

In 1907, when the Interstate Commerce Commission investigated the subject, these very bonds were selling for only a little more than the price at which they were issued, although they were just as good then as they ever had been. The exceptionally high prices from which the stockholders profited, or may have profited, in 1901–02, were purely fortuitous and were due mainly to the state of the money market, the low rates of interest which then prevailed, and the unprecedented demand for investment securities.

It must not be forgotten, moreover, that in investing cash to the amount of $20,792,200 in three per cent bonds, the stockholders took all the chances of interest rates, State legislation, and savings bank demand, and that such chances might have gone against them. In that case, their bonds might have been unsalable and they might not have been able to get their money back. They took risks and reaped profits, and there was little if any criticism of their action until seven years later, when the Government, through the Interstate Commerce Commission, began its campaign against that "undesirable citizen," E. H. Harriman.

So far as this particular transaction is concerned, the Federal authorities might, with equal reason, have begun proceedings against other railroad companies. In April, 1899, the Chicago, Burlington & Quincy sold to its stockholders at 75 three-and-one-half per cent bonds which went soon afterward above par, and some years earlier the St. Paul, Minneapolis & Manitoba sold to its shareholders at 10 an issue of mortgage bonds which later went above 100. It was at that time a frequently employed and never contested practice to give "rights" to stockholders by offering to them stocks or bonds at prices below their actual or possible market value, and it is still a common practice in other fields of business enterprise.

3. *The alleged over-capitalization.*

The question whether the Chicago & Alton Railroad was over-capitalized or not — that is, whether its capital stock exceeded its value — depends upon the definition given to the word "value." What is the "value" of a railroad? To this question three different answers have been given, namely:

(a) The value of a railroad is to be measured by the amount of money actually invested in it, from first to last.

(b) The value of a railroad is the present cost of building and equipping it, as new.

(c) The value of a railroad is the sum on which, as a "going concern," it can earn at least the current rate of interest.

The Interstate Commerce Commission seems to prefer the first of these definitions; some economists favor the second; while most railroad men adopt the third.

There seems to be no good reason for assuming that the value of a railroad differs in any essential way from the value of a farm or a factory. The value of a farm is to be ascertained by capitalizing its annual net return at the current rate of interest.

Two farms may contain exactly the same number of acres, and may represent precisely the same original investment, and yet one may have twice the value of the other. If a farm, during a series of years, shows its ability to earn, say, six per cent upon a capital of $10,000, then the value of that farm is $10,000 no matter what its original cost was. The owner may have bought it for $5000, but it would be manifestly absurd to say that its value is only $5000 when it yields crops large enough to pay the current rate of interest on $10,000. Its value is to be measured not by the amount of money originally invested in it, but by its earning capacity as a "going concern." The same is true of a factory.

There was once a horseshoe nail manufactory in northern New York which was started with a capital of $100,000. By managing skillfully, and by gradually putting $400,000 of earnings into new plant, improved machinery, money-saving inventions, etc., the owners finally made it earn $300,000 a year, or six per cent on $5,000,000. Was the value of that concern the $500,000 actually invested in it, or the $5,000,000 on which it could earn six per cent a year?

In June, 1915, the directors of the Ford Motor Car Company of Detroit increased the capital stock of that corporation from $2,000,000 to $100,000,000. Forty-eight millions were distributed in the shape of a stock dividend, and the remaining stock was held in reserve "for future dividends and the development of the company." [1] At the time of the increase of capitalization the actual assets of the company were $61,000,000, of which only $24,191,000 represented physical plant. Suppose that in future the company is able to earn six per cent on its inflated capitalization of $100,000,000. What, then, will be the value of the manufactory? Will it be worth $2,000,000 (the amount of its original capital stock), or $24,191,000 (the amount actually invested in plant), or $61,000,000 (the amount of its total assets), or $100,000,000 (the amount on which it can earn six per cent)? In explaining the transaction, James Couzens, vice-president of the company, said: "The purpose of the increase in our capital stock is to have the outstanding stock more nearly represent the value of the company" — meaning, of course, its value as a "going concern." If it could earn, with regularity and safety, six per cent on its expanded capitalization of $100,000,000, then its value would be $100,000,000 regardless of the fact that its original capital was only $2,000,000 and regardless also of the fact that its total assets fell nearly $40,000,000 short of its expanded capital. If the same reasoning is not applicable to the value of a railroad — why

[1] *New York Times* and *New York Sun*, June 5 and 20, 1915.

not? So far as the definition of "value" is concerned.
no distinction can reasonably be made between a
railroad and a manufactory. Both are to be valued
according to their earning capacity. Upon this
point political economists generally are agreed.
Professor H. R. Seager says:

As an investment, land is valued, as is any other
form of income-producing property, by capitalizing its
annual return at the current rate of interest. For example, if a given piece of land is found by experience to
bring in, on an average, a net rent of $1200, and the
current rate of interest is six per cent, its price will
normally be $20,000 or the sum which invested at six
per cent will yield the same return.[1]

In considering the value of a railroad as it affects the
security of its bondholders, Thomas L. Greene, vice-
president of the Audit Company of New York, says:

The whole property of a railroad company, considered
simply as real estate and old material, is worth but a
small fraction of the amount for which it is mortgaged.
The creditors of the company depend for their money
not upon the property considered as such, but upon the
business for which the company was organized; that is,
upon the transportation of passengers and goods. If
the earning capacity of that company becomes for any
reason impaired, the strong legal language of the mortgage will not save the holder of the company's bonds
from loss. In the end he must accept, as a basis for the

[1] *Principles of Economics*, by H. R. Seager, Professor of Political
Economy in Columbia University, p. 239.

revaluation of his securities, the earning power of the company as a carrier of traffic.[1]

This whole question of value, as it affects railroads, was discussed by Henry Fink, president of the Norfolk & Western Railroad Company, in a letter that he wrote to the Railroad Securities Commission in 1910, in reply to their request for information and opinions. His conclusion was that "the value of a railroad can be measured only by its earning capacity." His judgments, he added, were based on his own experience during sixty years of continuous railroad service.[2]

This view of railroad "value" has not only been accepted by the best economists and the most experienced railway administrators, but has repeatedly been sanctioned by the courts. In the Oklahoma case, Judge Hook said: "An established railroad system may be worth more than its original cost, and more than the mere cost of its physical reproduction." It has no value except as a going concern.[3]

This also was the view taken by the United States Supreme Court in the tax case of the C. C. C. &

[1] *Corporation Finance*, by Thomas L. Greene, vice-president of the Audit Company of New York (New York, 1913), pp. 35–36 and 38.

[2] *Federal Regulation of Railroad Securities and Valuation of Railroad Properties* (Roanoke, Va., 1910), by Henry Fink.

[3] *Railway Statistics of the United States*, by Slason Thompson (Chicago, 1914), p. 740.

St. L. R.R. Co. *vs.* Backus. In its opinion in that case the court said:

The value of property results from the use to which it is put, and varies with the profitableness of that use, present and prospective, actual and anticipated. There is no pecuniary value outside of that which results from such use. . . . Never was it held that the cost of a thing is the test of its value. Suppose there be two bridges over the Ohio, the cost of construction of each being the same, one between Cincinnati and Newport, and the other twenty miles below where there is nothing but a village on either shore. The value of the one will, manifestly, be greater than that of the other, and that excess of value will spring solely from the larger use of the one than of the other.[1]

Assuming then — or, rather, adopting the view of competent authorities — that the value of a railroad, and consequently its proper capitalization, should be based on earning capacity, "present and prospective, actual and anticipated," was Mr. Harriman justified in believing that he could make the Chicago & Alton pay interest and dividends on a capitalization of $101,000,000? [2]

The annual net income needed would be $3,533,-440, as follows:

Interest on $40,000,000 3% bonds...........	$1,200,000
Interest on 22,000,000 3½% bonds..........	770,000
Dividend on 19,544,000 preferred stock at 4% .	781,760
Dividend on 19,542,000 common stock at 4% .	781,680
$101,086,000	$3,533,440

[1] 154 U.S. 445.
[2] Owing to the necessity of spending for betterments four times as

Was it prudent and reasonable to anticipate that when the proposed betterments should be made, and the necessary equipment procured, the greatly improved road would be able to earn the annual net income of $3,533,440, which would be required?[1]

In the year when the syndicate bought the Chicago & Alton, the road, even in its run-down and half-equipped condition, earned $2,684,694 net, and it had earned, on an average, $2,734,534 net, for the six preceding years (1893 to 1898, both inclusive). It was only necessary, therefore, that annual net earnings should be increased by $798,906 in order to pay interest and dividends on all outstanding securities. Mr. Felton, a thoroughly competent judge,

much as President Felton estimated, the capital stock was later increased (upon the figuring of the Interstate Commerce Commission) to about $114,000,000, but the reference here is only to the original capitalization of $101,000,000 upon which Mr. Harriman's calculations were based.

[1] So far as fixed charges are concerned, the capitalization of the Chicago & Alton would seem to have been prudent and conservative. According to Professor Stuart Daggett, the average percentage of fixed charges to net income, in seven railroad reorganizations between the years 1893 and 1898 (the Atchison, Baltimore & Ohio, Erie, Northern Pacific, Reading, Southern, and Union Pacific) was 73.9. (*Railroad Reorganization*, p. 358.) In the Chicago & Alton, after reorganization, this percentage was only 72, and before 1907 it had fallen below 60.

Professor E. S. Mead says: "In most cases, no more than 20 per cent of the gross earnings of a railroad company should be represented by interest charges." (*Corporation Finance*, p. 65.) After the recapitalization of the Chicago & Alton, in 1900, the ratio of interest charges to gross earnings was 27.5; but in 1907, on the whole indebtedness then outstanding, it had fallen below 20.

estimated that by an expenditure of $5,200,000 in betterments the annual net earnings of the road might be increased at least $1,000,000. Mr. Harriman, an even better judge, believed that physical improvements and good management would bring the annual net earnings up to $4,000,000. How prudent and conservative these estimates were the result showed. In the year when the Interstate Commerce Commission investigated the recapitalization, the net earnings of the road were $4,415,974, a sum which was $415,974 above Mr. Harriman's estimate, and $681,440 above the estimate of Mr. Felton. If rates had not been reduced during the period of Mr. Harriman's administration, the increase in net earnings would have been even greater than this.[1]

[1] The reduction of ton-mile freight rates between 1899 and 1907 is given by the Director of the Bureau of Railway Statistics as follows:

Year	Receipts per ton-mile (in cents)
1899	.800
1900	.796
1901	.723
1902	.679
1903	.599
1904	.677
1905	.689
1906	.639
1907	.604

A part of this reduction, but according to Mr. Thompson only a small part, was due to the development of a large coal traffic, on

A case parallel in some respects to that of the
Chicago & Alton is furnished by the reorganization
of the Norfolk & Western Railroad in 1896. In
1895, before the reorganization and recapitalization,
the road and equipment were valued at $115,098,721
and the capitalization was $117,364,909 as follows:

Bonds.	$ 57,864,909
Preferred Stock.	50,000,000
Common stock.	9,500,000
Total capitalization.	$117,364,909

In the reorganization, the bonds were increased
by $4,635,000 and the common and preferred stock
by $30,000,000 making an expanded capitalization
of $151,999,909.[1] In commenting upon this infla-
tion, which amounted as above shown to nearly
$35,000,000, President Fink said: "Stocks issued in
such cases are in no sense fictitious. They represent
actual values, and are drafts, for value received, on
more prosperous times."

He then shows that although the Norfolk & Western was over-capitalized in 1896, in the sense that it

which the rates were low; but in commenting on the figures the
Director says:
"Whatever may be the popular impression as to the over-capitalization of the Alton, the above table furnishes proof that it had
no effect whatever in causing exorbitant rates, for these are nearly
25 per cent lower than in 1899." (*Cost, Capitalization and Estimated
Value of American Railways*, by Slason Thompson, Director of
Bureau of Railway Statistics, Chicago, 1907, pp. 186–87.)
[1] *Commercial & Financial Chronicle*, vol. LXII, 1896.

was not then earning dividends and fixed charges, it did begin paying dividends on its preferred stock in 1897, and on its common in 1901.[1] Its stock, in 1916, was quoted at 119, which showed that its earning power had much more than overtaken its expanded capitalization.

Mr. Harriman expected to do with the Chicago & Alton just what Mr. Fink did with the Norfolk & Western, namely, increase by means of extensive betterments its capacity for doing business and its earning power, and thus bring its net operating revenue up to the requirements of its enlarged capitalization. That he measurably succeeded in doing this is shown by the fact that when, after losing control of the road in 1903, he completely severed his connection with it in 1907, it was paying four per cent on its preferred stock and earning five per cent on its common. In other words, it was taking care of its entire capitalization, and was doing this with no increase of rates and with an enormous extension of its facilities for doing business and serving the public.

All these facts, however, were suppressed or ignored in the Interstate Commerce Commission's report. The Commissioners, from their point of

[1] "Over-capitalization," by Henry Fink; *Railway Age Gazette*, July, 1908.

view, might have been justified in expressing disapproval of Mr. Harriman's financial methods; but
they were not justified in concealing the fact that
these methods had more than doubled the capacity
of the road to serve the people. "Suppressio veri
suggestio falsi," and the concealment in this case
gave the impression that Mr. Harriman — in the
words of Senator Cullom — had "looted the road,"
regardless of the interests of the people and the territory that it served. The rebuilding of the Chicago
& Alton was one of the great railroad achievements
of the time; but in the report of the Commission
it is made to appear a piratical raid of unscrupulous financiers, who, for their own selfish purposes,
wrecked and looted a well-conducted and prosperous corporation. If the members of the Commission
could be put on the witness stand, as Mr. Harriman
was, and could be required, under oath, to tell "the
whole truth," they might find it difficult to explain
why, in a report that was supposed to cover all the
facts essential to an understanding of the case, they
said nothing with regard to the physical condition
of the Alton road when the syndicate bought it;
nothing about the intention of the old managers to
declare just such a dividend as that declared later by
the new managers; nothing about the sanction given
by courts and legal authorities to the capitalization

of past betterments; nothing about the practice of the time in the matter of reorganizations; nothing about Mr. Harriman's virtual reconstruction and reëquipment of the road; nothing about the increase of ninety per cent in gross earnings and eighty per cent in net earnings which resulted therefrom; nothing about the benefit that the public derived from the lowering of rates and the improvement of facilities; nothing about the relation between the earning capacity of the reorganized road and its expanded capitalization; and nothing about the resumption of dividends on the preferred stock in 1906. A report which conceals or ignores these pertinent facts is not a judicial review of the case, but merely a prosecuting attorney's brief.

The responsibility for the later condition of the Chicago & Alton cannot justly be thrown upon Mr. Harriman. The control of the road was wrested from him by the Rock Island, while he was in Europe in 1903, and he severed his relation with it altogether when the Rock Island transferred its holdings to the Toledo, St. Louis & Western in 1907. The financial measures adopted by the later management were ill-advised and unfortunate, and never would have met Mr. Harriman's approval. Partly to these measures, and partly to regulation, low rates, and depressed business conditions, the subsequent difficulties of the road were due. When Mr. Harriman resigned, it was not only paying its fixed charges, but was earning more than four per cent on both classes of its stock.

Before concluding this review of the Chicago & Alton reorganization, it seems necessary to answer specifically certain charges made against Mr. Harriman by two men who occupy positions of responsibility or authority; namely, Interstate Commerce Commissioner Prouty and Professor William Z. Ripley of Harvard University.

In an address delivered before the National Association of Manufacturers, in May, 1907, Commissioner Prouty said:

When Mr. Harriman, by dealings like those in the Chicago & Alton, enriches himself to the extent of many millions, he has not created that money. He has merely transferred it from the possession of some one else to himself.[1]

In the first place, there is no evidence to show that Mr. Harriman, as an individual participant in a syndicate of one hundred members, enriched himself to the extent of "many millions." In the second place, it may be said that when the Interstate Commerce Commissioners, by drawing money in the shape of salaries from the people of the United

[1] New York *Independent*, May 30, 1907, p. 1129.

States, enrich themselves to the extent of many hundreds of thousands of dollars, they have not created that money. They have merely transferred it from the possession of some one else to themselves. They may reply that for the money they have thus transferred from the people of the United States to themselves, through the United States Treasury, they have rendered valuable services — in other words, they have earned it. Mr. Harriman might have said the same, and with much more reason. By his "dealings" in the Chicago & Alton he almost entirely rebuilt the road; doubled its passenger accommodations; improved immensely its train service; increased by 134 per cent the hauling power of its locomotives; added 269 per cent to its capacity for moving freight; fostered old industries and created new ones all along its line, and enabled the people of Illinois to "create" tens of millions of dollars which they never could have created without the traffic facilities given them by Mr. Harriman's betterments. If the Interstate Commerce Commissioners could show anything like this equivalent for the money they have "transferred" from the United States Treasury to themselves, their claim to have earned their salaries would be unquestioned and unquestionable.

One of the most unfair, as well as one of the most

recent, of Mr. Harriman's assailants is Professor William Z. Ripley, Ropes Professor of Economics in Harvard University. In a volume entitled "Railroads: Finance and Organization," published by Longmans Green & Co. of New York, in 1915, Professor Ripley devotes a large part of his eighth chapter to the Chicago & Alton reorganization, and begins his account of it in the following words:

Practically all of the possible abuses and frauds described in the preceding pages under the caption of stock-watering are found combined in a single instance in recent years — the reorganization of the Chicago & Alton road by the late E. H. Harriman and his associates during the eight years following 1898.[1]

Most of the hostile critics of the Chicago & Alton transaction try to make their points by concealing or ignoring facts favorable to the defense. Professor Ripley not only conceals or ignores, but misstates. He says, for example, that the Chicago & Alton road, prior to the reorganization, was doing "a constantly expanding business." This, simply, is not true. The gross earnings of the road had decreased more than $2,500,000 in the eleven years that preceded the change of ownership. In 1887 they were nearly $9,000,000, while in 1898, the year before the Harriman syndicate acquired the property, they had fallen to $6,286,568. A business which declines to

[1] Chapter VIII, p. 262.

the extent of $2,655,000 in a little more than a decade may still continue to be a profitable business, but it certainly is not "a constantly expanding business." [1]

Professor Ripley states repeatedly (pp. 264–65) that the operations of Mr. Harriman and the syndicate were "covered up," "remained undisclosed," "were never disclosed," "were obscured in the published accounts," and "were thoroughly concealed." This, again, is simply not true. All the operations of Mr. Harriman and the syndicate, including the capitalization of past betterments, the declaration

[1] Professor E. S. Mead, who is a much more careful and trustworthy student of railroad affairs than Professor Ripley seems to be, states the fact accurately when he says (*Corporation Finance*, p. 251): "The earnings of the Chicago & Alton, prior to the reorganization, had been stationary for many years." They had been stationary for about five years, but had decreased thirty per cent in eleven years. The precise figures are given by Director Thompson of the Bureau of Railway Statistics as follows:

Year	Gross earnings
1887	$8,941,386
1888	7,511,465
1889	7,516,616
1890	7,065,753
1891	7,590,881
1892	7,730,610
1893	7,566,640
1894	6,292,236
1895	6,292,486
1896	6,840,283
1897	6,673,605
1898	6,286,568

(*Cost, Capitalization, and Estimated Value of American Railways*), by Slason Thompson, Director of the Bureau of Railway Statistics, Chicago, 1907, p. 183.

of a thirty per cent dividend, and the sale of the three per cent bonds to the stockholders at 65, were fully and accurately set forth in the listing application to the New York Stock Exchange, as well as in the leading railroad and financial publications of New York, including "Poor's Manual," "Moody's Manual," the "Manual of Statistics," the "Commercial & Financial Chronicle," the "Wall Street Journal," and the "New York Evening Post." [1]

In commenting upon this feature of the case, in a statement written in 1907 but never published, Mr. Harriman said:

Every essential fact connected with the recapitalization of the Chicago & Alton system, including the objects for which the new securities were issued, was fully disclosed and widely published, at the time, in circulars, financial papers, annuals, and reference books for investors, etc., etc. These publications, as well as the printed applications to the New York Stock Exchange, showed exactly for what consideration each class of securities had been issued, including the fact that the refunding three per cent bonds of the railroad company had been subscribed for by the stockholders at 65, and that a dividend of thirty per cent had been declared in May, 1900. The listing committee of the Exchange investigated fully, and unanimously recommended the

---

[1] *Poor's Manual* for 1900, pp. 654 and 657, and for 1901, pp. 661–02. *Moody's Manual* for 1901, p. 1195. *Manual of Statistics* for 1900, p. 61, and for 1901, p. 59. *Commercial & Financial Chronicle* in the five numbers for April 7 and 14; May 5 and 19; and November 17, 1900.

granting of official quotations to all the securities and their admission to dealings on the Exchange. This recommendation was approved, without any dissenting voice, by the Board of Governors of the Exchange, consisting of forty members of high standing. So far as I know, there has never been the slightest pretense that any of the original stockholders were deceived in any manner or form, or that any subsequent investor was in any way misled. All parties in interest have acquiesced, for seven years, with full knowledge. The transaction is now criticised, for the first time, and in a manner calculated to misrepresent and distort the facts as they existed in 1900 when the securities were created and issued.

Mr. Harriman's statement, supported though it be by all the railroad manuals and financial journals of New York, may fail to carry conviction to the mind of Professor Ripley; but it will be generally accepted by people who are more desirous of knowing the truth than of making out a case against the Chicago & Alton syndicate.

Professor Ripley accuses Mr. Harriman of "prejudicing the interest of shippers by creating the need of high rates for service in order to support the fraudulent capitalization" (p. 262). This charge is doubly misleading. In the first place, it erroneously assumes that rates are dependent upon capitalization, and in the second, it suggests that, as a matter of fact, Mr. Harriman did raise rates on the Alton in order to bolster up fictitious securities. Neither the assumption nor the suggestion is supported by the facts.

High capitalization, as a rule, does not result in high rates. On the contrary, the lowest average freight rates are in the parts of the United States that have the highest railroad capitalization.[1] That there is no interdependence of capitalization and rates has been repeatedly admitted even by the Interstate Commerce Commission. As long ago as 1899, Chairman Martin A. Knapp testified before the Industrial Commission that he had never seen a case in which rates seemed to depend upon capitalization, or to be influenced by it. "The capitalization of a railroad," he said, "cuts no figure in this rate question."

In an article entitled "Railroad Capitalization and Federal Regulation," Franklin K. Lane, while he was yet Commissioner, said: "Fundamentally there is no interdependence of capitalization and rate. The latter is not in law, nor in railroad policy, the child of the former."

Mr. Harriman, who had a much clearer understanding of the principles of rate-making than the Harvard Professor of Economics seems to have, said in the unpublished statement previously quoted:

[1] "The Railroad Situation of To-day," by Frank Trumbull: an address to the Western Society of Engineers, January 5, 1909, p. 7.

It is just as impossible to raise rates to any level that may be necessary to pay charges on increased capitalization as it would be for a manufacturer of steel, or of woolens, or of any other commodity, to raise his prices because he had a large debt upon which it was necessary to pay interest, or a large capital employed in the business. It would be suicidal for a railroad company to throttle or paralyze the industries along its lines by charging exorbitant rates. Even if there be no direct competition by parallel roads, every industrial plant located along a line of railroad is competing with plants located on other lines, and every railroad is forced to make such low and reasonable rates as will permit the industries in the territory tributary to it to make sales in competitive markets, and thus furnish the traffic from which the railroad company derives its earnings. It is impossible for a railroad company to sever its interests from those of its patrons. Its life blood is drawn from their prosperity, and it must furnish them with adequate and ever-increasing facilities at reasonable rates, wholly irrespective of its capitalization. If the calculations of the organizers of a railroad company turn out to be erroneous, and the capitalization is fixed at too high a figure, it is a misfortune for them and the other security-holders; but the widespread popular impression that a railroad company can extort money from the public at will, and in defiance of the laws of trade, simply for the purpose of paying interest or dividends upon increased issues of securities, is not justified by the facts.

In this brief statement there is more financial and economic wisdom, perhaps, than in a dozen volumes of Interstate Commerce Commission Reports, and more even than in some Supreme Court decisions.

The statement that the "unscrupulous management" of the Chicago & Alton did, as a matter of fact, "increase rates for service in order to support the fraudulent capitalization" is not true. The freight records of the Chicago & Alton for the period in question show a slight reduction in rates on grain, live stock, merchandise, and other classified commodities, with a very substantial reduction on coal. In 1899 the through rate on coal from the Springfield district was eighty cents. In 1907 it fell as low as forty cents. The average rate per ton per mile on the whole traffic (including coal) was reduced, as Slason Thompson has shown, about twenty-five per cent. The precise figures have been given on a previous page.

The most surprising of all Professor Ripley's misstatements is that which charges Mr. Harriman with "crippling" the Alton road "physically" (p. 262). Mr. Frank H. Spearman, who made the rebuilding of the Chicago & Alton the subject of a special article, described the "crippling" process in the following words:

Without delay or hesitation he [Mr. Harriman] set about making of the Alton the best possible road of its class, and its class is the first. He overhauled the system completely, and put it physically a little in advance of every competitor. To instance: For thirty years the Alton had been strong in a territory possessing the richest coal deposits in Illinois, and not until the Harriman forces took hold of the road had it ever developed a coal business. Not only has the new Alton been equipped with what it never had before, cars and motive power to handle this traffic, but its engineers, in rebuilding the line, show the lowest maximum grades from the Illinois coal fields into Chicago. Beginning with nothing, the new owners have, within five years, developed a coal traffic that already ranks second in volume among the soft-coal roads of its territory. . . . The Alton being once acquired, it became the policy of the new owners to increase the facilities of the public along their line for doing business. . . . The heaviest freight engines previously owned had been of fifty-five tons, and were capable, in condition, of hauling thirty cars, of twenty-five tons each; but the engines had been allowed to deteriorate until not above eighty per cent of that capacity could be obtained. The new engines, of the consolidation type, for freight traffic, weigh one hundred and sixty-five tons and haul one hundred freight cars. The passenger power consisted of forty- to fifty-ton engines, capable of hauling five to seven coaches of their day at high speed. Such engines have been replaced by modern engines of one hundred and thirty-five tons, while for especially heavy passenger service, of which the road has more than any line in its territory, exceptionally large engines have been provided, recent additions including the two most powerful express passenger engines in the world. . . . In freight car equipment, twenty- and twenty-five-ton capacity wooden gondola cars were replaced by fifty-five-ton capacity steel gondolas, and the proportion of the weight of car to load was reduced one third at a stroke. Acquiring a line that had always enjoyed a heavy passenger traffic, the new owners, where they had found fifty-feet coaches, built coaches seventy feet long, and

by ingeniously installing seats of a modern type, as well
as more comfortable than those of earlier models, they
have succeeded in accommodating in the new cars twice
the number of passengers provided for in the old. . . .

What it means to make over a railroad for such
modern traffic requirements is reflected sharply in the
work put upon the construction department. Working
out of Chicago, track elevation was pushed until every
railroad grade-crossing, from the terminal station to
the suburban yards, has been eliminated. The grades
receiving the heaviest of the traffic, as it centered
toward Chicago, were reduced until they gave the rebuilt road the lowest maximum grade of any road entering Chicago from the western coal fields. At the very
outset the work of double-tracking was begun. To provide for heavy cars and engines, heavier rails have been
spread south and west until to-day over one half the
total mileage of the entire system shows new steel.
The work falling on the bridge department was continuous and exacting. While shops were being enlarged,
engine-houses rebuilt, and turn-tables lengthened, the
track elevation at Chicago called unceasingly for via-
ducts, and the traffic conditions everywhere on the
system demanded new bridges for the motive power.
. . . On less than a thousand miles of trackage three
hundred and eighteen bridges were replaced within four
years. Of these, one hundred and fourteen bridges
were wholly done away with by the cast-iron pipe and
the concrete arch — the progress in the use of concrete
work being one of the most striking features of recent
bridge construction. But besides the great bridge across
the Missouri [the old million-dollar steel bridge was
"scrapped"] and four solid-floor creosoted trestles, one
hundred and twenty-two steel bridges also were installed.

The elimination of curvature, pushed till the maximum had been reduced to four degrees, is still in

progress, and so far has bad curvature been taken care of that an engineman familiar with a division five years ago would hardly recognize the right of way in the daylight. Long restful stretches of straight track have been developed until there are now on the system many tangents of from fifteen to twenty miles; there is at least one tangent of twenty-nine miles; and one extraordinary stretch of forty-five miles of track, straight as an arrow's flight. . . . To strengthen the work of the operating department, the railroad world has been drawn upon for the most effective safety devices in the operation of trains. Long stretches of track, in one instance covering a distance of sixty-five miles, are provided with continuous electric signals which protect moving trains, stations, grades, and curves. Previously to the rebuilding there were comparatively few interlocking signals on the whole line to protect railroad grade-crossings.[1]

According to Professor Ripley, the nefarious purpose of the "main conspirator" in making all these improvements was to "cripple" the road "physically"!

During the period of Mr. Harriman's administration, he spent $11,262,763 on roadway and structures, and $11,064,454 on new equipment, making a total of $22,327,219 for permanent betterments, a sum equivalent to about $22,000 per mile. The road thus "physically crippled" increased its gross

[1] "The Rebuilding of an American Railroad," by Frank H. Spearman (in *The Strategy of Great Railroads*, New York, 1914, pp. 50, 223, 225-26). This article was originally published before the work of rebuilding had been finished.

earnings from $6,286,569 in 1898 to $12,809,426 in 1907, and its net earnings from $2,684,694 to $4,415,974. How it was able to do this, in its "physically crippled" condition, Professor Ripley does not explain.

Those who have made a serious study of Mr. Harriman's activities know that he never "physically crippled" a railroad in his life. On the contrary, he never touched a railroad that he did not physically improve. From the Sodus Bay & Southern to the Union Pacific and the Alton, he made every railroad that he controlled serve the public better than it had ever served it before. No railroad corporation, moreover, ever defaulted on its bonds, or failed to earn its fixed charges, under Mr. Harriman's management.[1]

[1] Hearings before the Interstate Commerce Commission in the Chicago & Alton Case, p. 73.

CHAPTER XXVIII

REPLY TO ACCUSATIONS

THE foregoing account of the Chicago & Alton reorganization was originally published, as a separate article, in the "North American Review" for January, 1916. In the April number of the same periodical Professor Ripley and Mr. Roosevelt made a joint reply, in which the former renewed his attack on Mr. Harriman and the latter disclaimed responsibility for the investigation of the Harriman lines by the Interstate Commerce Commission. Inasmuch as the unfair and one-sided presentation of the Chicago & Alton case by the Commission did more than any other one thing to prejudice the public against Mr. Harriman, it seems necessary to consider briefly the additional arguments by which Professor Ripley tries to sustain it.

No public question or private transaction can be profitably discussed unless the essential facts involved therein are accurately set forth. In his book entitled "Railroads: Finance and Organization," Professor Ripley made the following erroneous or misleading statements:

(1) That the Chicago & Alton Railroad, when the

Harriman syndicate bought it, was doing "a constantly expanding business"; (2) that the syndicate made a profit of $23,600,000 out of its financiering; (3) that the operations of the syndicate were "concealed," "covered up," "never disclosed," and "obscured in the published accounts"; (4) that the reorganization of the road created "the need of high rates for service in order to support the fraudulent capitalization"; (5) that as a result of the recapitalization the road was "physically crippled"; and (6) that Mr. Harriman was a "conspirator," whose management of the property was "unscrupulous," "fraudulent," "piratical," and "predatory." [1]

In the preceding chapter an attempt was made to prove that each and every one of these statements was erroneous. Does Professor Ripley, in his reply, question the proofs, or attempt to make good his original assertions? Not in any way whatever. He brings up sundry new matters, and shows conclusively that the capitalization of the Alton was largely increased — a fact that has never been disputed — but he does not join issue on any of the points raised. So far, therefore, as silence can give consent, he virtually admits that the Harriman syndicate did *not* make $23,600,000 out of its finan-

[1] *Railroads: Finance and Organization*, pp. 77 and 262–66.

ciering; that the Alton road, when the syndicate bought it, was *not* doing "a constantly expanding business"; that the reorganized còmpany did *not* raise rates "to support the fraudulent capitalization"; and that the property was *not* "physically crippled" as the result of Mr. Harriman's operations. Now that the ground has been cleared to this extent, it may be profitable to consider the first account and the latest account given by Professor Ripley of this Chicago & Alton transaction.

The earliest public reference that Mr. Ripley made to the case is to be found in a single paragraph of the Report of the United States Industrial Commission of 1901. The Report is signed by the Commissioners, not by Professor Ripley, but the latter says he wrote it, and doubtless he did. As it shows what he first thought of the "Alton business," and what the Commission thought of it, at a time when all the details of the reorganization were known or readily accessible, the paragraph is here quoted in full:

An excellent illustration of inflation of capitalization is furnished by the recent reorganization of the Chicago & Alton Railway Company. The old Alton management was extremely conservative. The stock had never been watered, and represented, before the recent deal, less than the probable cost of duplication. The company was capitalized at about $30,000,000, including

$22,000,000 of stock and about $8,000,000 bonds. It had a net earning capacity of $2,900,000 a year, paying regular dividends of seven or eight per cent on its common stock. In 1899, the road was bought by a syndicate, which paid $175 a share for the common stock and $200 a share for the preferred stock, making a total cost to the purchaser of $40,000,000 for the $22,000,000 of stock. The road was recapitalized at $94,000,000, or $54,000,000 of bonds and $40,000,000 of stock. The new bonds were floated at three and a half per cent. The fixed charges of the road as reorganized amount to $1,963,000 per year. On the basis of the former earning capacity of the road, which averaged considerably more than three thousand dollars net per mile, it is estimated that the company will have no difficulty in earning its fixed charges and paying a dividend on the preferred stock. The increase of capitalization in this case is defended on the ground that the road will not have to earn any more than formerly in order to pay interest and dividends on the new capital. It seems clear, however, that the doubling of the capital stock and the increasing of the bonded debt nearly sevenfold must impose a burden upon the rates that will tend to prevent any reduction which might otherwise take place, and afford a convenient reason for refusing to advance wages.[1]

This is probably the most nearly accurate account of the financial reorganization of the Alton that Professor Ripley has ever given; but it contains no suggestion of "fraud," "piracy," "crippling," or "scuttling." On the contrary. it treats the transaction as an ordinary case of inflation, and admits

[1] *Report* of United States Industrial Commission, vol. XIX, p. 407.

that the reorganized company will probably "have no difficulty in earning its fixed charges and paying a dividend on the preferred stock." The only criticism made — and that a very mild one — is that the expanded capitalization may "tend" to prevent a reduction of rates and an increase of wages — two things that we now know it did not do.

Professor Ripley may say, in explanation of the marked difference between his first statement and his later statements, that at the time when he wrote the former the details of the reorganization were not known, because they had been "obscured," "concealed," or "covered up." But this explanation will not bear even the most superficial scrutiny. Every essential fact connected with the reorganization had been published in the financial journals of New York long before Professor Ripley wrote his first account of the transaction. All that the Interstate Commerce Commission did, six years later, was to make a show of uncovering things that had never been covered. But if all the facts were known — as they were — in 1901, why did not Professor Ripley make his charges of "fraud," "conspiracy," "crippling," and "scuttling" at that time? No one would suppose, from reading his Industrial Commission Report, that the Alton transaction involved anything worse than injudicious over-capitalization.

When did he discover that the reorganization was "unscrupulous," "fraudulent," "piratical," and "predatory"? Not, apparently, until the Interstate Commerce Commission and its counsel began proceedings against Mr. Harriman as presumably a malefactor in 1907. If, as suggested by an English economist, "Professor Ripley believes that the utterances of the Interstate Commerce Commission are inspired," he might naturally be expected to follow the Commission's lead; but there seems to be no other plausible explanation of the marked difference between the account that he gave of the Alton transaction *before* the Commission made its report, and the accounts that he has given *since* that time.

His latest statement of the Chicago & Alton case is contained in his article in the "North American Review" for April, 1916. The unproved and unprovable assertions on the first page, with regard to Mr. Harriman's influence and power, do not seem to call for serious criticism. Everybody knows that Mr. Harriman was a prominent figure in the great fields of transportation and finance; but few believe, or can be made to believe, that he controlled "the greatest banking institutions" in the country; that he did what he liked with "the vast resources of the New York life insurance companies"; that "laws were enacted at his will"; and that "state and national conventions" assembled only to "take his orders." Able and influential Mr. Harriman undoubtedly was; but he never exercised the almost supreme control over railroads, banks, insurance companies, legislatures, and political conventions that is here attributed to him. When, therefore, Theodore Roosevelt intervened, as Mr. Ripley says he did, and "thwarted his [Mr. Harriman's] purpose to become an absolute dictator in transportation affairs," the President would seem to have acted without sufficient knowledge, or upon inadequate provocation. But would it not have been well for Mr. Roosevelt and Mr. Ripley to agree in advance upon their joint defense? Mr. Roosevelt says it is "monstrously iniquitous" to suppose that his "personal disagreement with a railroad president" had anything to do with the prosecution of Mr. Harriman by the Interstate Commerce Commission. Then comes Professor Ripley with the declaration that it was "Theodore Roosevelt" who "blocked the path" of the ambitious railroad president and "thwarted his purpose." Who, then, really did do it? According to Mr. Ripley it was Theodore Roosevelt; but the latter seems to disclaim responsibility. This conflict of testimony leaves the question in doubt, and possibly we may never know who it

really was that brought about the investigation of
Mr. Harriman's past activities, and thus saved the
country from an "absolute dictatorship in transportation affairs."

Professor Ripley's restatement of the Chicago &
Alton case from his 1907 point of view does not
seem to need extended comment. Neither does
the page of statistical proof that the capitalization
of the Alton was expanded. All this ground has been
covered before. The only new matters brought up
are: (1) the alleged disapproval of the Alton reorganization by Mr. Harriman's own counsel; (2) the
amount of the new capitalization ($62,000,000) that
Mr. Ripley says did not represent "one dollar of
consideration"; (3) the increase of capitalization as
compared with the "net average capitalization of
the railroads of the United States"; (4) the failure
of the Alton Railway Company to report the thirty
per cent dividend to the Interstate Commerce Commission; (5) the responsibility for the present financial condition of the Alton Company; (6) the mortgaging of thirty-four miles of unbuilt road; (7) the
alleged attempt to "cover up" the discount on the
three per cent bonds by means of deceptive bookkeeping; and (8) the alleged "concealment," in
general, of the syndicate's operations.

1. *The alleged disapproval of the Alton reorganization by Mr. Harriman's own counsel.*

Professor Ripley quotes Mr. Paul D. Cravath, of Mr. Harriman's counsel, as saying:

> But . . . we are now dealing with the period which immediately followed the depression of 1893 . . . when very different standards were being applied from those applied now, and when many things were not only permissible, but were approved, which, under existing conditions and under the conservative influences which have come from success and from our rapid development, are now regarded as at least unwise.

Upon this Mr. Ripley makes the following comment:

> The foregoing admission that the Alton reorganization may be "now regarded as at least unwise" — a piece of bad business — few will question nowadays.

Mr. Cravath did not admit that the Alton reorganization was "at least unwise." He said that "many things were approved" twenty years ago which "are now regarded as at least unwise." His reference was to changes in business standards, not to the Alton reorganization as a whole. Speaking of a single feature of that reorganization — the issuing of common stock to represent anticipated earnings rather than intrinsic value — Mr. Cravath also said:

> According to present practice this was unsound finance; but it was never dishonest finance. According to the standards of the time it was entirely defensible.

2. *The $62,000,000 of the new capitalization which, it is alleged, did not represent "one dollar of consideration."*

Professor Ripley says that a $40,000,000 three per cent mortgage was placed upon the property, "to take up $8,500,000 worth of first mortgage bonds, to make improvements — only $18,000,000 was, however, actually expended for this purpose — and for 'other corporate purposes.' This left a net increase of $62,000,000 of stock and liabilities without one dollar of consideration" (p. 541). Mr. Ripley's arithmetic is somewhat baffling. Eighteen millions from forty millions does not leave sixty-two millions. He apparently intends, however, that the $18,000,000 shall be subtracted from the gross increase of $80,000,000. This leaves, he says, "a net increase of $62,000,000 without one dollar of consideration." The clear implication is that this increase was all "water." But Mr. Ripley's statements do not agree with one another, nor do his computations work out. He quotes, and seems to accept as true, the old Alton Company's report for 1894, showing that the capitalization of the road "represented less than sixty per cent of the actual cost of the property" (p. 540). As the old capitalization was $34,000,000, and as this sum was "less than 60 per cent of the actual cost of the property," the

road, before the syndicate bought it, must have
been intrinsically worth more than $57,000,000. If
we add to this real intrinsic value the sum of $18,-
000,000 which Professor Ripley admits Mr. Harriman spent in betterments, we have an actual cash
value, in 1906, of $75,000,000. This, subtracted from
the total capitalization of $114,000,000, leaves only
$39,000,000 of "water," instead of Professor Rip-
ley's $62,000,000. But even this estimate of the
"water" is much too large. According to Mr. Slason
Thompson, Director of the Bureau of Railway News
and Statistics, the reproduction cost of the Alton
in 1907, including the largely enhanced value of
terminals, right of way, etc., would cover all of the
new capitalization except the common stock.[1] Even
the common stock represented the potential earning
capacity of a rebuilt and reëquipped road, and the
company was actually earning five per cent on it
when the control of the property was transferred to
the "Clover Leaf" in 1907.

3. *The increase of capitalization.*

Professor Ripley says that after the Harriman
syndicate bought the Alton its total capitalization,
within seven years, was "expanded from $33,951,000
to more than $114,000,000 — an increase of se-

[1] See *Cost, Capitalization, and Estimated Value of American Railroads*, by Slason Thompson (first edition, Chicago, 1907), p. 187.

curities exceeding $60,000 per mile, that being about
the average net capitalization of the railroads of the
United States at the present time" (p. 540). According to the Bureau of Railway Statistics, the
average net capitalization of all the railroads in the
North Atlantic States was $102,931 per mile.[1]
Three of the most important railroads of the country, namely, the Baltimore & Ohio, the Delaware
& Lackawanna, and the Reading, are capitalized
respectively at $106,000, $115,000, and $169,000
per mile, net.[2] The expanded capitalization of the
Alton per mile, according to Mr. Ripley's figures,
was less, in 1907, than that of the Lackawanna, or
the Reading, and did not greatly exceed the average
of all the railroads in the North Atlantic States.

4. *The failure of the Alton Railway Company to re-*
port the thirty per cent dividend to the Interstate
Commerce Commission.

Professor Ripley sets forth this omission with
the emphasis of italics; but, as a matter of fact, there
was no requirement of law which made it necessary
for the Alton Railway Company to report this
dividend. The fact that it had been declared was
made public in all the leading financial journals of

[1] See *Cost, Capitalization, and Estimated Value of American Railroads*, by Slason Thompson, p. 98.

[2] See *Railroads: Finance and Organization*, by William Z. Ripley,
p. 75.

New York, consequently it could not have been hidden from the Commission, nor from anybody else.

5. *The responsibility for the later financial condition of the Alton Company.*

Professor Ripley says that "the road has failed to earn even its fixed charges since 1912 by about $6,600,000, the deficit growing larger year by year." If this means that the deficit grew larger every year from 1912 to 1916, the statement is not true. The "New York Times," commenting upon the annual report of the Alton Company for 1915, says:

The Chicago & Alton failed by $1,690,156 to meet charges, but this deficit is $1,072,133 smaller than the 1914 deficit.[1]

But this, perhaps, is an excusable inaccuracy. It is much less pardonable to say, as Professor Ripley does, that the Alton was "financially assassinated" by the Harriman syndicate in 1899 (p. 541).

When Mr. Harriman and President Felton severed their connection with the Alton, after the transfer of control to the Toledo, St. Louis & Western in 1907, the road was paying the stipulated dividend of four per cent on its preferred stock and earning five per cent on its common. It was, therefore, not only

[1] *New York Times*, October 22, 1915; also *Railway Age Gazette*, October 29, 1915.

a solvent but a prosperous road. What happened afterward? Between 1907 and 1912, under the Shonts management, the gross earnings increased 13.5 per cent, while the net earnings fell off 27.8 per cent. The result of the later management may be shown in tabular form as follows:

	1907	1912
Gross earnings	$12,809,426	$14,535,722
Net earnings	4,415,974	3,188,865
Operating ratio	65.5	78

It thus appears that the road, in 1912, was doing $1,726,296 more business than in 1907, while, at the same time, it was earning $1,227,109 less money, net, owing largely to the fact that it had increased its operating expenses from 65.5 to 78 per cent.

If the year 1907 (the last year of the Harriman-Felton management) be compared with the year 1915, the result is equally instructive.

	1907	1915
Gross earnings	$12,809,426	$14,245,624
Net earnings	4,415,974	2,660,584
Operating ratio	65.5	81.3

In this period of eight years the volume of business increased more than eleven per cent (11.21), while the net earnings fell off nearly forty per cent (39.67). This in itself is quite enough to account for the Alton's later financial condition, and for this the Harriman syndicate cannot possibly be held responsible. Mr. Harriman left the road on a dividend-

paying basis in 1907, and two years later he died.
Mr. Ripley says that the reorganization was an
"opportunity industrially lost by the people because
privately exploited by a few" (p. 541). If getting
better transportation at lower rates is a loss to the
people, the people have unquestionably lost; but,
from the economic point of view, improved service
at reduced cost would seem to be a gain.

6. *The mortgaging of thirty-four miles of unbuilt road.*

At the time when the Chicago & Alton Railway
Company was organized, it was thought expedient
to secure the right to build, in the future, a short
cut, or air line, between Springfield Junction and
Murrayville, which would reduce, by about five
miles, the distance between Kansas City and Chicago. The projected cut-off was to be only thirty-
four miles long, and the survey showed that it could
be built over easy grades, not exceeding in any place
sixteen feet to the mile. The estimated cost was
about $600,000, and it was thought that this sum
could easily be saved out of earnings. When it was
proposed to put a mortgage on a part of the road, to
secure a part of the bond issue, the question came
up: should such mortgage be made to cover this
legally authorized but as yet unbuilt cut-off? Counsel for the company and counsel for the trustee both

advised that the short branch line be included, because it would be better to subject it to the lien of the mortgage then being executed than to create another mortgage lien at a later time. Upon this advice Mr. Harriman and his associates acted; but in order to proceed openly and above-board, they distinctly said, in their listing application to the New York Stock Exchange:

This line has been surveyed but has not yet been constructed. By advice of counsel it was included in the description, so as to fasten the lien of the mortgage thereon as soon as constructed [1]

At the time when the Interstate Commerce Commission investigated the Alton reorganization, about $1,000,000 had been spent on this Murrayville cut-off and it was nearly done. It was completed in July, 1907, and opened to traffic in August.

By quoting selected parts of the testimony of the Rock Island Company's controller, Mr. Charles W. Hillard, Professor Ripley tries to make it appear that in this mortgaging of an unbuilt branch line there was something crooked, if not illegal. As a matter of fact, however, the mortgaging of a short stretch of unbuilt line was not only a legal but a very common practice. At a later stage in the hearing Controller Hillard himself said:

[1] See *Commercial & Financial Chronicle*, November 17, 1900.

I would like to make a little explanation. I fear the language I used in answering the question propounded yesterday was not as it should have been. It has been taken as a criticism of making a mortgage on a road before it was constructed. That I know to be a very common thing. . . . I know it to have been true for many years. I have done it myself.[1]

If Professor Ripley had wished to be perfectly fair, he would have quoted this part of Controller Hillard's testimony as well as the parts that he selected, but, then, of course, he could not have made the impression that he was apparently trying to make.

7. *The alleged attempt to "cover up" the discount on the bonds.*

By again quoting a selected part of the testimony of Controller Hillard — a part drawn from him by the improper leading questions of the Commission's counsel — Professor Ripley tries to make it appear that an ordinary and customary treatment of items in double-entry bookkeeping was an attempt to conceal the sale of the three per cent bonds to the stockholders at a discount of thirty-five per cent. The matter in question was the propriety of charging the discount against the surplus of $12,444,000 obtained by capitalizing sums spent for past betterments. The Rock Island controller — a more or less

[1] Official testimony, pp. 21–22.

critical but apparently a fair and candid witness —
tried to explain to the Commission that this treatment of the items was "a matter of" bookkeeping
"judgment." "Having done what they did do,"
he said (that is, having capitalized past betterments), "they had a perfect right to credit this $12,-
444,000 to profit and loss; and then the discount
on bonds was a proper charge against profit and
loss." [1] The witness disapproved the capitalization
of sums spent for past betterments; but he saw
nothing wrong in the bookkeeping. By skillful
elimination and substitution, however, Professor
Ripley makes Mr. Hillard seem to condemn the
method of keeping accounts. In the testimony relating to the bookkeeping, Professor Ripley quotes
Commissioner Lane as asking the following question,
and Mr. Hillard as making the following reply:

Commissioner Lane: If those things could be done . . .
would not a practice of that kind destroy the integrity
and uniformity of railroad accounts generally?
Mr. Hillard: It would upset the whole system.

The reader naturally supposes that the question
of the Commissioner and the reply of the witness related to the method of bookkeeping — that is, to
the setting off of the bond discount against the
$12,444,000 surplus, for the alleged purpose of con-

[1] Mr. Hillard's testimony, p. 11.

cealment. In fact, however, they related to a wholly different matter. In Professor Ripley's quotation they are made a part of Mr. Hillard's testimony on a question of bookkeeping. In the official record they appear as a part of his testimony on the question whether a later board of directors can properly reverse the action of an earlier board. Professor Ripley puts two scraps of testimony together as if they belonged together; but in the official record they are four pages apart and relate to wholly different matters. Mr. Hillard did not say that the Alton's bookkeeping methods would "upset the whole system" of railroad accounting. He said that if one board of directors should pay for betterments out of revenue, and a later board should reverse that action and charge those same betterments to capital, such a practice would "upset the whole system." [1]

It is proper enough, in quoting the testimony of a witness, to omit such parts of it as may not bear on the matter in hand; but it is not proper, by eliminating four pages, to make a witness seem to say what he did not say. Commissioner Lane's question and Mr. Hillard's answer are made by Professor Ripley to discredit the bookkeeping; while, in reality, both related to an entirely different subject which had

[1] Mr. Hillard's testimony, pp. 12, 16.

been taken up after the question of bookkeeping had been dropped. Such garbling of an official record is not permissible.[1]

Professor Ripley, however, resorts to improper elimination, not only when he quotes the testimony of Mr. Hillard, but also when he quotes the testimony of Mr. Harriman. In the latter case he eliminates fourteen pages; and if after reading in the official report the first part of his quotation you wish

[1] The testimony, as Professor Ripley gives it, is as follows (omitting all except enough to show the context):

"*Mr. Kellogg:* But charging the discount on the bonds against this would cover it up on the books, would it not?

"*Mr. Hillard:* Yes.

"*Mr. Kellogg:* It would tend to obscure it, would it not

"*Mr. Hillard:* Yes, so far as the public were concerned (p. 12).

"*Commissioner Lane:* If those things could be done . . . would not a practice of that sort destroy the integrity and uniformity of railroad accounts generally? (p. 16).

"*Mr. Hillard:* It would upset the whole system" (p. 16).

The testimony as the official record gives it is as follows:

"*Mr. Hillard:* Each board of directors has a perfect right to appropriate that [the money earned]. They have the option to pay it in dividends, or set it aside; and when they have exercised that option it is final. No subsequent board of directors can revoke it.

"*Commissioner Lane:* If those things can be done, and revoked from time to time as the directorate changes, would not such a practice destroy the integrity and uniformity of railroad accounts generally?

"*Mr. Hillard:* It would upset the whole system" (p. 16).

In order to make Commissioner Lane's question and Mr. Hillard's answer (about changes in the directorate) fit into the place to which Mr. Ripley transfers them (the discussion about the bookkeeping) the professor found it necessary to omit the Commissioner's words: "and revoked from time to time as the directorate changes." Upon such manipulation of official testimony it is hardly necessary to comment.

to find the last part, you must skip from page 117 to
page 131. Five asterisks are hardly enough to indicate the omission of five or six thousand words.
The matter under investigation was the failure of the
Alton Company to pay dividends on its common
stock. Mr. Kellogg asked Mr. Harriman: "Don't
you think that when stock of a railroad company is
put out there is some obligation, at some time, to
pay something on it?" Professor Ripley quotes Mr.
Harriman as replying merely: "Yes, sir" (p. 117).
Then the Professor puts in five asterisks and coolly
jumps fourteen pages to another question! (p. 131).
What Mr. Harriman really said was: "Yes, sir —
wait a minute!" — showing that he wished to make
an explanation. Mr. Kellogg, however, would not
listen, and was already asking another question when
Mr. Harriman again said: "Wait a minute!" The
witness finally got a chance to explain; but his
"Wait a minute!" and his explanation are in the
fourteen pages that Mr. Ripley omits.

Such manipulation of documentary material is not
creditable to a professor of economics, nor is it fair
to Mr. Harriman.

The whole question of alleged "concealment," by
means of "deceptive bookkeeping," seems to be
conclusively settled by the wide publicity given in
the press to the discount on the bonds, which, ac-

cording to Professor Ripley, it was the purpose of the syndicate to conceal. No sane and reasonable man juggles with his books in order to conceal a certain fact, while, at the same time, he publishes that fact broadcast in the newspapers. The sale of the three per cent bonds to the stockholders at a discount of thirty-five per cent was made known to the public through all the leading financial journals of New York. The circular offering the bonds to the stockholders at 65 was noticed in the "Commercial & Financial Chronicle" of July 22, 1899, and again in the issue of April 14, 1900. Reference to it may also be found in the "Manual of Statistics" for 1900, p. 61; in "Moody's Manual" for 1901, p. 1198; in the listing application to the New York Stock Exchange, November 17, 1900; and in various letters and circulars issued and widely distributed by the Alton Company in the summer of 1899. To every broker and well-informed investor the fact was not only known but perfectly understood. In commenting, seven years later, upon this feature of the reorganization, the "Commercial & Financial Chronicle" said:

The sale of the three per cent refunding bonds at 65 has been heralded in the press as if it marked the uncovering of some hidden item; and surprise has been affected at the idea that the bonds should have been disposed of at such a low (as assumed) figure. The truth is, these bonds were offered for subscription to the stockholders of the company at the figure given, and announcement of the offer was conveyed to them through circulars, Stock Exchange listing applications, and in various other equally public ways. If any one cares to pursue the inquiry he will find a news item concerning this subscription offering in one of our issues nearly seven years ago, namely, in the "Chronicle" of April 14, 1900, p. 739. In our Investor's Supplement, which is a reference book containing a standing record of facts, this particular feature of the reorganized company was noted in number after number, year by year, until July, 1905.[1]

Nothing but a fixed determination to blacken Mr. Harriman's reputation could have led counsel for the Government to charge the Alton syndicate with a resort to "deceptive bookkeeping" as a means of concealing the thirty-five per cent discount on the three per cent bonds. Mr. Kellogg knew, or ought to have known, and Professor Ripley now knows, or ought to know, that instead of trying to "cover up" the discount, the syndicate was giving it the widest possible publicity through the leading financial journals of the country.

8. *The alleged "concealment," in general, of the Alton syndicate's operations.*

Professor Ripley says: "So adroitly was every-

---

[1] Editorial in the *Commercial & Financial Chronicle* for March 2, 1907, just after the Alton investigation.

thing concealed that not even the Rock Island 'crowd' — not unskilled in the ways of Wall Street — suspected the actual situation until they had acquired a half interest in the road.

That the "Rock Island crowd" should have been ignorant of the condition of the Alton when they bought a half interest in it is practically impossible. If they had had no other sources of information than the files of the "Commercial & Financial Chronicle," they would have found therein every fact that it was necessary for them to know, not only with regard to the financial condition of the road, but with regard to all the operations of Mr. Harriman and his associates.

The whole charge of "concealment" may best be refuted, perhaps, by means of quotations from the journal above named. In the course of the Alton investigation, counsel for the syndicate and counsel for the Commission both agreed that a file of the "Commercial & Financial Chronicle" should be put in evidence, and that either side should be at liberty to refer to it as an authority on financial transactions.[1]

The "Chronicle's" references to the Chicago & Alton reorganization began as early as February 4,

[1] Mr Harriman's testimony in the Alton investigation, pp. 188 and 386.

1899, when it made public the fact that the road had been purchased by the syndicate, and that "the deal would be financed by Kuhn, Loeb & Co." As the earlier steps in the reorganization have never been questioned and are not now in dispute, it is not necessary to quote references made to them in the numbers of the "Chronicle" for February 11, February 25, March 4, March 18, April 1, April 8, May 20, May 27, June 24, July 1, and July 15, 1899. The later references begin with the number for July 22, 1899, when the syndicate issued a circular offering the three per cent bonds to the stockholders at a discount of thirty-five per cent. This is one of the matters that Professor Ripley says was "covered up," and that he thinks the Interstate Commerce Commission uncovered in 1907. The "Chronicle" published it in July, 1899, and explained what the syndicate proposed to do with the proceeds of these bonds.

One week later — July 29, 1899 — the "Chronicle" announced that Goldman, Sachs & Co. had arranged to purchase from the syndicate $10,000,000 of these securities. This is another "concealed" matter that the Interstate Commerce Commission triumphantly brought to light seven years after the "Chronicle" had made it public.

On the 7th of April, 1900, the "Chronicle" an-

nounced the incorporation of the Chicago & Alton
Railway Company, and said that it would lease the
Chicago & Alton Railroad Company for a period of
ninety-nine years. "A new corporation was necessary," the "Chronicle" explained, "because the
charter of the old company would not permit the
merger of the new acquisitions" (the Quincy,
Carrolton & St. Louis Railroad and the Peoria
Northern Railroad). Professor Ripley, however,
gives a different explanation, based on the theory of
more "covering up." He asserts that the purpose of
the syndicate in creating a new corporation was to
"obscure the income account" of the old company,
and that it was merely a shrewd "device." But he
furnishes no evidence in support of his assertion, nor
does he show that the "income account" of the old
company ever was "obscured."

On the 14th of April, 1900, the "Chronicle"
printed the annual report of the Alton Company for
the year ended December 31, 1899. This report
showed that the company had capitalized the sum
of $12,444,000 which had been spent for betterments,
and had previously been charged to revenue.

May 5, 1900, the "Chronicle" noted the fact that
another mortgage had been executed to secure
$22,000,000 of three and a half per cent bonds, and
one week later — May 12, 1900 — it explained that

this mortgage was a lien on the stock of the old company, as well as on the track and equipment of the Peoria Northern.

On the 12th of May, 1900, the "Chronicle" announced the declaration of a thirty per cent "extra" cash dividend on the stock of the old company, and said that this dividend represented "the accumulated surplus earnings of the company which had not been distributed to the stock," but had been "diverted from it."

May 19, 1900, the "Chronicle" clearly stated the fact that the thirty per cent dividend covered a part of the surplus of $12,444,000 obtained by capitalizing sums spent for betterments in previous years. It also gave an explanation of the relations between the Alton Railway Company and the Alton Railroad Company, and set forth the terms on which the latter had been leased to the former. Finally, it gave the amounts of the new securities that had been distributed proportionately among the members of the syndicate, and a little later stated that the market value of the cash and new securities so distributed was $1115.75 for every $1000 subscribed.

November 12, 1900, the "Chronicle" published in full the listing application to the New York Stock Exchange, in which every feature of the reorganization that could possibly interest or concern an investor was fully and clearly described.

First and last, in the two years 1899 and 1900, the "Chronicle" published no fewer than thirty-six editorials, statements, circulars, reports, notices, or news items, relating to the Chicago & Alton reorganization; and if there was any fact "uncovered" by the Interstate Commerce Commission in 1907 that had not been uncovered by the "Commercial & Financial Chronicle" six years earlier, it is impossible to find it.

Professor Ripley says, in his latest article, that "everything hinges" on the questions "whether frank and full publicity prevailed," and whether those who bought the Alton securities from the syndicate "purchased them under a misapprehension as to their value" (p. 543). The evidence above set forth, which is taken wholly from a journal recognized by the Commission itself as an authority, seems to show conclusively that every feature of the Alton reorganization was laid frankly and fully before the public, and that no investor who bought Alton stocks or bonds could possibly have "purchased them under a misapprehension as to their value."

Who, then, was hurt by the operations of Mr. Harriman and his associates? Not the old stockholders, because, as even Mr. Ripley admits, they received "top-notch prices" for their stock; not the new stockholders, because they are accused of making even more profit than they should have made; not the subsequent investors, because they bought with full knowledge of what they were buying; not the shippers, coal miners, farmers, and manufacturers along the line of the road, because they got infinitely better transportation at much lower rates; not the road itself, because it was so improved by Mr. Harriman that its efficiency was more than doubled. Who, then, were the injured? Apparently only Professor Ripley, Theodore Roosevelt, and the Interstate Commerce Commission.

The only question that remains unsettled is whether Professor Ripley, in his book and in his articles, has accurately presented the facts of the Alton reorganization. The evidence seems to show that he stated them with reasonable accuracy in the report that he wrote for the United States Industrial Commission in 1901, but that he has persistently misstated them ever since the Interstate Commerce Commission began its attack on Mr. Harriman in 1907.

In concluding this review of the Chicago & Alton case, and of Professor Ripley's statements concerning it, it seems necessary to say something with

regard to the way in which the Federal investigation of 1907 was conducted by the legal counsel who
represented the Interstate Commerce Commission.
In an article published in the "Market World &
Chronicle" for March, 1915, Major Henry L. Hig-
ginson, of Boston, said that the Government should
instruct the various commissions "not to proceed
against corporations as a criminal lawyer proceeds,
but as judges, fair-minded, open-minded, and in-
dustrious in learning the facts with regard to which
they judge." [1]

Was this the spirit in which the Chicago & Alton
investigation was conducted by the Interstate Commerce Commission? Certainly not! A correspondent
of the London "Economist," who was present at the
taking of testimony in New York, described the
proceedings in the following words:

The members of the Commission surprised many
present at the last New York session by their manifestly
hostile spirit toward Mr. Harriman and witnesses allied
with him. It had been imagined that the Commission
was there purely to secure such testimony as it might;
and that it appreciated the fact that it was in no sense
acting as a court having charge of any one accused of
crime. Yet, from the manner and form of questions put
by several of the Commissioners, it was difficult to
understand how they regarded it so — if indeed they
did. Neither is it any violation of fact to explain that

[1] *New York Evening Post*, March 20, 1915.

the Commission's lawyers acted toward Mr. Harriman and Mr. Kahn quite as if they were prosecuting attorneys who had at last got before the bar of justice some well-known malefactors. Not only did they seek at times to prevent witnesses from replying freely to questions, but they were truthfully accused of seeking to so put questions and so insist upon replies as to leave misleading impressions. [1]

These words were not written for an American newspaper prepossessed in favor of Mr. Harriman. They were written for one of the best-known financial journals of England, and were to be read by the people of Great Britain. Is it an unfair, or unreasonable, conclusion from these facts that the Commission and its counsel were not trying to investigate impartially the Chicago & Alton reorganization, but were endeavoring to make out, if possible, a case of criminality against Mr. Harriman? The so-called investigation was a one-man hunt, if ever there was one. This fact was well understood by the better informed part of the public, and in June, 1907, the "Economist" said editorially:

The report was afloat last week that after a conference between the President and the members of the Interstate Commerce Commission it was decided that no violation of law by Mr. Harriman had been discovered under which action could be taken against him. ... It will be too bad for the Government to fail of

[1] London *Economist*, March 16, 1907.

accomplishing anything after all this talk. If they cannot put him through for railroad manipulation, why don't they charge him with carrying concealed deadly weapons, or breaking the Sabbath, or shooting game out of season? Anything to catch him. It won't do to give it up in this weak way.[1]

But if the conviction of Mr. Harriman as a lawbreaker was the object of the one-man hunt, it was a complete failure. The Interstate Commerce Commission had to report to the President, as stated by the "Economist," that "no violation of law by Mr. Harriman had been discovered," and that legal proceedings against him would not be expedient.

This was evidently the conclusion reached also by the Rock Island Company, and the Toledo, St. Louis & Western Company, which controlled the Alton successively between 1906 and 1912. Their managers certainly were not partial to Mr. Harriman, nor coöperative with him, but they never attempted by litigation to bring him or his associates to account for anything done in the course of the Alton reorganization. The question of legality, therefore, would seem to be conclusively and finally settled. The whole transaction, in the words of Mr. Paul D. Cravath, "was legal from beginning to end."

Such also was the judgment of the best English

[1] *Economist*, Chicago, June 1, 1907.

and American authorities at the time when the Alton investigation was made. In a long editorial, published April 27, 1907, the "Commercial & Financial Chronicle," an authority officially recognized by the Interstate Commerce Commission, referred to the Alton reorganization in the following words:

We know of no railroad transaction which has been so generally and so sweepingly condemned. And it is difficult to see why this should be so. In its main features this reorganization did not differ essentially from numerous other reorganizations, none of which have been criticised. We can explain the general expressions of disapprobation on no other theory than that the facts are but imperfectly understood — or not understood at all — owing to the sedulous efforts that have been made to create erroneous impressions with regard to the same. Newspaper headlines and editorial and other comment, gave the impression that in this reorganization a few leading financiers got together, secured control of the property and looted it, at the same time fleecing the security-holders; while in all the years since then the road has been engaged in robbing its patrons by charging them exorbitant prices for transportation service rendered them. Nothing could be further from the truth. [1]

The London "Statist" of April 6, 1907, published an interview with Mr. Robert Fleming, one of the most eminent English authorities on American railroads, in which the English banker said he could see nothing illegal or improper in the Alton transaction.

[1] *Commercial & Financial Chronicle*, April 27, 1907.

In commenting on the increase of capitalization, he pointed out the fact that inflation of the same kind, in England, has repeatedly been sanctioned by both Houses of Parliament. The "Ordinary" shares of the Midland Railway, for example, were thus increased from £38,000,000 to £76,000,000. Mr. Fleming also said that the whole net profit of the Alton syndicate, in which he participated merely as an investor, "was only eight per cent — about five per cent per annum — nothing very extraordinary surely." [1]

Another eminent English authority on American railroads, who is at the head of one of the most famous financial houses of the world, said that he "did not understand the outcry [in the Alton case] because nothing had been done that required apology."

Mr. H. T. Newcomb, a well-known American economist and statistician, who was in the employ of the Interstate Commerce Commission for seven years as railroad expert, published an article in the "Railway World" for September 17, 1909, in which he expressed his opinion of the Alton transaction, and of Mr. Harriman, in the following words:

Animadversions upon the methods which accompanied the rebirth of Chicago & Alton did not begin

[1] London *Statist*, April 6, 1907.

until nearly ten years after the episode had passed into history. They could not have originated out of the state of public opinion of the year (1898) in which the reorganization occurred, nor were they at any time based upon any valid and substantial detriment to the traveling and shipping public, or any real damage to provident investors. Even when official agitation against railway managers and financiers as a class had aroused a superficial public sentiment which sought out opportunities to suspect and to condemn, it was impossible to convince the thinking majority that the substitution of an active and vigorous management for the rigid unprogressiveness of the administration of the able but unprogressive President Blackstone had been really injurious to any one, or that the readjustment of capital issues incident to the physical reconstruction which followed change of control could impose additional charges upon travel or transportation. The facts cannot be repeated too often, or be too much emphasized. Between 1897, the year before the reorganization, and 1907, the Alton's average charge per passenger, per mile carried, declined from 21.16 mills to 20.25 mills (4.3 per cent), and the average charge per ton per mile for freight was reduced from 8.93 mills to 6.04 mills, or 32.2 per cent. At the same time, the amount of work done in the public service more than doubled, and the typical unit of service became of higher quality, travel became safer and more comfortable, transportation more expeditious.

Nearly the whole mileage of the company was relaid with heavier rails; passenger car capacity was doubled freight car capacity was trebled; and aggregate tractive power increased more than twofold. This is plainly a process of cheapening transportation by substituting lower capital cost for the part of the former operating or labor cost of moving persons and property. Yet, in spite of these changes, which required an expenditure for betterments exceeding one half the former cost of the property, the proportion of gross freight rates from operation, paid to capital of all sorts in 1905, was but 27.37 per cent, an increase of almost exactly one eighth of one per cent from 27.24 per cent in 1899.

The reconstruction of the Alton was a fundamental industrial necessity, which was certain to be undertaken by some one, and there is nothing in the manner in which it was accomplished, or in the results attained under his management, that is not creditable to Mr. Harriman.

CHAPTER XXIX

THE SAVING OF THE ERIE

ONE of the last opportunities that Mr. Harriman had to render a great public service was offered to him in the spring of 1908, when the country was just beginning to recover from the panic of 1907. That panic and the business depression which followed it were largely the result of President Roosevelt's attack on business combinations in general and Mr. Harriman's railroad combinations in particular. When the Administration undertook to disrupt the consolidation of the Union Pacific with the Southern Pacific, and when, a little later, Judge Landis imposed a fine of $30,000,000 on the Standard Oil Company, security-holders everywhere took alarm. If the Government intended to break up all capitalistic combinations, regardless of the time that they had been in existence, and if the courts were going to confiscate property by imposing fines of such magnitude, corporate securities would soon lose a large part of their investment value.

President Roosevelt assured a delegation of bankers, headed by J. P. Morgan, that no general raid on business was contemplated, and that nothing would be done to increase the prevailing distrust.[1] The attack on the Harriman Lines, however, still continued, and railroad security-holders, naturally enough, said to themselves: "If the Government is going to break up the Harriman combination, which has been in undisturbed existence for seven years, why is it not likely to break up the Hill combination, or even the Vanderbilt combination?" The result was an increasing feeling of apprehension, which soon extended from Wall Street to the country at large and finally culminated in the panic of that summer and fall.

By the spring of 1908, confidence in corporate securities was beginning to be restored; but in financial circles generally there still remained a feeling of uncertainty and depression. Just at that critical time, the Erie Railroad Company was threatened with serious embarrassment, if not insolvency, on account of its inability to meet its maturing obligations. For several years it had been satisfying its most urgent financial needs by issuing short-term notes. During the period of depression that followed the panic, the renewal of short-term obligations became very difficult, and in order to provide for the payment of $5,500,000 in notes that would mature April 8, 1908, the company planned to issue $15,000,000 in new

[1] *Commercial & Financial Chronicle*, March 16, 1907.

notes, payable April 8, 1911, and bearing interest at six per cent. Of these new notes, $5,500,000 were to be exchanged for the old ones, and $5,000,000 to be sold at par, while the remainder were to be reserved for future use. A syndicate, headed by J. P. Morgan & Co., agreed to underwrite $5,000,000 of the new notes, provided the holders of the $5,500,000 of old notes would exchange them for the new ones at par. The holders of the old notes, however, showed a decided disinclination to make the exchange, and J. P. Morgan & Co. were not willing to take up the old notes and at the same time assume the risk of the new issue. A receivership seemed to be inevitable, and on the afternoon of April 7th a call was issued for a conference, to be held that evening in J. P. Morgan's library, for the purpose of considering the emergency.

There had been, for several days, a feeling of apprehension in the financial district with regard to the maturity of these notes. No provision whatever had been made for paying them, and everybody knew that unless $5,500,000 could be raised, in some way, the Erie, on the following morning, would be put into the hands of a receiver. This, Mr. Harriman thought, would bring about a renewal of the panic; would cause the failure of many other companies, already financially embarrassed, and would prolong indefinitely the prevailing business depression.

When the gentlemen invited to the conference assembled in J. P. Morgan's library, there were present several members of the Morgan firm; a number of Erie directors, including Mr. Harriman; H. McK. Twombly, who represented a large Erie interest and who was also prominent in New York Central affairs; and Francis Lynde Stetson, general counsel for the Erie Company, as well as for the firm of J. P. Morgan & Co.[1] After making a brief statement of the object of the meeting, Mr. Stetson exhibited a printed bill in equity, ready for filing in the United States Circuit Court, setting forth the insolvency of the Erie, and other pertinent facts and praying for the appointment of a receiver. When a question was raised as to whether such action was necessary immediately, Mr. Stetson replied that it was, and referred at length to a New York statute making it unlawful for a corporation of that State to continue in business after defaulting in payment of its obligations upon maturity.

Then ensued a general discussion of ways and means of raising the money. Morgan & Co. firmly refused to lend it, partly because they had already agreed to underwrite $5,000,000 of new notes, and partly because the addition of $5,500,000 in cash to this obligation would render the security inadequate.

[1] J. P. Morgan himself was absent in Europe.

Finally, Mr. Harriman offered to furnish one half of the $5,500,000 if the other parties in interest would lend the other half. Then most of the gentlemen present withdrew to another part of the library to consider this proposition. Mr. Harriman, meanwhile, sat in front of the open grate, smoking and looking into the fire. After a few moments' reflection, he said to a friend and business associate, who had accompanied him to the meeting, that if his proposal to furnish half of the $5,500,000 should be declined, he felt disposed to advance the whole amount himself. His friend, who had not approved even the offer to lend one half, then ventured to advise strongly against such action. His argument was that Mr. Harriman had no responsibility for the Erie, and would not be blamed or criticized, even if it should fail. The mere fact that he was a director did not make it necessary for him to come to the rescue, because he constituted only a small minority of the board, and his personal interest in the company was so small as to be almost negligible. Besides that, the Erie was over-capitalized and practically insolvent; the outlook for it seemed hopeless, and if he (Harriman) loaned it this money, the chances were that he would never get it back.

Harriman listened thoughtfully, while he smoked and gazed into the fire. Finally, when his friend had finished, he said that what concerned him was the general situation, rather than the Erie Company or his own personal interest. The business depression, he said, had about run its course, and if the Erie notes were paid, the revival would set in. On the other hand, if the Erie defaulted and went into a receivership, the effect on the general situation would be disastrous, because other companies that were in a precarious condition would probably go the same way, and the existing business depression would be prolonged indefinitely. To this his friend replied that inasmuch as his (Harriman's) companies were fairly prosperous and in a strong financial condition, he had nothing to fear, so far as his responsibility to them was concerned, and it would be extremely unwise to jeopardize so large a personal fund, and expose to risk of loss $5,500,000 of his own money, merely for the betterment of the "general situation." Harriman made no response to this, but continued to gaze into the fire.

After a long separate consultation, the other members of the conference returned and announced their unwillingness to put up any part of the necessary amount. Mr. Harriman then said: "Rather than see such a disaster as the receivership of the Erie under existing conditions, I am disposed to furnish the entire amount myself, provided you will lend me the money. I could borrow it from others downtown if there were time to take the matter up and make the necessary arrangements."

For the purpose of discussing this new and surprising development in the situation, the other parties to the conference again withdrew. After long consideration of the matter they returned and said that if, as Mr. Harriman thought, he could borrow the money downtown, they preferred to have him do that. Mr. Harriman replied that as the hour was then late (nearly 2 A.M.), he could do nothing before daylight and he had not fully made up his mind to try. He said, however, that he would think it over, and if he decided to make the effort he would take the matter up early in the morning. Meanwhile, he asked that the filing of the receivership papers and all other prejudicial measures be deferred. This was agreed to, and counsel for Morgan & Co. and the Erie stated that the company would not be declared in default before three o'clock in the afternoon. It was also agreed that when notes should be presented at the bank where they were payable, payment should not be refused, but the holders should be requested to present them again later. Thereupon the conference broke up and Mr. Harriman drove home at 2 A.M.

Early the next morning (about seven o'clock)

Judge Lovett, Mr. Harriman's legal counsel, was called to the latter's house by telephone. When he arrived there, an hour later, he found Mr. Harriman in bed, suffering intensely from an acute attack of the rheumatism, or other malady, which had long caused him severe pain, at intervals, and which kept his body more or less bent a large part of the time. His condition, on this particular morning, was made worse by a storm of cold rain, mixed with snow, which prevailed outside, and also by the loss of sleep and the strain of the previous night. He was evidently suffering severe pain, and it was clearly impossible for him to go downtown, even if he were able to get out of bed. He told Judge Lovett that he had made up his mind to lend the Erie Company the $5,500,000 needed to take up the notes falling due that day, if he could raise the money on such short notice, and if the Erie Company would agree to keep F. D. Underwood as president until the loan should be paid. He requested Judge Lovett to go downtown with his personal financial secretary, Mr. Tegethoff; open his (Harriman's) strong box in the safe deposit vault, and after getting out the necessary securities, take them to President Vanderlip, of the National City Bank, explain to him the situation, and ask him to lend Mr. Harriman $5,500,000 on certain specified collateral.

The capital and surplus of the National City Bank, at that time, were not great enough to enable it, under the limitations of law, to lend as much as $5,500,000 to a single individual, and it was therefore necessary to distribute the loan among several banks. Mr. Vanderlip, who had hastened downtown in compliance with a request by telephone, expressed a desire to be helpful to Mr. Harriman and said he believed he could arrange the loan; but the amount was so considerable that it would take a little time — probably half an hour or more.

Foreseeing the difficulty of raising so large a sum at short notice, Mr. Harriman had asked Judge Lovett to see also Mr. George F. Baker, president of the First National Bank, and ask him for a loan of $1,000,000 in case it should be needed. Mr. Baker was a director of the Erie and had been present, during a part of the time at least, at the conference of the previous night. He and Mr. Harriman were on friendly terms, personally, but they belonged to different financial groups and had never before done any business together. When Judge Lovett asked Mr. Baker to lend Mr. Harriman $1,000,000, he replied without a moment's hesitation: "I will lend Harriman one million, or two millions, or three millions, if he wants them." It did not prove to be necessary, however, to call upon Mr. Baker for the assistance so generously offered. When Judge Lovett returned directly to the National City Bank, he found that Mr. Vanderlip had already made arrangements to provide the entire amount. Mr. Harriman warmly appreciated Mr. Baker's offer of $3,000,000, in case that amount should be needed, and when, sometime later, Judge Lovett told him what Mr. Baker had said and described the way in which he said it, Mr. Harriman expressed the highest admiration for Mr. Baker, not only as a great banker, but as a considerate and generous man, always ready to help when help was needed and justified.

As soon as the money had been secured, Judge Lovett, in pursuance of Mr. Harriman's directions, went to the office of Morgan & Co., where Mr. Stetson and the Erie directors had assembled, and arranged with them for the adoption of the necessary resolutions and the payment of the notes. A transcript of the proceedings, with due credit to Mr. Harriman, was then made and furnished to the press, together with copies of all letters relating to the transaction.

The announcement, before noon of April 8th, that the Erie notes would be paid with funds provided by Mr. Harriman, created a profound sensation in the whole financial district. Nobody doubted Mr. Harriman's ability, or the soundness of his judgment, and when it became known that he had put up $5,500,000 of his own money as an evidence of his confidence in the future, everybody felt that the tide had turned — and it had. A general improvement in business conditions followed almost immediately. The stock market became buoyant, under the leadership of Erie; public confidence revived; hope took the place of discouragement, and the whole financial horizon cleared.

In commenting, three days later, on this change in the situation, the "Commercial & Financial Chronicle" said:

Mr. Harriman has saved the Erie road from a receivership. In so doing he has taken a heavy load from off the market and ought to receive the gratitude of the public. . . . Just at this time, it [a receivership] would have been a disaster of no small proportions. . . . The tender of cash to take up the old notes relieved the market for the time being, so that the Erie securities led a material advance, which the general market followed.[1]

The "Financial World" said:

Harriman's rescue of the Erie, when its own bankers had apparently deserted it, will long be remembered as a master stroke of courage and resourcefulness, which saved not only the Erie, but the general financial situation, from serious embarrassment.[2]

In reviewing, in 1909, the services rendered by

[1] *Commercial & Financial Chronicle*, New York, April 11, 1908.
[2] *Financial World*, New York, September 3, 1909.

Mr. Harriman to the public, Mr. H. T. Newcomb
said:

A service of a different character was last year's rescue
of the Erie from impending bankruptcy and as a consequence, the prevention of a probable sympathetic de-
moralization in the financial markets of the world which
might have grown to the dimensions of a widespread
panic. Early in April, 1908, Mr. Harriman struggled un-
successfully throughout an all-night conference to convince great business men that something ought to be
done to save the Erie from inability to meet maturing
promissory notes aggregating $5,500,000. Retiring un-
successful from that conference, but not convinced that
his own judgment was erroneous, Mr. Harriman finally
determined to act independently, and, at his own risk,
to supply the necessary funds. Thus, single-handed,
with characteristic self-confidence, he prevented a de-
plorable incident in the dangerous after-panic period
which, if it had taken place, would undoubtedly have
carried in its wake the bankruptcy of several great corporations that, with the respite thus obtained, have
been restored to stability and solvency.[1]

The effect of Mr. Harriman's action upon his own
reputation was hardly less marked than its effect
upon financial conditions. Before that time he had
been looked upon, in many parts of the East, as a
man who selfishly played his own hand for all he
could make out of it, regardless of the public welfare
or the rights of others. He had been blamed for the
panic that followed the Northern Pacific "corner";

[1] "Harriman the Efficient," by H. T. Newcomb; *Railway World*,
New York, September 17, 1909.

he had been criticized for suddenly raising the dividend rate of the Union Pacific to ten per cent; he had
incurred hostility by taking part in the investigation
of the Equitable Life; he had been condemned for
alleged participation in the political activities of
Governor Odell; and finally he had been characterized by the President of the United States as an
"undesirable citizen" and a "wealthy corruptionist," whose railroad combinations were such a menace to the public welfare that they must be disrupted
by Federal prosecution. No wonder the uninformed,
or misinformed, part of the public regarded him
with suspicion and dislike! But the saving of the
Erie changed all this in a single day. It seemed to
throw a flash of revealing light upon all his misunderstood activities in the past, and made thousands
of business men doubt whether they had ever known
the real Harriman at all.

The revulsion of feeling thus brought about
changed completely the attitude of the people
toward the man whom they had so long misjudged.
He was universally praised for his courage, foresight,
and public spirit, and from that time until the day of
his death, a year and a half later, respect and admiration for him steadily increased. Wall Street, at
least, will not soon forget the indomitable courage
and almost clairvoyant vision of that frail, seriously

ill man, who, after spending more than half the night in a vain effort to make others see the situation as he saw it, took the matter up again in the early morning, and in complete disregard of the judgment and advice of everybody, marshaled his forces from a bed of sickness and pain, and with his own personal resources carried to successful accomplishment a task that nobody else would undertake, and that was universally regarded as absolutely impossible.

Mr. Harriman's business judgment, as well as his forecast of the future, was more than justified by the result. Not only did the country enter soon upon a new period of prosperity, but the railroad company that he had saved from bankruptcy paid in full, at maturity, the renewal notes that he had taken, and eventually succeeded in extricating itself from all its financial difficulties. Eight years later, the "New York Evening Post" said:

In his annual report, published to-day, F. D. Underwood, president of the Erie, points out that the recent sale of convertible bonds will permit the company to retire the last of the outstanding notes which, in March, 1914, amounted to $34,500,000. Erie has been able finally to work off its burden of floating debt, only because E. H. Harriman performed almost a miracle, exactly eight years ago next month, by going down into his pocket to pay off the notes maturing at that time. The receivership papers had been drawn up and all but signed. Since then, the company has been financing by hand-to-mouth methods, that is, by issuing and extending short-term notes. Underwood, who stood with Harriman in opposing the receivership, will probably feel like having some kind of a celebration when the last of these notes are actually cancelled." [1]

[1] *New York Evening Post*, March, 31, 1916.

CHAPTER XXX

LAST YEARS

DURING the later years of his life Mr. Harriman suffered almost constantly from ill-health, due, very largely, to overwork and long-continued nervous strain. Several of his friends tried to persuade him to retire from business, or, at least, to throw upon the shoulders of others some of the burdens that he was trying to carry alone. James Stillman said to him, as early as 1905, that he, himself, intended to give up active work and that he thought he (Harriman) ought to do the same. Several years later, in June, 1909, when Mr. Harriman was in Europe trying to regain his lost health, he met Mr. Stillman there and said to him one day, in a reminiscent mood: "You were right, Stillman, all the time. I ought to have quit and laid back. But it is too late now. I am in deeper than ever and must go on, on."

In the fall of 1907, when Jacob Schiff was about to sail for Egypt in order to get rest and recreation, he urged Mr. Harriman to follow his example, or, at least, to safeguard his health by giving up some of his responsible positions and taking life more easily.

He understood Mr. Harriman to say that he would do so, and two or three months later he wrote him, from a steamer on the Nile, the following letter:

Luxor, Egypt, February 2, 1908

DEAR MR. HARRIMAN:

Here I am, on board of a Nile steamer, thinking of you, while the imposing ruins on the shore remind me how hollow everything earthly is; how we strive so often for naught; how short a time we live and how long we are then dead. Take my advice, my good friend, do not work so constantly and do not go back on what you told me on the eve of my departure — that you would give up the different presidencies and content yourself with the chairmanships of the various boards and executive committees, placing on them, moreover, men of experience to share responsibilities with you. I wonder whether you have done anything in this direction? . . .

I am

Very sincerely yours

JACOB H. SCHIFF

On this letter, when he received it, Mr. Harriman made the following note: "I told him, in confidence, what I had in mind eventually to do; but I made no promise. His advice is good if matters are looked upon only from a selfish viewpoint."

Mr. Harriman's persistence in working up to the limit of his capacity was due partly to great confidence in his own powers of endurance; partly to keen interest in world-wide affairs, and partly, perhaps, to an overestimate of the duty that he owed to those who had put immense sums of money into his enter-prises and were relying upon him to direct them. Personally, he had little more to gain — nothing more that was worth the sacrifice of health; but some of his plans had not yet been fully worked out, and there was no one to whom he could entrust the execution of them with the certainty of successful accomplishment. "I would give up the whole busi-ness," he said to one of his associates, "if I could be sure my plans would be carried out."[1] But there was no one in sight who seemed capable of carrying them out, and he therefore continued to work at his self-imposed task long after he would have been justified in relinquishing it if he had "looked at matters from a selfish viewpoint." He did take such vacations, however, as it was possible to take with-out getting too far away from a telegraph line.

He spent most of the summer of 1907 [says John Muir] at his Pelican Bay Lodge on Klamath Lake, in southern Oregon. On his arrival in San Francisco he said to me:

"You're going to the Lodge with us, are you not?"

"Yes," I replied, "I shall be very glad to pay my respects to Mrs. Harriman and the family, but I cannot afford to spend the summer there."

"Why?" he inquired.

"Because I am busy."

[1] "Edward Henry Harriman," by Alexander Millar, secretary of the Union Pacific Railroad Company, *Journal of Commerce*, New York, June, 1910.

"What are you doing?"

"Writing a book."

"Well, you come up to the Lodge and I will show you how to write books. The trouble with you is that you are too slow in your beginnings. You plan and brood too much. Begin, begin, begin! Put forth what you wish to say in the first words that come to mind — just as you talk — until all that's to go into the book is got down. Then correct, transpose, add, strike out, and change as much as you like. Hammer away at it until it suits you. Come on and get something begun."

So I went to the famous Lodge, intending to stay a few days or a week; but when I spoke of leaving, Mr. Harriman said I must stay and work, and directed his private secretary to follow me and put down everything I said. So I was fairly compelled to make a beginning, in dictating to a stenographer, which proved rather awkward at first, but in a couple of months a sort of foundation for more than one volume was laid.

The Lodge was beautifully located at the head of Pelican Bay beside its famous crystal springs, the magnificent Klamath Lake in front of it, bordered with meadows and bounded in the distance by dark, forested mountains and hills — a fine place for recreation and rest — air, water, and scenery reviving. The weather was mostly cool and bright, just right for soothing exercise, walks in the woods, and boating on the lake, which most of the time was mirror-like, reflecting the sky and the fringing meadows and forest-clad mountain shores.

On our return from boat excursions a beautiful picture was outspread before us about an hour before sundown, especially toward autumn, when the colors were ripening — the shining lake enlivened with leaping trout and flocks of waterfowl; the stream from the great springs like a river with broad brown and yellow meadows on either hand; and the dark, forested mountains, changing to blue in the background, rising higher and higher, with Mt. Pitt, highest of all, pointing serenely heavenward through the mist of the sunset purple and gold.

But even here Mr. Harriman did not enjoy complete rest, for he called his lieutenants about him, and through them and a telegraph wire kept in touch with all his work and world affairs in general. Nevertheless, we hoped for lasting benefits from the mountain air and water — nor were we wholly disappointed.

When at length we left the Lodge, I accompanied him to Portland. At the stations along the road he was hailed by enthusiastic crowds, assembled to pay their respects, recognizing the good he had done and was doing in developing the country and laying broad and deep the foundations of prosperity. Alike enthusiasm marked his reception in Portland, and on the return trip a large body of Shriners, on their way to Eugene, stopped his train by taking possession of the track, climbing over the railing of his car, and literally took him by force and carried him away through the crowd on their shoulders, with cheers and hurrahs as straight from the heart as any I ever heard. The popular tide had turned, sweeping away hatred and the old, hard railroad mistrust and suspicion. He was at last coming into his own, after as hard a fair-play battle as ever man won.[1]

The tide of popular prejudice against Mr. Harriman began to turn first in the West, where the people could not help seeing the beneficent results of his work. In the East, however, it continued to run

[1] *Edward Henry Harriman*, by John Muir (New York, 1911). (Privately printed.)

against him for more than a year, mainly for the reason that in reinvesting the money that came to the Union Pacific through the liquidation of the Northern Securities Company, he had bought large blocks of stock in other railroad corporations — purchases which amounted in the aggregate to about $130,000,000.[1]

These transactions [says Mr. Kahn] first became known to the public through the investigation of the Interstate Commerce Commission, which gave them a doubly suspicious appearance (they would, as a matter of course, have been disclosed anyway in the next annual report of the Union Pacific), and lent color to the impression that Mr. Harriman was aiming at a gigantic illegal monopoly of the railroad industry. This, taken together with the simultaneous unfair and hostile presentation of the old Chicago & Alton transaction, added to the latent irritations, enmities, and apprehensions which his career and ways had aroused, and fanned by the skillful and insidious publicity work of the Harriman Extermination League, unchained a veritable cyclone of criticism, condemnation, and defamation upon him. Mr. Harriman, on the witness stand, did nothing to set things right; he always made an indifferent witness. being impatient, resentful and defiant under examination, reluctant to explain so as to make things plain to the ordinary understanding, and disdaining to defend himself against accusations and innuendo. An inflamed public sentiment lent ready credence to the allegations, accusations, and insinuations which were spread broadcast in the press, from the platform, in political assemblies, even from some pulpits. A kind of hysteria of

[1] See Vol. I, chap. XVI, p. 398.

fury against him swept over the land; he was denounced and anathematized as a horrible example of capitalistic greed and law-breaking. The legal machinery of the Nation and of several of the States was set in motion to discover some breach of the law, however technical, of which he might be held guilty and convicted. Fairness and charity were thrown aside. All the good work he had done counted as nothing. Anything said in defense, or even explanation, was contemptuously and indignantly brushed aside. To say a good word for him was as much as one's reputation was worth. His punishment was clamored for. His expulsion from financial life was demanded. Anybody who would not dissociate himself from him became *particeps criminis*, a sharer of his guilt, in jeopardy of sharing the doom which was to overtake Harriman. And very few there were who remained loyal to him, and still fewer who dared believe that he would ever recover his old position of prestige and influence. Even amongst those who remained friendly to him and honestly meant well by him, the greater number advised him to bow before the storm, temporarily resign from the presidency of his companies and retire to Europe for a year, giving as a reason the admittedly unsatisfactory condition of his health.

Amidst all this terrifying din, amidst this avalanche of vituperation, misrepresentation, threatening and assault, amidst the desertion of some friends, the lukewarmness of others, amidst the simultaneous strain and stress of a financial panic (during which, moreover, he did more than his full share in the work of support and relief), Mr. Harriman stood firm as a rock, calm, silent, and dignified, his courage never daunted, his spirit never faltering, strong in his faith in himself and in the potency of truth, right, and merit, strong in the approval of his own conscience as to his motives and actions. He did not complain, he asked nobody's help, he made no appeal for sympathy, he told no one that he was weak and ill and that the continuous nervous strain was a fearful tax on his impaired health, he stooped to no weapon not sanctioned by the rules of gentlemanly warfare, though plenty of them lay ready to his hand and though his opponents were troubled by no such scruple, he offered no compromise, no concession, he did not budge an inch, he never for one moment took his hand off the helm — and thus he rode out the storm. The spectacle of a man undaunted, opposing his solitary strength and will to overwhelming odds, is always a fine and inspiring one. There have been contests far more important and spectacular and for far greater stakes, but I doubt whether any more superb courage in bearing and daring has ever been demonstrated than was shown by Mr. Harriman in those long months of incessant onslaught. This sounds rhapsodical and exaggerated, but it is not. Only one who saw him in that period from close by, as I did, who had the privilege of hearing him "think aloud," as he used to call it, can appreciate the marvel of the lofty, indomitable spirit which animated, one might almost say which kept together, that weak, frail, sick, suffering body. [1]

It may possibly be thought that Mr. Kahn, as a close associate of Mr. Harriman, exaggerated the violence of the attack made upon him; but a dispassionate and uninterested observer, who could not have been biased by personal or friendly considerations, said of it:

He [Mr. Harriman] came up against influence and

[1] *Edward Henry Harriman*, by Otto H. Kahn; an address delivered before the Finance Forum in New York, January 25, 1911.

combinations that would have destroyed most men similarly situated. He was confronted with the entire power of the Federal Administration at Washington, actively and openly aided by apparently invincible Wall Street alliances, and secret enemies in his own camp almost as strong. How he ever escaped ruin, in the face of the tremendous interests combined for his discomfiture, is the marvel of latter-day financial history.[1]

The fight lasted [Mr. Kahn says] for a full year. Gradually the aspect of affairs began to change; gradually the effect of Mr. Harriman's brave and dignified attitude and masterful strategy began to tell. One fine morning it became known that in the face of universal discouragement, single-handed, directing matters from a sick bed, he had saved a very important railroad from bankruptcy [the Erie] by one of those strokes of combined boldness and wisdom which had become familiar to those who knew him best and which, in this instance, marked the end of the 1907 panic. From that time on his star rose rapidly again, the people at last began to recognize that in his great constructive genius they possessed a national asset of no mean value; they also recognized that the man, his motives and purposes, had been grievously maligned and misunderstood, and, with characteristic impulsiveness and generosity, they started to give him plentiful evidence of their change of heart. The Harriman Extermination League broke up; the more generous of its members frankly acknowledged his great qualities, admitted that he had been wronged, and became whole-hearted adherents; others, from self-interest, made haste to climb on his bandwagon; only a few irreconcilables continued to sulk and frown, but no longer dared attack him.[2]

[1] W. G. Nicholas, in the *Washington Evening Star*, August 9, 1908.
[2] *Edward Henry Harriman*, by Otto H. Kahn (New York, 1911).

The Government, however, continued to thwart Mr. Harriman's plans, so far as it had power to do so. For seven years it had allowed the Union Pacific–Southern Pacific combination to exist, without molestation or interference; but in the early part of 1908, the Federal authorities seemed suddenly to discover that, under the Sherman Anti-Trust Law, the virtual consolidation of these two great systems was a "combination in restraint of trade," and they consequently brought suit in the United States Circuit Court for the purpose of disrupting it, and of getting a decision that would make it illegal for the Union Pacific to buy or own stock in four other railroad corporations, namely, the San Pedro, Los Angeles & Salt Lake, the Atchison, Topeka & Santa Fé, the Great Northern, and the Northern Pacific. These corporations were not under Mr. Harriman's control, but it was apparently thought that if the Union Pacific were allowed to own stock in them, the result would be coöperation, rather than competition, and competition, at that time, the Government was determined to enforce. Although this suit was not decided during Mr. Harriman's lifetime, the threatened disruption of the great coördinated system that he had worked so long to create must have added to the burden of anxiety that he had to carry during his last years. [1]

[1] The first decision, in the United States Circuit Court, was in

Between 1905 and 1909, much of Mr. Harriman's time and thought were given to certain plans that he had long had in mind in connection with the Arden estate. It had always been his intention to build a house for himself on the property, as soon as he could determine what location would be best for it; but until all parts of the estate had been made accessible by forty miles of bridle-paths and roads, it was not possible to compare the advantages of one site with those of another. In the spring of 1905, when he had secured title to all the high lands that were desirable and had cut roads to them through the woods, he decided to build on the crest of the forested ridge that rises steeply from the valley of the Ramapo River on one side and the wooded ravine of Forest and Cranberry Lakes on the other. It was an ideal site for a country residence, on account of the beautiful views that it commanded in every direction; but the farmers who lived in the vicinity declared that the building of a big house, thirteen hundred feet above the sea, on a waterless and almost inaccessible mountain-top, would prove to be an impracticable if not absolutely impossible undertaking. The difficulties involved, however, only

favor of the Union Pacific; but the case was carried by appeal to the United States Supreme Court, and there, three or four years later, the judgment of the lower tribunal was reversed and the Union Pacific was ordered to relinquish its control of the Southern Pacific Company.

gave Mr. Harriman a keener interest in the project. His first step was to build up the steep side of the mountain a funicular or cable railway by which workmen and materials could be quickly and easily carried to the summit. He then cleared away the forest on the crest of the ridge; blasted out of the granite a site for house, lawn, and garden, using the rock in building the house, and began drilling a deep artesian well for water. At the same time a carriage road was built in gentle, well-graded zigzags up the mountain-side, so that the summit could be reached either by road or by rail. The distance from the house to the Arden House station of the Erie, by the cable incline, was not more, perhaps, than a thousand feet; but by the carriage road it was three miles and a half. Automobiles, however, might go either way, as they could be lifted on a horizontal platform by the line of cable in less than ten minutes. The new Arden House was not built by contract. The plans for it were drawn by Carriere & Hastings[1] under Mr. and Mrs. Harriman's personal direction, and the building, which was made largely of granite from the mountain on which it stood, was erected by their own force of workmen under the supervision of their own manager.

---

[1] Mr. Hastings, of this well known firm of architects, was a warm personal friend of the Harrimans.

In more than one respect the new house was in a class by itself. Not only did it stand on the most commanding site in Orange County, but it was, in every detail, the highest possible expression of American taste and art. Mr. Harriman was an ardent lover and admirer of his native country, and when he undertook to create for himself a permanent home, he determined that it should be made wholly of American materials and should serve as a proof of American ability to reach the highest standard of excellence in architecture, decoration, and tasteful effect. Nothing therefore was used, in the house itself or in its furnishings, that was not a product of American industry and skill. The carved woods, the marbles, the paintings, the tapestries, the sculptures, and the great organ in the gallery over the beautiful and spacious hall, were all made in the United States and the spirited marble bas-relief over the principal fireplace, which represented a mounted Plains Indian attacking a buffalo, was the conception and the work of an American artist.[1] Almost everything in the house was specially designed and made, under Mr. and Mrs. Harriman's direction, for the particular place that it was to occupy, so that the interior, as a whole, not only represented American skill and American products

[1] Charles Cary Rumsey.

THE ROSE TERRACE OF THE PRESENT ARDEN HOUSE

at their very best, but was the harmonious embodiment of personal ideals in form, color, proportions, and effective arrangement.

By the time the Harrimans returned from Klamath Lake, Oregon, the work was well under way, but the house was not so near completion that the family could move into it until the summer of 1909. It was then one of the most beautiful country residences in the vicinity of New York, chiefly on account of its magnificent site. Standing on a heavily wooded ridge, thirteen hundred feet above the sea, its western windows and terraces overlooked the cultivated, thickly settled valley of the Ramapo River, with the blue mountains of the Shawangunk Range in the distance, while on the other side nothing met the eye but a deep, wild, forested ravine, in which, hundreds of feet below, there were two or three small blue lakes, but not a sign, far or near, of human habitation or human life.

When Mr. Harriman bought the property that afterward became the Arden estate, it already contained two or three times as much land as he really needed; but instead of contenting himself with his first purchase, he continued to buy more at every opportunity until, in 1905, he owned about thirty square miles. His main object in doing this was to save the beautiful wooded hills on the west side of the Hudson River from falling into the hands of timber speculators and lumbermen and preserve them intact for the use and benefit of the public. This object he kept steadily in view for many years; but his plans did not take definite shape until the spring of 1909, when he decided to offer the greater part of his holdings to the State as the nucleus for a great public park. On the 1st of the following June, just as he was about to sail for Europe, he outlined his wishes and intentions in a letter to Charles E. Hughes, who was then Governor of the State:

I am sorry to sail away without having a conference with you regarding the Park matter. I want you, however, to have some idea of what I have in mind, which is about as follows:

I plan to set aside about 12,000 acres [nineteen square miles] of what I at present own, and, with this, to donate something like $1,000,000 for the acquisition of the necessary interior properties and the property lying over toward the Hudson River, and I have thought that possibly some of the other property-owners might join with me in this move, making it possible to secure practically the whole wild area between the Ramapo and the Hudson Rivers, extending from West Point down to below Stony Point, and again north of West Point, taking in the Crow's Nest. I feel that if this should be accomplished, the State's prison should be moved again to the other side of the river, so as not to destroy the natural beauty which can never be replaced.[1]

[1] The State Legislature, a year or two before this time, had appropriated money for the purchase of a large tract of land near Bear Mountain, where it was proposed to erect a penitentiary. As this

This, of course, is a matter which interests the whole future population of New York State and particularly of New York City and the other cities adjacent to it. As the population increases, this area will be all the more necessary as a place upon which tuberculosis camps can be established and outdoor life be enjoyed, providing great benefit to every one.

I am giving this little tale to my secretary on the dock just before leaving, as I am anxious to have you understand my ideas upon the subject.

To the above letter Governor Hughes's secretary wrote the following reply under date of June 25, 1909:

Governor Hughes directs me to say that he was very glad to receive the statement with regard to Mr. Harriman's plans, and to know that Mr. Harriman contemplates such a great public benefaction. The creation of a public park embracing a wide expanse of this beautiful highland country, controlling a great watershed, and reserving for public uses a territory so accessible to New York City, would be of incalculable benefit to the people. The Governor hopes that Mr. Harriman will see his way clear to carry out this splendid project at an early day, and that the whole area to which reference is made may be secured for a public park.

With regard to the site of the new prison, it must be borne in mind that the matter is not within the control of the Governor. The site has been selected, and a commission constituted by law has authority to proceed with the erection of the prison.

would mar the beauty of the park which Mr. Harriman hoped to see created, he was strongly opposed to it and used what influence he had against it.

The site cannot be changed without legislative authority, and if there were good and sufficient reasons for changing the site, it would be of great importance that the matter should be taken up before a contract is let for the erection of buildings upon the location which has been selected.

Governor Hughes appreciates Mr. Harriman's suggestion as to the great advantages such a reservation would present for health camps and for outdoor life, and the vast possibilities which would be opened up for those who are crowded within the great city so near at hand. The Governor hopes Mr. Harriman will soon be able to give the matter further attention, and will be glad to hear from him further as he perfects his plan, which means so much for the public interest.

Mr. Harriman was not able to carry out personally the scheme that he outlined in his letter to Governor Hughes. When he returned from Europe, about three months later, he was desperately if not hopelessly ill, and death came before he had taken the action that he contemplated. His wishes and intentions, however, were faithfully carried out by his wife, to whom all of his property was left. Before the end of the following year, the great health and pleasure resort that he had in mind was brought into existence, as a northern extension of the Palisades Interstate Park; the New York Legislature gave to it the wild land near Bear Mountain which it had bought as a site for a prison; private individuals coöperated, as Mr. Harriman hoped they would, by

contributing money, as well as by relinquishing
ownership of lands that were needed to round out
and complete the proposed reservation, and on the
29th of October, 1910, Mr. Averell Harriman, acting
in behalf of his mother, presented to the Board of
Park Commissioners one million dollars in cash and
ten thousand acres of land, as the gift of his father
to the people of the State. In his presentation address Mr. Averell Harriman said:

In accordance with a long-cherished plan of my
father, to give to the State of New York, for the use of
the people, a portion of the Arden estate, and acting in
behalf of my mother, I now present to the commissioners of the Palisade Park the land comprising the
gift. I also hand you my mother's contribution to the
expense of future development of the Harriman Park.
It is her hope and mine that, through all the years to
come, the health and happiness of future generations
will be advanced by these gifts.

The great Hudson River reservation, of which the
Harriman Park forms a part, now serves as a recreation and health resort for hundreds of thousands of
New Yorkers every year. In the summer of 1919,
it contained twenty-nine tent settlements, where
more than fifty thousand people, mostly women and
children, spent an average of eight days each; it
furnished camping sites for sixteen hundred Boy
Scouts, and its play and picnic ground at Bear

Mountain was visited, in the course of the season, by more than half a million people.[1]

The Palisades Interstate Park was created more than twenty years ago, as a means of saving the picturesque basaltic cliffs on the lower Hudson from the quarrymen who were beginning to destroy them; but it comprised only a narrow strip of land along the western side of the river. The much larger Bear Mountain Park, which was afterward merged in it, owes its existence mainly to the initiative and far-sighted wisdom of Mr. Harriman, who first saved the beautiful wooded hills of Orange and Rockland Counties from denudation and ruin by purchasing them himself; then conceived the idea of making them the nucleus of a great forest park, to serve as a health and pleasure resort for the people of New York, and finally gave to this park more than half of his Arden estate, with a small fortune in cash for its future extension and development.

President W. C. Brown, of the New York Central Railroad Company, said, soon after Mr. Harriman's death: "The Union Pacific and Southern Pacific Railroads, both transformed by his masterful hand from financial and physical wrecks to the magnificent properties that they are to-day, will perhaps be the

[1] *New York Times*, March 1, 1920.

most enduring monuments to his marvelous executive ability and constructive genius." [1]

This of course is true; but hardly less enduring
will be such monuments as the Boys' Club, the fertile oasis of the Imperial Valley, and the Harriman
forest park, which will long be sources of health,
pleasure, or profit to multitudes of people.

In the spring of 1909, Mr. Harriman's health,
which had been failing for several years, became so
impaired that he decided to go to Europe for medical treatment and rest. On the 1st of the following
June, soon after his return from Mazatlan, where
he went to inspect the Mexican division of the
Southern Pacific system, which had just been finished
to that point, he sailed with his wife for France.
After spending a few days in Paris, he went by rail
to Vienna, and upon the advice of physicians there
proceeded to Bad Gastein, an old and celebrated
health resort in the Austrian duchy of Salzburg,
whose hot mineral springs have been regarded, for
more than a thousand years, as very useful in cases
of nervous prostration and general debility. At Bad
Gastein he spent a large part of the summer, deriving some benefit, perhaps, from the mineral waters,
but more, probably, from the mountain air and
complete rest. Up to this time he does not seem to

[1] *New York Sun*, September 10, 1909.

have regarded his physical condition as in any way serious, still less alarming. On the 21st of July he wrote a long letter to Jacob H. Schiff in which he said:

This is a queer little place, and has been and is doing us much good. I have no trouble except my back, which will always be stiff, but not dangerous in the least. The only necessity is to give my nerves a chance to become normal, and this I am doing and intend to continue in the work.

Mr. Harriman's "trouble," however, was more serious than he supposed. No doubt he was suffering from overwork and undue nervous strain; but the deep-seated ailment that sapped his strength and made his condition serious was gastric ulceration, a disease whose symptoms are often so indefinite or obscure as to make accurate diagnosis extremely difficult, especially at first. When he returned to the United States, on the 24th of August, 1909, he was noticeably worse, but, in spite of pain and weakness, he continued to dictate letters and manage his business affairs with as much wisdom and decision as ever. But he never left Arden House again. On Sunday, the 5th of September, he had a collapse, and on Thursday, September 9th, he passed away, calmly and quietly, in the sixty-second year of his age. He was buried in the shady churchyard of the Arden parish, only a short distance from the house that had been his summer home for more than twenty years.

THE FRASER BAS-RELIEF

CHAPTER XXXI

CHARACTER AND BUSINESS METHODS

IN a statement made to a Washington correspondent of the "New York Times" in December, 1919, Secretary Franklin K. Lane said, in forecasting the future of the United States:

Coöperation is to be the word of this century, and coöperation will mean that power to do will be lodged in some one's hands. There can be no effective administration by mob, or by any mass of men. Coöperation must therefore not only be based on a mutual desire for a common end, but also on common confidence in leadership. . . . *We shall keep the premiums for those who have initiative, imagination, resourcefulness, leadership, self-confidence, and the confidence of others.* [1]

The preëminence of E. H. Harriman in the fields of transportation and finance was gained by precisely the qualities that Secretary Lane has named — initiative, imagination, resourcefulness, leadership, self-confidence, and the confidence of others. No man in his generation possessed these qualities in a higher degree, and few other men, in the judgment of his contemporaries, equaled him in the thinking power, the sheer intellectual ability, that made these qualities effective and fruitful. Julius Kruttschnitt,

[1] *New York Times*, December 28, 1919.

chairman of the executive committee of the Southern
Pacific Company, who worked with him for many
years in the upbuilding and development of the so-
called "Harriman Lines," said of him: "He had the
most wonderful intellect I ever knew." [1]

William F. Herrin, vice-president and chief counsel of the Southern Pacific Company, who was also
one of Mr. Harriman's co-workers, laid particular
stress upon his intellectual ability, of which he said:

The first notable quality which any one must have
realized in dealing with him was his incisiveness, his
ability to quickly get at the very point to be considered
and upon which the question under consideration must
turn. His clearness and penetration made him impatient
of ordinary mental processes, and he frequently reached
the kernel of the matter before the person presenting
it had finished his statement. His analysis was rapid
and unerring, and his synthetic process equally notable. Hence the whole scope of any subject was before
his mind. No important detail escaped his observation,
and his final judgment was unimpeachable. In view of
the many questions he dealt with and their magnitude,
it seems marvelous that any one man, in the period of
Mr. Harriman's life, could have accomplished what he
did; and this only emphasizes the intensity and extraordinary power of his mental processes. In the qualities
I have mentioned he excelled any man I have ever
known. [2]

[1] Testimon before Judge Bledsoe in the suit of the United States
against the Southern Pacific Company for the recovery of oil lands.
(*New York Sun*, January 24, 1917.)

[2] *Personal Impressions of Edward Henry Harriman*, by William F.
Herrin. (A privately printed brochure, San Francisco, 1911.)

The late James Stillman, president of the National City Bank, who knew Harriman intimately and who coöperated with him in the most important of his many great enterprises, said of him, two years after his death:

I have been acquainted with all of the prominent men of this country during the past forty years, and I can truly say that Harriman, in his conception of vast achievements and his skill, energy, and daring in bringing them to realization, far surpassed any other man I have ever known. His brain was a thing to marvel at; and yet, if you could take it apart, as you would a clock, you would find its mechanism extremely simple. Nevertheless, it could make the most complex problems understandable and solvable.[1]

H. T. Newcomb, the well-known statistician and economist, who also noticed Harriman's ability to make "the most complex problems understandable and solvable," said:

The thing which is unique, unequaled, is the magnificent and prophetic plan of which every one of these [Harriman's] triumphs was a coördinate and harmonious part. The comprehensive breadth of his far-seeing imagination seized upon facts and conditions remote from one another, seemingly unrelated and incapable of being brought into effective juxtaposition, and out of an apparently heterogeneous mass conceived an orderly arrangement, a unified plan, an efficient, coördinate whole. And once such a conception had been formed

[1] Unpublished interview of James Stillman with G. W. Batson September 10, 1911.

and its realization determined upon, the method of its execution was painstaking, persistent, consistent, and indomitable.[1]

This ability to grasp a multitude of facts and bring them into harmonious and effective relationship with one another by sheer thinking power was the characteristic that seems to have made the deepest impression upon Mr. Harriman's associates and co-workers. To all of them he was, primarily, a great intellectual force. But it was not this alone that made him a born leader of men. Growing out of it and dependent partly upon it were the courage, self-confidence, and indomitable will power that inspired confidence in others and made his influence so nearly irresistible. He reasoned more widely, clearly, and accurately than other business men did, and then he impressed the results of his thinking upon other minds by the dynamic force of his personality. In commenting upon this, Mr. Otto H. Kahn has said:

I was asked sometimes, when things that had seemed utterly improbable of realization were finally accomplished by Mr. Harriman, to give a reason why the parties concerned had yielded to him. What was the inducement? What the motive of their action? Why had they finally done what they had declared they

---

[1] "Harriman the Efficient," by H. T. Newcomb (at one time associated with Professor H. C. Adams as expert adviser of the Interstate Commerce Commission), *Railway World*, September 17, 1909.

would not do, or what there was no plausible explanation for their doing? My answer was: "Simply because Mr. Harriman had set his will and mind at work to make them do it." He once said to me, early in our acquaintance, "All the opportunity I ask is to be one amongst fifteen men in a board room." Yet he had neither eloquence, nor what is ordinarily called tact or attractiveness. His were not the ways or the gifts of the "easy boss." Smooth diplomacy, the talent of leading men almost without their knowing that they are being led, skillful achievement by winning compromise, were not his methods. His genius was the genius of a Bismarck, of a Roman Cæsar; his dominion was based on rugged strength, iron will and tenacity, irresistible determination, indomitable courage, tireless toil, marvelous ability, foresight almost prophetic, and, last but not least, upon those qualities of character which command men's trust and confidence. His rule was frankly the rule of the conqueror who has made his place by the superiority of his powers and is ever prepared to hold it against all comers. He was unable either to cajole or dissemble. He was stiff-necked to a fault. It would have saved him much opposition, many enemies, many misunderstandings, if he had possessed the gift of suavity, of placing a veneer over his dominating traits, so as to make the fact of his rulership less overt and thereby less irksome. Sometimes, when even some of his associates would chafe under his undisguised autocracy, I ventured to plead with him that the results he sought could just as surely be obtained by less combative, more gentle methods, while, at the same time, avoiding bad blood and ill feeling. His answer was invariably:

"You may be right that these things could be so accomplished, but not *by me*. I can work only in my own way. I cannot make myself different, nor act in a way foreign to me. They will have to take me as I am, or drop me. This is not arrogance on my part. I simply cannot achieve anything if I try to compromise with my nature and to follow the notions of others." [1]

One cannot estimate rightly the usefulness to the world of a man of such dominating personality and great intellectual power without taking into consideration his aims and purposes. If he employs his natural gifts in the making of money, as most business men do, what ultimate end has he in view? Does he seek wealth merely for the satisfaction of getting and possessing it? Does he strive to amass a great fortune for the sake of the pleasure, luxury, influence, and social distinction that it can give him? Or has he in view other ends to which the making of money is only incidental? Harriman himself always said that he valued money, primarily, for the power that it gave him to do constructive or creative work. It was not possible to do such work — at least on a great scale — without capital, and he therefore strove to amass wealth; but it was primarily the work, not the money, that interested him. On the trip to Alaska, almost at the beginning of his great career, he said to his friend, John Muir:

I never cared for money except as power for work.

[1] *Edward Henry Harriman*, by Otto H. Kahn (New York, 1911), pp. 7–8.

What I most enjoy is the power of creation, getting into partnership with Nature in doing good, helping to feed man and beast, and making everybody and everything a little better and happier.[1]

Eight years later, when the greater part of his life-work was done, he said in a letter to the rector of All Saints' Church, Omaha:

Accumulation of money must come with success in developing enterprises and should be looked upon only as evidence of the success of the undertaking. The satisfaction lies in the fact that the enterprise *is* successful and will be of permanent benefit to humanity. Without capital it could not be begun, or carried on after completion.[2]

Many of Harriman's private and personal letters show how much importance he attached to the permanent usefulness of his work in the upbuilding of the country and the development of its resources. It was this, in large part, which inspired his efforts and which recompensed him for the months and years of toil that he gave to the formation and execution of his far-reaching plans. In a letter that he wrote to Jacob H. Schiff, shortly after the tenth anniversary of the reconstruction of the Union Pacific, he said:

[1] *Edward Henry Harriman*, by John Muir (New York, 1911), p. 36.
[2] Letter to Rev. T. J. Mackay, rector of All Saints' Church, Omaha, September 16, 1907.

Your reminder of our having passed together the first decade of the Union Pacific and its successful regeneration has gratified me very much. It is to me the greatest satisfaction to feel that we "still stand together" and that we are looking forward as well as backward. Of course it has been nerve-wearing and has taken some of our vitality, and I have sometimes questioned whether it has been worth while. Maybe it would not have been if only the Union Pacific and ourselves had been the gainers. But where would have been those whom the Union Pacific serves, if we had not struggled, improved, improved again, enlarged and made better, and so increased its capacity as to permit the development of every enterprise, and the establishment of new ones, in all the territory adjacent to it and to the systems under its influence? Besides that, its methods induced like methods in the management of other important systems. Where would we all now be without them? It has all made for advancement in civilization and will some day be understood, so as to induce, by legislation, coöperation and expansion instead of contention and competition. There is still much improvement to be worked for in the future, and I hope we shall still be found "standing together" when the opportunities and responsibilities present themselves.

That Harriman would not have toiled as he did during the last ten years of his life if he had not been working for objects that seemed to him "worth while," and if he had not been able to see the tangible results of his labor, is unquestionably true; but results, in the shape of useful work accomplished, were not his only, or even his chief, incentive. The driving force behind his various activities was the keen pleasure that the mere exercise of his transcendent powers gave him. Incidentally, he amassed a large fortune; but he did not strive merely to make money, nor even to achieve results that would benefit the world. He worked strenuously and constantly up to the week of his death largely, if not chiefly, because the matching of his brain against difficulties, the thinking out and execution of great plans for the attainment of what seemed to him desirable results, were the breath of life to him. He was, primarily, a great intellectual force expending itself constantly in material achievement for the simple reason that in so expending itself it was fulfilling the very law of its being.

That Mr. Harriman was a good and patriotic citizen is shown by his thirty years of personal work for the Boys' Club; by his scientific expedition to Alaska; by his long-continued support of Dr. Trudeau's sanitarium for consumptives and laboratory for the study of tuberculosis at Saranac; by his fight with the Colorado River for the protection of the Imperial Valley; by his work in San Francisco after the earthquake and fire, and by many other enterprises and undertakings of which less is generally known. But in all of these activities he was quite as much a dynamic force seeking an outlet in achievement as he was a doer of good for the mere sake of the good. "His real purpose was to do big constructive things; his real sport to pit his strength and brain against those of other men, or against difficult tasks; his real reward was the consciousness of worthy accomplishment, the sense of mastery, the successful exercise of power." Mr. W. F. Herrin understood him rightly and judged him accurately when he said:

Although he was a very wealthy man, a man of enormous powers of acquisition, it may truly be said of him that he did not value money for its own sake, but only as a means of accomplishing other ends and purposes. The mere gaining of wealth interested him much less than the activities which attended its acquisition; in other words, he looked upon money as he did upon the locomotives, rolling stock, rails, and other materials out of which he constructed and operated his railways; and these materials were quite as much valued by him as the money with which he purchased them. He played the game of life upon a large scale and it was the intense activity of this game and the ultimate ends accomplished by it which were of value to him.[1]

To intimate friends, in hours of confidential talk, Mr. Harriman himself said that the exercise of his powers in constructive work — and especially difficult work — was the thing in life that interested him most. One night in New York, when he and James Stillman happened to attend the same per-

[1] *Personal Impressions of Edward Henry Harriman.* (Brochure previously cited.)

formance of grand opera, Harriman came to Stillman's box during one of the entr'actes and said,
"Stillman, I want to see you a minute." Stillman
arose, and Harriman, saying, "Come this way,"
went down to the cloak-room and thence to a
brougham which was waiting. They entered the
brougham and proceeded to drive to Harriman's
house, which was then in East Fifty-Fifth Street.
On the way Stillman said: "Well, Harriman, what
do you want of me?" To which Harriman replied:
"Wait a few minutes; we will soon be there." In
due course of time they arrived at Harriman's
house and went upstairs to the library. There Stillman again inquired expectantly: "Harriman, what
is it?" Without making any reply Harriman got
out a box of cigars, passed them to Stillman, and
then went to the grate and poked the fire. Surprised
and a little impatient, Stillman finally said: "Well,
Harriman, I am still waiting; what is it you want?"
"Oh!" said Harriman, "you must have been tired
of that opera. I know I was, and I thought we might
pass the time better at home."

After some talk about the performance from which
they had just come, Stillman said: "Harriman, what
is it that interests you most in life and gives you
most pleasure?" Harriman thought a moment and
then, looking up, said: "Well, I think it is to plan

some big piece of helpful work that everybody says can't possibly be done, and then jump in with both feet and do it." [1]

Harriman's interest in a piece of work grew as the difficulties that it presented increased. Nothing daunted him, nothing discouraged him, and his confidence in his ability to surmount the most formidable obstacles was never shaken. Indeed, the more difficult the task the more enjoyment he derived from the struggle to accomplish it. Two and a half centuries ago, Viscount Halifax, one of the foremost English statesmen of his time, said: "A difficulty raiseth the spirits of a great Man; he hath a mind to wrestle with it and give it a Fall. A Man's Mind must be very low if a difficulty doth not make a part of the Pleasure." [2] These words might have been written with a character like Harriman's in mind.

Harriman's phenomenal success in the field of transportation is attributable not only to his extraordinary intellectual ability, which would doubtless have made him distinguished in any field, but also to his intimate acquaintance with both practical railroading and finance. "If I were asked what is the key to Harriman's success," said one of the greatest bankers in New York ten or twelve years ago, "I

[1] Unpublished interview of James Stillman with G. W. Batson, previously cited.
[2] *Recollections*, by John Morley, vol. I, p. 155.

should say it is the fact that he is the only man I have ever known who is just as familiar with the physical as the financial side of his properties. Morgan is a great banker, but he knows nothing about the physical side of a railroad. Hill is a great traffic man and railroad builder, but he is a baby when he gets into Wall Street. Harriman knows both ends of the game and knows them well. He started in life as a floor trader and developed into a banker, and when he took hold of the railroad business he put aside the banking and financial end and spent long, hard, and patient years in learning the traffic and operating side. Then he took the two and counterbalanced them. Now he is his own banker and his own traffic manager, and the combination is irresistible." [1]

But, it may be asked, how did Harriman learn "the traffic and operating side" of the railroad business? He had not been graduated by a special or technical school, he was not a student of books, and he had never served as an engineer or operating official on any transportation line. Where did he get the facts and the practical knowledge that enabled him to deal so effectively with the technical problems of railway management and operation?

[1] "Owners of America: E. H. Harriman," by Charles P. Norcross, *Cosmopolitan Magazine*, July, 1909, p. 160.

When these questions were asked of a prominent railroad man who knew Harriman well, he replied: "Harriman had an all-seeing eye and an insatiable curiosity. Nothing escaped his attention, and when he saw anything that he did not fully understand, he went to the man or men who knew most concerning that particular thing and asked questions about it until he got to the bottom of it. No perfunctory or makeshift explanation satisfied him. The man who gave him information had to know his subject thoroughly and accurately down to the ground. His technical knowledge of railroading, therefore, was gained partly by observation and partly by detailed personal inquiry continued through a long term of years."

In all probability, Harriman never consciously formulated in words the principles upon which he acted in getting a railroad education; but if he had expressed them in precepts, they would have appeared, perhaps, in something like this form:

Observe attentively everything in sight, big or little, important or unimportant, good, bad, or indifferent.

If in what you see there is anything that you do not fully understand, question people who know until the matter is perfectly clear in your mind.

Finally, remember all things, of all kinds, that are

related in any way to your work and think about them incessantly.

It has been said that Harriman was impatient of details, and that he seldom read a letter of more than a page or two until after it had been "boiled down." This is partly true. Trivial details, or details that he already knew, did not interest him and he was unwilling to waste time in going over them; but no man ever gave closer attention to details that were significant or vital. He noticed them and inquired about them constantly; and when he took hold of the Union Pacific in 1898 he had a knowledge of practical railroading that had been gained by fifteen years of observation and study as a director of the Illinois Central. But he never regarded his railroad education as finished. When maps, plans, profiles, estimates, traffic schedules, and details of equipment were sent to him by Union Pacific officers in the field, he toiled over them and thought about them until his mind had completely absorbed and assimilated them. Then, when an important question into which these details entered as factors, came up for discussion at a meeting of the directors, his understanding and complete mastery of the whole subject were so overwhelmingly manifest that, again and again, the board gave him *carte blanche* by adopting unanimously the brief resolution: "Referred to the chairman of the executive committee with authority to act."

The cardinal principle of Harriman's philosophy of railroading was briefly but clearly set forth in a talk that he had with J. B. Berry, chief engineer of the Union Pacific, in 1898. "The only way to make a good property valuable," he said, "is to put it in the best possible condition to do business." [1] Upon this principle he always acted from the time when he bought thirty-four miles of run-down, unprofitable railroad in northern New York in 1883 to the time when he managed or controlled 23,000 miles of road with a capitalization of $1,500,000,000 in 1906. And putting a property "in the best possible condition to do business" meant, with Harriman, the lowering of grades, straightening of curves, rebuilding of bridges, and, if necessary, complete reëquipment with new rolling stock. It made no difference whether the betterments would cost a few hundred thousand dollars, or a few hundred million dollars; the improvements must be made before the property could be regarded as being "in the best possible condition to do business."

In obtaining the capital for such betterments Mr. Harriman was governed by two rules which he formulated early in life, namely:

[1] "Notes of Association with E. H. Harriman," by J. B. Berry. (An unpublished manuscript.)

MR. HARRIMAN IN HIS OFFICE

(1) Develop railroads with cheap money.

(2) Never borrow from the substance of a road.

By the first of these rules he meant that loans should be negotiated only when money seeking investment is abundant and interest rates are low, and by the second that it is a ruinous policy to try to economize by letting property deteriorate for lack of proper maintenance.

"The formula of development with cheap money," says John Moody, "became one of the foundation principles of Harriman's career. 'I have known him,' said one of his closest associates, 'to wait nine months, in negotiations for placing bonds, to save a charge of one eighth of one per cent a year.' As his operations rose into the hundreds of millions, this formula became a matter of great consequence." His second rule — "Never borrow from the substance of a road" — was almost equally important. "He believed," says Mr. Moody, "that every dollar gained by letting a road run down cost two dollars to replace. He had learned this in following out his purpose to understand the business of a great railroad thoroughly by actual operation." [1]

In developing his railroad properties on the financial side, Harriman never paid out in dividends

[1] "Masters of Capital in America," by John Moody and G. K. Turner, *McClure's Magazine*, December, 1910, pp. 338–39.

money that could be used to advantage in making betterments, nor did he ever fail to keep a large sum in reserve for emergencies. When the Union Pacific was earning money rapidly, but was paying only five per cent on its common stock, Gishart Farrer, of London, wrote him urging an increase in the dividend rate. To this he replied:

In 1898, when I first came into the Union Pacific, the shareholders were just finishing the payment of an assessment. Now they are insatiable for big and ever bigger dividends. I intend to prevent if possible a recurrence of the assessment condition. . . . The property will have to husband its resources for protection against the aggression of its neighbors, both north and south as well as in the middle, and also for the extensions necessary to enable it to get its proper share of business.

In pursuance of this far-sighted policy, Harriman paid only four per cent on the common stock of the Union Pacific and nothing at all on that of the Southern Pacific until 1906. Nearly all the earnings of both roads were either put back into the properties, or held in reserve for emergencies. It was this policy that gave him such perfect confidence, in the panic of 1907, when he wrote Prince André Poniatowski in Paris:

We can meet any condition. We are stronger than banks, or bankers. If the French market wants anything, this is its chance, and it is the chance of a lifetime.

The Union Pacific has the credit, the securities, and the income, and will be the first to push forward.

Finally, in the management of his railroads Harriman never failed to keep in mind the interests of the people whom they served. As Mr. Kahn has justly said:

Shippers and others using the Union Pacific lines were benefited alike with the stockholders. Indeed, whenever there was a question between increased returns to the stockholder and increased efficiency to the railroad, Mr. Harriman invariably chose the latter course. As a matter of fact, he cared altogether more for the approbation of the people served by the lines of his railroads than for the applause of the financial or any other part of the community. [1]

Fully realizing that the prosperity of his roads was largely dependent upon the good-will of the public, he strove in every way to secure that good-will, not only by helpful and efficient service, but by courtesy and prompt attention to complaints.

In the years when the railroads were indifferent to public opinion [says Mr. Cornwell], and disregarded all attempts to make friends of their clients (a method of procedure which brought on more than half the troubles which the railroads met later), one of the principal causes of grumbling and bitterness was the difficulty which shippers had in getting their claims attended to. These were relegated to the red-tape route, and it some-

[1] *Edward Henry Harriman*, by Otto H. Kahn (New York, 1911), p. 12.

times took years to get a settlement. The policy of courtesy, devoted attention to the wants of the customer, and insistent determination to make friends of the public, was inaugurated by Mr. Harriman on his Pacific lines and is now more and more becoming a part of railroad methods.[1]

Mr. Harriman himself outlined this policy in an article entitled "The Railroads and the People" which he wrote for "The Independent" in March, 1907. In that article he said:

The railroad that does not seek to build up the territory through which it passes by offering good service pursues a policy that can only bring it to grief in the long run. It dries up its territory; the territory does not produce anything, and then there comes a day when there is nothing for the railroad to carry. It is like knocking the piers out from under a bridge, and a railroad can no more afford to disregard such natural conditions than a bridge-builder. . . . The Union Pacific system has spent $250,000,000 in improvements and extensions since 1900; has laid 7500 miles of new track, and replaced, all together, 14,000 or 15,000 miles of track. These things are indications of the service rendered in building up the country, and I want to do what I can to develop such a feeling of coöperation between the people and the railroads that the Union Pacific and the other systems may not be shut off from further contributing to the country's development.[2]

[1] William C. Cornwell in *The Bache Review*, December 24, 1915, p. 3.
[2] "The Railroads and the People," by Edward Henry Harriman, *The Independent* (New York, March 28, 1907), p. 703. So far as known, this is the only magazine article that Mr. Harriman ever wrote.

Public appreciation of Mr. Harriman's work came late, but it came at last. In January, 1911, the "Commercial & Financial Chronicle" of New York said editorially:

Though Edward H. Harriman died less than a year and a half ago, the country is already beginning to appreciate more clearly than it did during his strenuous lifetime what he accomplished and what he aimed to do for the people of the United States. Doubtless as time passes, affording a truer perspective, bringing fresh facts to light and brushing away animosity, the public judgment will crystallize so strongly in his favor that he will be awarded a high place among the geniuses who have done so much for the constructive development of the country.

A little earlier the "Commercial Times" of Chicago said editorially:

Think of the masterful one whose ashes repose in the tomb at Arden — review that man's life and achievements, recall the dominion he possessed over the faith, hopes, actions, and beliefs of thousands of men controlling capital and credit — and reflect that he left no heir to his kingship of affairs. Edward Henry Harriman, above all else, was a fountain head of faith, whose like had not been known in this country since the days of the golden spikes that marked the marriage of the oceans. He had that superhuman assurance which welcomed sublime hazards and rejoiced in opportunities that ordinary men called ruinous. His genius was doing the impossible; and he did it by showing men their destiny of wealth, through faith and daring, not for selfish ends, but for the welfare of the masses that neither see into the future nor act in advance of the present.

CHAPTER XXXII

RECOLLECTIONS, ESTIMATES, AND APPRECIATIONS

IN the first year or two after the death of Mr. Harriman, a number of his friends or business associates wrote for the press, or for private circulation, personal recollections of their intercourse with him, estimates of his character as they had observed it during long terms of years, or brief tributes to his memory inspired by feelings of affection and respect. As these writings show the man as he appeared to those who had the best opportunities of knowing him, and as they reveal or emphasize many different sides of his character, they may not be out of place in the concluding chapter of this biography.

Among the men who coöperated with Mr. Harriman in his various railroad enterprises, none played a more important part than Jacob H. Schiff, senior partner in the banking house of Kuhn, Loeb & Co. Their acquaintance began in 1884, soon after the election of Mr. Harriman as a director of the Illinois Central Railroad Company; but they were not closely associated until 1897, when a committee headed by Kuhn, Loeb & Co. undertook the reorganization of the Union Pacific. In that work Mr. Harriman participated, and in the spring of the following year he was made chairman of the reorganized company's executive committee. From that time until 1909 the two men worked together in financing and upbuilding the Union Pacific and Southern Pacific systems.

About a year after Mr. Harriman's death, Mr. Schiff wrote an "appreciation" of him in which he said:

I knew the late E. H. Harriman for almost a quarter of a century, having become more intimately acquainted with him during the period of the reorganization of the Union Pacific Railroad in 1896-97. The task which my firm had undertaken in this connection was a difficult one, due to a great extent to the complications resulting from the company's considerable indebtedness to the United States Government, and also to the many conflicting interests involved. Finding that Mr. Harriman was not in harmony with certain portions of the plan, I arranged a conference with him at which he frankly and without reserve told me that, recognizing what could be made out of the Union Pacific with proper management, it was his ambition to secure its control, in order to assure to himself the extraordinary opportunity to build it up; that, because of this, he wanted to become actively interested in the reorganization, and that he would bend all his efforts toward succeeding in this. Knowing something of E. H. Harriman's persistency and energy, we concluded that it was in the interest of a prompt and successful reorganization to secure his coöperation rather than to work at cross-purposes with him. As a result of brief negotiations, Mr. Harriman agreed to coöperate with us, upon the understanding that he should be given a potent voice in the management of the company upon completion of its reorganization. In fulfillment of this he was made a member of the executive committee as soon as the new company came into existence, and after a short while he was elected to the chairmanship of the committee. At successive periods thereafter, in order to assure a homogeneous management, he assumed the presidency of the Union Pacific and its affiliated companies.

E. H. Harriman's great achievement in building up "a rusted streak of iron" — as the Union Pacific had been aptly termed at the time of its reorganization — into one of the greatest and most profitable railroad systems on the continent is so very recent that it appears needless here to state in detail facts so well known and understood. The same might be said concerning his success in bringing back into the system valuable connecting lines which had been lost as a consequence of the company's breakdown, and the adding and bringing under Union Pacific influence new lines, which were considered and have since proven to be of much importance and great value.

The question has often been discussed as to what it was that brought about the great success of E. H. Harriman. Small in stature, bodily rather frail, frequently subjected to great physical suffering, his influence upon those he came in contact with was such that they readily accepted his judgment and bowed to his indomitable will. There can be little doubt that this was primarily in consequence of a ready recognition on the part of his associates and co-workers that his views were almost always sound. He was a positive genius in matters of railroad management, and his understanding of the complex questions which came up in connection with his varied activities was instantaneous. His courage was without limit, and when he was once convinced of the correctness of a view — which, however, he never hesitated to change if he could be shown to be in error — nothing could turn him from the way he deemed right and proper in order to assure the accomplishment of his purpose. His wisdom and courage in emergencies were amazing. Indeed, his capacities appeared to grow with the magnitude and difficulties of the situations he was at times called upon to aid in solving.

What, however, more than anything else attached so many men of mark to E. H. Harriman, and induced them to stand by him under all conditions, was his unquestioned loyalty to those who were his business associates, or his friends in private life. No one who trusted himself to Mr. Harriman, or who frankly went to him for advice, suffered disappointment. With very few exceptions, those who worked with him in his many important enterprises, whether as members of boards of directors, as managing officers, as heads of departments, or even in minor positions, never separated from him lightly thereafter, and their devotion to him constantly grew. In fact, in many cases, men whose opposition or enmity he had incurred in his earlier career finally became co-workers in his enterprises, or solicited his co-operation in undertakings of their own, after they had become acquainted with his great ability and trustworthiness.

He passed away a martyr to his energy and to the loyalty with which — even to the hour of his death — he looked after the large interests he had undertaken to represent. To those who knew him well, and who had the privilege of being intimately associated with him, the memory of his strong personality and forceful character will continue as an inspiration. He was always a builder, never a puller-down, and by his death the country has lost one of its greatest constructive forces.[1]

Among the prominent men who were intimately associated with Mr. Harriman in the last decade of his life, none perhaps was nearer to him, and none certainly more fully enjoyed his confidence, than R. S. Lovett, general legal counsel for the Harriman lines. In a private letter, written without any thought of publication, but quoted here with permission, Judge Lovett says:

There are at least three aspects of Mr. Harriman's character that ought to be brought out in any biography of him:

1. Beyond all question in my mind, he was a genius, as pronounced and unique as Napoleon. He had all the idiosyncrasies of genius. He would conceive things so extraordinarily clever or wise that one almost felt they must result from inspiration; and on the other hand — but fortunately very rarely — do other things inexplicable even to himself. Such is the habit of genius. I have likened him to Napoleon. This occurred to me often during association with him. It seemed to me that he possessed in an extraordinary degree all the qualities of a great military commander — the genius of insight, unerring intuition, amazing quickness of decision, resourcefulness, boundless courage, command of the confidence of others, persistency and yet endless patience when necessary, and above all, push, drive, and determination. His mental processes were unlike any I have ever known. He never arrived at his conclusions

[1] "E. H. Harriman: An Appreciation," by Jacob H. Schiff, August, 1910. (An unpublished manuscript.)

by reason, or argument, or any deliberative process that I could observe. His judgments seemed to be formed intuitively. The proposition was presented and he saw it. It was much like turning a flashlight on an object. If interested, he *saw it;* and did not care and probably did not know how it was revealed. And his vision and measure of it was almost unfailingly clear and correct. This mental method and effect was to me a most striking evidence of his genius — that he was indeed, in many respects, a superman. Incidents almost without number of the play of his extraordinary mentality could be recounted.

2. Another aspect of Mr. Harriman's character not to be overlooked was the difference between his superficial manner and his heart. His brusqueness was the dominant aspect of his manner in business intercourse. It sometimes amounted almost to rudeness. The pressure of time, the need for every minute, and the multitude of matters weighing upon him when downtown, were responsible to a considerable degree, but I believe the physical pain constantly suffered by his small, bent body every hour was responsible more than anything else for this brusqueness. But he had no quarter for a strong, well, able-bodied man capable of taking care of himself. His clerks and others about him, well and able to work, were taxed to the limit of their capacity when there was anything to do — and there generally was much. But the moment one became ill, or met with misfortune or sorrow, Mr. Harriman's consideration and sympathy went out in an extraordinary way. His whole attitude toward such person was reversed immediately. It was not done ostentatiously, or even graciously, but as if he were trying to conceal his feelings, which nevertheless were unmistakable. When one of those with whom he came in personal contact was discharged, however justifiably, even by his own order, he would relent

and require reinstatement. The result was an accumulation of more or less inefficient helpers about the office, who were to some extent a personal trial to him, when every possible facility for his great work should have been at hand. It was almost impossible, through interference by him, for those in charge of his offices to get rid of incompetent or undependable clerks. I recall one telephone operator of slow methods who was dismissed and actually paid off on three separate occasions by Mr. Harriman's own order to the office manager, only to be reinstated the next day, to renew the slow methods which were such a torture to him. Indeed, his sympathy and his spirit of helpfulness toward the unfortunate, and his tolerance in spite of his brusqueness, led to the retention on his personal staff of some types until their undependability caused some of his associates anxiety and, in at least one notable instance, led to the betrayal of his confidence and the sale of his secrets. These incidents may seem of trifling importance in a great career, but their significance lies in what they reveal of the true heart and feeling of the man, in spite of a brusque manner and fierce aggressiveness.

3. Any biography of Mr. Harriman which omits his family life misses the point and loses the light of the whole story. I know of no one who can deal with it adequately, for of course members of his family are ineligible for the task. Family friends knew of it in a general way, but perhaps, after all, some of those who were associated almost constantly with him in business, year in and year out, and often with him at his homes — town and country — where much of his business was transacted, were best able to judge of the consistency of his attitude. They soon learned that no business, however great its magnitude nor how urgent its importance, caused him to neglect his home or his household, or to forget the most unimportant engagement

with his wife, or the smallest plans for his children. It was not unusual for him in the midst of transactions of such importance as to make men dizzy from concentration, to stop in order to speak a word on the telephone or send a message to Mrs. Harriman about some engagement or matter of family interest. His attitude toward her was more than devotion. It was profound admiration, respect, and unfailing attention and courtesy. Many times, through the years, business was interrupted or preceded by an order for flowers in commemoration of some anniversary. And as for his children, their welfare and education came before everything. Absolutely nothing was allowed to interfere with a visit to their schools, or the prosecution of any investigation or enterprise affecting their training or welfare. It really is not too much to say that their interests were paramount with him, at all times and under all circumstances.

Mr. Epes Randolph of Tucson, Arizona, who managed for many years the Harriman lines in Arizona and New Mexico and who, as president of the California Development Company, directed the fight with the Colorado River for the preservation of the Imperial Valley, said of the chief under whose orders he acted:

I doubt if Mr. Harriman was more genuinely admired, or more thoroughly appreciated, anywhere throughout the land than he was here [in Arizona]. The sad message announcing his death had scarcely reached me when people began to pour into my office to express their sorrow. Nor were these visitors confined to any particular class. Men from the humbler walks of life, as well as those most prominent, came, and their sorrow was genuine. To this day I never visit the west coast of Mexico, nor go into the Imperial Valley, that I do not hear Mr. Harriman's name mentioned with little short of reverence. It is but natural that the people should feel as they do. Mr. Harriman was doing work — great work — the world was his workshop — and he was then developing their country. They were benefited; they felt a personal interest in their benefactor; they respected him, admired him, rejoiced in his life and sorrowed in his death.

I have read much that people have written about Mr. Harriman, and Mr. Muir's tribute is the best; but it is not fully satisfying. He does not compass the man. He emphasizes his gentler characteristics, which were beautiful, but he does not picture the man in his manifold elements of greatness. The man described is not the Harriman, *facile princeps*, whom I knew and whose memory I revere. He is best entitled to the epithet of Great. How great, no man can say. He was always superior to occasion. I know of no other man of whom this can be truthfully said.

Mr. Harriman was predestined to create; he accepted the stewardship, and earnestly, joyously, and fearlessly went about his appointed work, its consummation making for the good of mankind. He was intensely human. His attitude toward his fellow creatures was beneficent, yet his aim, primarily, was not philanthropy. He amassed wealth, yet he loved not money. Men and money to him were but materials to be used as means to an end, the end the loftiest — the upbuilding of the estate; the reward, the satisfaction of fulfillment.

At the time of his death, knowledge of him, his work and his motives was becoming disseminated among men, and he was coming into his own — universal appreciation. It is a calamity that his span of life could not have been lengthened to the period allotted to man. He has gone to his rest, but his spirit lives, his work goes on. His monument is still in the building and his name will be spoken by people yet to be born.[1]

On the expedition to Alaska Mr. Harriman made the acquaintance of a number of eminent writers and scientists, among whom were John Burroughs, Dr. C. Hart Merriam, then chief of the United States Biological Survey in Washington, and John Muir, the well-known geologist, explorer, and naturalist of California. Dr. Merriam's recollections of Mr. Harriman's life and activities on this trip have been given in a previous chapter. In his estimate of Mr. Harriman's character he said:

The enjoyment of Nature shown by Mr. Harriman on the Alaska expedition was a strong characteristic. He was a lover of unspoiled country and was fond of hunting and fishing. After visiting various parts of the United States, he purchased a tract of wild land on the Upper Klamath Lake in Oregon, where he could go with his family to gratify the cravings for sport with rod and gun and at the same time find needed rest in the depths of the primeval forest. To this remote and beautiful retreat he once took two celebrated lovers of Nature — John Muir, who had previously been his guest on the Alaska expedition, and the late William Keith, the great California painter.

The same spirit that led him to establish a summer camp in the wilds of Oregon determined the location of his country home near New York; for while the pressing

[1] Extract from private letter, November 20, 1911.

demands of an exacting business life made it necessary
for him to be within easy reach of the great city, his
love of the country drew him to the rugged hills and
extensive forests of Orange County where he gradually
acquired an immense wooded domain. And when he
came to build his final Arden home he insisted that
wild Nature be allowed to reach the very walls of his
massive mansion. He was willing to tolerate a formal
court, but outside the outer wall a tree should not be
cut nor a bramble broken.

From the summer of 1899 until the year before his
death, I saw Mr. Harriman at infrequent intervals, but
under a variety of conditions — as when occupied with
matters of business at his New York and San Francisco offices; when traveling in his private car; when
at his hotel in Washington and San Francisco; when
with his family at his New York home and his country
place at Arden; and a few times as a caller at my residence in Washington. During these various meetings
the estimate I had formed of him on the Alaska expedition was confirmed and I became more and more
impressed by the greatness of his mind and the power
of his personality. Among his marked attributes were
simplicity, directness, fairness, courage, thoughtful-
ness, determination, and breadth of view. His conversation covered an amazing range of subjects, while his
active mind showed a philosophic grasp of many of the
problems that disturb our political and industrial
worlds. In his personal relations he was kind, considerate, and generous. In matters of business he was
shrewd and cold, asked direct questions, said little, and
kept his plans to himself until ready to act.

It is not for me to speak of his family life, but I may
be allowed to say that in our personal intercourse he
was frank and companionable. His quiet, thoughtful
manner was in itself attractive and there was about

him a certain sympathetic kindness which drew one to him.

He differed from most men in high positions in his knowledge of details and in the personal attention he gave to minor matters of organization and administration; and it was his custom to personally control the operations of his roads and other activities. He was interested in various engineering enterprises having for their object the betterment of existing means of transportation; was a believer in the development of electric power for railroads, and spoke with just pride of the achievements of his pet roads — the Union Pacific and Southern Pacific — particularly in bridging Great Salt Lake and in checking the ruinous overflow of the lower Colorado River.

In matters of business the scope of his thoughts knew no bounds. He loved to sit under the trees and think. He once showed me a tree by the little lake near his old country home where it was his habit to sit by the hour, looking off into the forest and thinking — working out in his mind the vast projects upon which he was engaged or which he had in contemplation. His vision swept quickly over the field of the average man, and pushing out into realms beyond discovered opportunities for development and for initial enterprise. His mind was of the constructive type, always on the lookout for new combinations and reorganizations, in order — as he often said — that the work might be done more economically and the public given better service. He believed that the prosperity of a people depends first of all on the adequacy of its means of transportation — that growth of population, industry, and general welfare go hand in hand with the development of transportation facilities. In extending and improving the service of his railroad and steamboat lines, therefore, he felt that he was doing a double good — that he was acting in the interest of the people as well as of the particular railroad or steamship line more immediately concerned. In all of this work he was governed not so much by the needs of to-day as by those of the future — as he foresaw them. He was a patriotic American, proud of his country and ambitious for its development. In building his great stone mansion at Arden he forbade the use of any but American materials and would not allow any of these to be sent abroad for finishing.

One of the best-known examples of his public spirit is his gift to the State of New York of a large tract of forest land for a public park, accompanied by a cash contribution of a million dollars for its care and development. This and other substantial gifts and endowments in contemplation at the time of his death have since been provided by Mrs. Harriman.

He was strongly opposed to wastefulness, extravagance, and false charity, and believed that much time and money are thrown away on unworthy objects. On the other hand, he was ready to help a good cause. When asked whether or not he approved of doing a certain thing, or of doing it in a certain way, his usual answer was, "If it is worth doing, if it will be useful, do it, and do it in the best way. If it is worth doing at all, it is worth doing well." When he saw a competent man engaged in routine or clerical work, he was very apt to remark, "Never do what a clerk or assistant can do for you; save your time and strength for work which others cannot do."

His quiet manner was not to be misunderstood. He always meant what he said, and when giving directions expected to be obeyed implicitly and promptly. In negotiations with rivals his manner was sometimes imperative — possibly imperious. He would not submit to dictation or defeat. He felt his power and at times enjoyed exercising it. An agreement once made he considered inviolable. The man who broke his word or failed to live up to his agreement he held in contempt. He believed in "a square deal and *fair play*" and laid special emphasis on the fair play.

The qualities which led to his success were common sense, tireless industry, initiative, daring, far-sightedness, judgment in weighing business propositions, tenacity of purpose, insight into the capacity and integrity of men, cleverness in planning combinations, a genius for organization, adroitness in placing responsibility, acumen in foreseeing contingencies, and almost superhuman executive ability — qualities that make men great.

In whatever enterprise he embarked he soon became the dominating force; his masterful mind and tremendous will power made him the leader; he was a natural ruler. He was taken off in the noontime of his mental vigor — just as the world was awaking to an appreciation of his genius.[1]

John Muir, who knew Mr. Harriman for a period of ten years and who occasionally spent weeks at a time in daily association with him, was deeply impressed by his kindliness, friendly affection, and considerate sympathy. An anonymous newspaper writer once said: "If Mr. Harriman had more red blood and a warmer heart he might be a great statesman." To Muir, Morris, McGuinness, Trudeau, Bishop Morrison, and all who knew him intimately in private life, warmth of heart and affectionate loyalty in friendship were among his distinguishing

[1] "Recollections and Impressions of E. H. Harriman," by C. Hart Merriam. (An unpublished manuscript.)

characteristics. In a little booklet published for private circulation two years after Mr. Harriman's death, Muir said:

Of all the great builders — the famous doers of things in this busy world — none that I know of more ably and manfully did his appointed work than my friend Edward Henry Harriman. He was always ready and able. The greater his burdens, the more formidable the obstacles looming ahead of him, the greater was his enjoyment. He fairly reveled in heavy dynamical work and went about it naturally and unweariedly like glaciers making landscapes — cutting canyons through ridges, carrying off hills, laying rails and bridges over lakes and rivers, mountains and plains, making the Nation's ways straight and smooth and safe, bringing everybody nearer to one another. He seemed to regard the whole continent as his farm and all the people as partners, stirring millions of workers into useful action, plowing, sowing, irrigating, mining, building cities and factories, farms and homes.

Nothing he had was allowed to lie idle. A great maker and harvester of crops of wealth, and of course a great spender, he used his income as seed for other crops of world-wealth in succession, sowing broadcast for present and future good, pouring back his gains again and again into new commonwealth currents to create new benefits, or to increase the fruitfulness of old ones after he himself had passed away. Fortunes grew along his railroads like natural fruit. Almost everything he touched sprang up into new forms, changing the face of the whole country. . . .

I saw him in the spring of 1903 in San Francisco just before he started back home, and only a few weeks later, when I was on my way to Europe and Asia, I visited him at the Hotel Netherland, New York, where he was

recovering from a dangerous surgical operation. After
cheery greetings he said he was getting well and would
soon be up and at work. "You must have suffered ter-
ribly," I said. "Oh, never mind that; you know there
is always more or less pain connected with surgery, but
I made the quickest time across the continent that ever
was made. I made it in less than three days from
San Francisco to New York, and I did n't hurry the first
day, either. Troubles seldom come singly. Now we are
getting out of them all — strikes on the roads, scarlet
fever in the family, etc. — and this evening, for the first
time since these troubles commenced, we are going to
dine together in my room. Join us and you will see all
the family." But a prior engagement prevented, and I
had to sail the next morning for Liverpool. Noticing I
looked tired, he ordered a glass of milk for me and bade
me remember there is such a thing as an electric cable,
that he was president of two steamship companies, and
when I got round to China and Japan, if I should happen to need anything, to let him know. And when I
replied that I was already unconscionably in his debt,
he said, "Oh, you can't keep accounts of that kind; pass
them along anywhere whenever you get the chance."

Just as I was leaving St. Petersburg for the Crimea
and the Caucasus, I received a long letter from him,
stating that it had occurred to him after I left that a
letter to his agents in Japan and China might be of use
to me. No heart could escape the influence of this sort
of kindness from one overladen with so many cares.
That he should have thought of me at all under such
crushing circumstances was an unmistakable token of
affection, and brought more clearly to view his noble-
hearted loyalty and depth of character, on which all
sound friendship is founded. . . .

The serene strength of his mind was manifested by
being always equal to whatever might happen, or to

whatever he wished to do. None I ever knew faced the storm and stress of the world's affairs more calmly and resolutely, nor have I ever known another with such power of performance. He was quiet and reserved in manner, and to those who judged him only from newspaper reports, or from meeting him in formal business matters, he often seemed unsympathetic; but never so to those who were permitted to see beneath the surface.

He was flashing quick to see the best of things and the best of people. I never saw him bitterly or stormily angry or unjust. None I ever knew had a greater capacity for kindness. He was a shrewd judge of character, had strong sense, broad humanity, and like underground irrigating streams did much in quiet, hidden ways for clubs, schools, churches, public parks, neglected children, etc., always ready to lend a hand.

To him I owe some of the most precious moments of my life. The memory of heart-to-heart talks that pleasant summer at Klamath Lake I shall always treasure with reverent affection, together with those of our last days at Pasadena, when, in the midst of his own crushing cares, he lavished whole-hearted sympathy and care on my sick child. I never knew a warmer heart. Our last meeting was in Los Angeles, at a public reception, where I was delighted with the good wishes and respect accorded him by the multitude that pressed around him to shake his hand. But when the meeting broke up, leaving him weary and pale, there fell a foreboding shadow that I could never shake off.

He will not be forgotten. Respect and admiration for his wonderful talents, and love for the greatness of his heart and service, are every day growing. And although scarce any one as yet is able to make anything like a fair estimate of his life and character, almost everybody comes at last to know a good man.[1]

[1] *Edward Henry Harriman*, by John Muir (New York, 1911). (Privately printed.)

Political economists, as well as naturalists, recognized the value and importance of Mr. Harriman's creative work. In a letter to the director of the Bureau of Municipal Research in New York City, in January, 1912, Dr. L. S. Rowe, Professor of Political Science in the University of Pennsylvania, said:

Mr. Harriman's career furnishes the best instance of one of the fundamental characteristics of the great leaders of industry in the United States and distinguishes them from European men of affairs. The ambition to do real creative work, rather than a mere desire to acquire wealth, was the keynote of Mr. Harriman's activities. In this respect he stands forth as a creative genius, certainly one of the greatest that this country has produced. I have always felt it to be one of the weaknesses of our American democracy that the Government cannot command the thought and effort of such men in the solution of our great social and political problems.

As a rule, men whose business interests are conflicting seldom praise each other; but the following tribute is from E. D. Kenna, a distinguished lawyer who was formerly vice-president and general solicitor of one of the railroads with which the Harriman lines were in active competition, namely, the Atchison, Topeka & Santa Fé.

Contemporary history seldom does justice to any one of prominence; but time is a great corrector of errors when the facts essential to a true estimate of character are accessible. It is a genuine pleasure, therefore, for

those who admired Mr. Harriman, to know that who-
ever may investigate impartially hereafter the Chicago
& Alton reorganization will find in it nothing derogatory
to the reputation of the greatest man of business our
country has produced. Mr. Harriman never controlled
a property — including the Chicago & Alton — that
was not every day increasingly better for his control,
and he shared with every stockholder the immense advantages of such control.

It was the unique distinction of Mr. Harriman that
he made a great fortune by serving both railway shareholders and the public better than they had ever been
served before, and, consequently, it is not strange that
his reputation has been at times assailed, privately by
less successful men of affairs, and publicly by dema-
gogues, because of jealousy and hatred. But it would
have been a great public gain if we might have been
spared Mr. Harriman a few years longer and lost his
detractors.

No one has better opportunities for judging a man
in private and public life than his family physician.
Other men see him at his office, or in a directors'
meeting, when he is engrossed in business affairs,
and when, perhaps, he shows only the harder, sterner
side of his character; but the medical practitioner
sees him at various times — in his office and at
his home, in sickness and in health — and finally
comes to know him intimately in all the relations of
life.

Dr. Lewis R. Morris, who went with Mr. Harriman to Alaska and was his family physician for

many years, has given his recollections and impressions of him in the following words:

In writing a reminiscence of a man whom you have known as intimately as a physician grows to know a patient, you are at once confronted with the various and different characteristics, both mental and physical, which he presents. This is especially so if you have made it a habit to study the character and mental habits of your patients, as well as the physical conditions, while you are studying their maladies. These varied characteristics are especially prominent in a great man, a genius, a man of large affairs, a man who, by the force of such characteristics, has accomplished much in this world. The greater the man, the more he accomplishes, the more these various traits become prominent, and not only one, but several, will stand out and form, as it were, a harmonious chord of the theme of his life and work; this was particularly so with Edward Henry Harriman.

To succeed was the dominant feature of Mr. Harriman's character, and the mental processes which make for and spell the word success were the most prominent, namely, indomitable will, untiring energy, keen foresight, a correct judgment of men and conditions, extraordinary power of organization, a fine sense of justice, a firm belief in his country, its institutions and its future — in every sense of the word a patriot — and perfect honesty. . . .

The world will remember Mr. Harriman for the great achievement in building up the great railway systems in the West with which his name was connected, and the other great enterprises throughout the country in which he was interested. He was a firm believer in the institutions and future of the country, and nothing could have been more patriotic than his refusal to put himself right before the public when attacked by its Chief Magistrate, when he had in his hands all the proof, because he could not bring himself to attack his President, or to belittle him in the eyes of the world. Only those near him knew how hard it was for him to bear this unwarranted and untruthful attack.

Physically, Mr. Harriman was a short, slight man of dark complexion, with a dark, quick, and penetrating eye; quick in his movements, and in fact impressed you as a man of a highly organized nervous type, and with an enormous force of nervous energy. In his younger days he had been a good boxer, and until the last few years of his life, for his size and weight, he had wonderfully well-developed muscles. He was a good rider and driver, was very fond of horses and had bred and owned many fast ones. Of his features, his eyes attracted your attention at once and held it; being particularly bright, liquid and piercing, and he seemed to take in everything. . . .

The characteristics shown to those nearest him were often not known to those who had only business relations with him. His charities, which were many and varied, were never done in the public eye, and were essentially of the best and most practical kind. His family and friends will remember him best not as the organizer and upbuilder of railroad systems, but as a true, sympathetic, and kindly friend, and a devoted husband and father. In my experience of over twenty years as a family physician I have never seen a more perfect family life than he led. No day was so short, or so full of affairs, that he did not find time for the children before his dinner at the end of the day; and when conferences with men of affairs had lasted at his house through the afternoon, and the children's hour came, the men and affairs had to give way to his children. No man ever passed to his children a better heritage of uprightness and honor.

STAMBOUL

Finally, as a neighbor of his in Orange County aptly and in all sincerity put it, in talking of Mr. Harriman to me in the smoker of an Ontario & Western Railroad train near Middletown, New York — he being unaware that I knew Mr. Harriman — "We people up in Orange County considered E. H. Harriman to be the best example of a Christian gentleman." There can be no greater tribute to any man than this, and this is the man as his best friends knew him.[1]

Among the men who made the acquaintance of Mr. Harriman in his early manhood and who maintained a close friendship with him throughout his life was the Reverend J. D. Morrison, formerly rector of St. John's Church, Ogdensburg, New York, and now Bishop of Duluth. In a paper giving his recollections and impressions of his lifelong friend. Bishop Morrison says:

My acquaintance with Mr. Harriman extended over a period of more than twenty-five years. I officiated at his marriage in St. John's Church, Ogdensburg, New York, in 1879, when he deprived my parish of the services of a young lady who had been a leader in every good work, especially in helpful ministries to the ignorant, the distressed, and the poor. After that, from time to time, I saw him at his home, or in his office when I visited him in New York, and once I was with him for a brief season in the Adirondack Mountains. Gradually I came to know him with ever-deepening respect and regard. Living remote from the great business world, I knew very little of its affairs, and it was a chance re-

[1] "A Successful Life: Edward Henry Harriman," by Dr. Lewis R. Morris. (An unpublished manuscript.)

mark at dinner, in a house in the city of New York, that first made me aware that he had become a man of great influence and power. Nothing in his attitude or manner, as I had met him year after year, had indicated any consciousness of his greatness. It was so to the end. I was never conscious of any change. I always found him the same kindly friend, with keen insight and swift judgment, and with momentary flashes of quiet humor. He never failed me in his approval of righteousness and integrity, or in sympathy with real distress. When I was called to occupy my present position [bishopric of Duluth] in 1897, although he rather disapproved my going West, he never ceased to take a warm interest in my work, and his strong helpful hand aided me greatly in carrying the burdens of a new missionary diocese.

He was an enthusiastic lover of nature, and his ideal of a holiday was to go away into the forest with rod and line and camping kit, to catch and broil his own supper, and spend the night at the camp-fire beneath the stars. Years ago, when I met him in the Adirondacks, he was almost like a boy in his enjoyment of nature, his freedom from care, and his glad exhilaration of spirit.

As I saw him at infrequent intervals during many years, he was always a steadfast friend, whose outlook seemed to be toward the things that are high, pure, and true.[1]

Early in his young manhood, while he was still a clerk in the Stock Exchange house of D. C. Hays, Mr. Harriman made the acquaintance in the Adirondacks of a young physician named Edward L. Trudeau, who afterward became widely known as

[1] "Recollections and Impressions of Edward H. Harriman," by Right Reverend J. D. Morrison, Bishop of Duluth. (An unpublished manuscript.)

the founder and manager of a sanitarium for consumptives at Saranac Lake. The two young men were almost exactly of the same age; both were enthusiastic lovers of unspoiled nature, and both were fond of hunting, fishing, and camping out. Brought together at first by similarity of tastes, they soon became well acquainted, and for a period of nearly forty years thereafter they were close and intimate friends. Their careers in life were very different and they did not see each other often; but their friendship never cooled, they kept constantly in touch with one another, and Mr. Harriman made it a point to attend, if possible, the meetings of the sanitarium trustees, which were held in the Adirondacks every year. In his autobiography, published shortly after his death, Dr. Trudeau gave the following account of this long-continued friendship:

However divergent our paths and interests in life proved to be, and in spite of the fact that we saw each other only at rare intervals, the old friendship between us through a lifetime remained the same, and Mr. Harriman never neglected an opportunity to show me that it was so. In spite of his fame and power and riches, his manner toward me never changed in the least. If I called on him when I went to New York, and found as usual many influential financiers and great railroad presidents waiting for an interview with him, he would keep them all waiting, no matter who they were, until he had taken time to greet me and hear how things were going in the Adirondacks. His friendship for me was always expressed in deeds, and not in words. At intervals in life, when great sorrows swept over me and nearly crushed me, I felt at once his helpful hand and strong, sustaining personality, and all that a good friend could do to help me he quietly did for me.

When my health broke down almost completely in 1902, he urged me to go to California in February for a two months' trip. He placed at our disposal a private car, in charge of one of the best stewards on the Union Pacific Railroad, provisioned it thoroughly, put orders on board to other roads to convey us wherever we might want to go, and told me to go and rest and amuse myself for a while. Unfortunately, I was taken ill in Redlands, and although we enjoyed every minute of the trip, it seemed to do my health little good.

Beset on all sides by keen enemies who plotted his overthrow, and by seeming friends who were too often ready to betray his confidence, Mr. Harriman no doubt learned the wisdom of keeping his own counsel and trusting very few men. He showed me, however, on many occasions, that he trusted me, and I believe he never had any reason to think that his confidence had been misplaced. People often tried to learn his views on financial matters by questioning me; but I could always tell them frankly that if there was one thing that we did not discuss when we were together it was business and his railroads.

He had a keen sense of humor and I think was often amused by my ingenuousness about business matters. We both belonged to a little fishing and hunting club at Little Rapids, with two other friends of mine. Mr. Harriman rarely went there, but insisted, as did my other two friends, on holding his membership for many years, paying his share of the expenses of the little club, because he knew that I loved to go there with my family for rest and recreation when the strain of work

was too much for me. On one occasion I wanted to add
to our small land-holdings so as to get more hunting
and fishing ground, and asked him if he would care to
invest a few thousand dollars in such wild land. He said
he would, and listened to me as I enthusiastically dilated
on the advantages of the proposed purchase. When I
ended by saying, "It seems well worth the money to
me, but you must decide, as I don't want you to get
stuck if you buy it," he smiled as he touched me on the
arm and said, "Ed, don't you ever worry about my
getting stuck."

He left for Alaska a few days later with the expedition he had organized, which he had invited Mrs.
Trudeau and me to join, taking my son Ned with him.
To show how keen his memory was for detail, and how
good a friend he was to me, in spite of the pressure of
the great responsibilities to be adjusted and arranged
for before his departure for so long an absence and the
cares of preparation for his large expedition, he did not
forget me. A few days after his departure, I had a note
from his secretary saying Mr. Harriman had left instructions that if I decided to buy any land, I could
draw on his office for any sum needed up to $40,000.
I was afraid of "getting him stuck," however, and did
not avail myself of his friendly offer.

I never knew a calmer or more self-contained man
than Mr. Harriman, and until physical complications
broke down his health, he seemed absolutely unruffled
by the stress and strain of the great business struggles
in which he constantly took so prominent a part. I remember I happened to be in town on the day before
Wall Street's great panic in 1907, and I got a telephone
message from him saying he was going down to his
country place at Arden early in the afternoon, to stay
overnight, and asking me to accompany him and we
could have a drive together. We spent the afternoon

driving together, and at ten o'clock started for bed. As we parted at the foot of the stairs I said: "Goodnight to you; I hope you will have a good night's sleep and that things will straighten out in Wall Street tomorrow." He smiled and said: "Ed, I never stayed awake a night in my life about business, and I'm not going to begin now." Next morning at the breakfast table he was as fresh and cheery as usual, though he knew better than any one else that the very foundations of great business concerns, and of Wall Street itself, would totter on that day, and that ruin might come to the most powerful.

He became a trustee of the Sanitarium at my request, and remained on the board until his death in 1909. He always gave the work while on the board his time, interest, advice, and support, and in several instances induced his friends to join him in subscriptions to the Endowment Fund. He loved a joke, and always pretended to me that his responsibilities as trustee of the Sanitarium were a great burden — greater than any others he had — and that he must sacrifice all other business to be present at these meetings, which he nevertheless found time to attend, no matter how pressing his engagements. He would always make it a great point to come from New York to Paul Smith's to attend the summer meetings, which were always held in the Adirondacks, and after the meetings he usually remained and visited me for a few days. On the one occasion when he was in Japan during the summer, he sent me a cable on the day of the meeting which was characteristic of him: "Sorry I can't come to the meeting. It is a long way round to you, but not so far in a straight line through the earth. Best wishes."

When Dr. Trudeau's son, Ned, died from pneumonia,

among many others, Dr. James, Linsly Williams, Mr. Harriman, and Lawrence Aspinwall were with us through all that terrible evening when Ned lay dead in the next room, and they did everything that love, sympathy, and helpful friendship could do to steady us and relieve us in doing what had to be done. The next afternoon, at the Grand Central Station, we found two cars Mr. Harriman had arranged for, attached to the Adirondack train. In one Ned's body lay, buried under a roomful of flowers and surrounded by his Yale chums who sat up all night by him as the car sped through the darkness toward the little churchyard under the tall pines at Paul Smith's.

In speaking again of the little hunting and fishing lodge in the Adirondacks, Dr. Trudeau says:

When Mr. Van Woert died, Dr. James bought his share and Ritz sold his to Mr. Harriman, and these good friends, who had little or no time to give to amusement and Little Rapids, and never went there, nevertheless divided the expenses of the place for years, because they knew how much I loved to go there.

Early in the history of Dr. Trudeau's Sanitarium, Mr. Harriman and Dr. Walter B. James raised $82,000 to add to its endowment, and as long as he lived Mr. Harriman never failed to come to its support when it was in need of help.[1]

In 1909, when Mr. Harriman's health was failing rapidly, he went to Europe for the last time, to get a little rest, to drink the medicinal waters of Bad Gastein, and to consult certain eminent medical

[1] *An Autobiography*, by Edward Livingston Trudeau (New York, 1916), pp. 90–96, 198, 276, 293, and 302.

authorities in Austria-Hungary with regard to his physical condition. In Vienna he made the acquaintance of Nelson O'Shaughnessy, Secretary of the American Embassy, who has given the following account of Mr. Harriman's last days — the days when he was already entering into the dark shadow of death:

I am impelled to record, albeit imperfectly, in some form more permanent than unwritten memories and sentiments, the deep impression left upon me by the great personality of Mr. Harriman. During those last months of struggle with physical suffering, when I had an opportunity, perhaps unequaled, of appreciating his moral qualities, nothing struck me so much as the complete absence in him of personal animosities. He seemed entirely without ill-will toward those whose judgments he knew had wronged him. He understood better than any one his own power of accomplishment, and had the feeling characteristic of all really strong natures that the prime necessity is to push on, despite opposing ideas, combinations, or persons; but never did he at any time entertain rancor toward individuals on account of their opposition, or of their inadequate comprehension of his great economic purpose.

In spite of the strain of conscious and unconscious combat with illness, his mind during those last months was formulating new plans, not for his own immediate advantage, for he had long since passed all milestones of personal gain, but for the rounding-off and conservation of the great system which he had brought into being. His direct and synthetic mind had both the power to foresee and to provide for future events; for him achievement was never finality.

On several occasions he said to me with that indescribable glance of his eye, "Ours is the greatest country
in the world and I intend to do my share to make it
greater." This seemed the pervading aspiration of the
last months of his life. Once, at Gastein, he remarked
in a rare moment of depression, "No one man is missed,"
and when I answered, "A work is carried on, but with a
difference, or what is the meaning of personality," he
replied with a look that revealed the consciousness of
his own strength, "It is true that men do not struggle
alike with the forces of destiny."

I was almost awed by his boundless imagination. He
saw things as they could become and possessed the yet
rarer gift of ability to bring them into being, combining
in his single person the man of perspicacious faith and
the man of works. I was conscious too of that great
power of his of commanding the allegiance of those with
whom he came into contact, a power proceeding not
less from his unfailing recognition and appreciation of
ability in any form, than from the conviction with
which he inspired those around him that his aims were
beyond the personal and broader than the interests of
any one individual. No leader ever commanded the
entire devotion of his followers unless he embodied for
them some personal ideal, and I felt when with him that
he was in truth a leader of men and a master in the
choice of instruments, from whom he demanded the
best and also received it.

I shall never forget the picture of him on the Sem-
mering, the map of our great West laid out before him,
visible through the open window the slopes of the
Styrian Alps, down which the oldest of mountain railroads winds its way to the historic valley of the Danube.
It was the old and the new, the things to come evolving
out of those of the past — and who shall say what vast
projects for the better communication between the sons

of men his fertile genius might not have engendered and brought to fruition had but a further span of life been allotted to him?

I shall add nothing more to these imperfectly recorded impressions. A great friend came into my life and was soon taken away; but my intercourse with him has left me under the spell of his commanding personality and bequeathed to me, as it were, an inheritance of clearer thought and greater courage, arising from the example of his intellect, energy, and fortitude.[1]

[1] "Impressions of E. H. Harriman," by Nelson O'Shaughnessy, Secretary of the American Embassy, Vienna. (An unpublished manuscript.)

THE END

CHRONOLOGY OF E. H. HARRIMAN'S LIFE

CHRONOLOGY OF E. H. HARRIMAN'S LIFE

1848. Born at Hempstead, New York, February 20.

1851. Family moved to Jersey City.

1854–1860. Attended public schools, Jersey City.

1860–1862. Student in Trinity School, New York.

1862–1868. Messenger boy, "pad-shover," clerk and chief clerk in office of D. C. Hays, stockbroker, New York.

1870. Opened broker's office of his own on corner of Broad Street and Exchange Place, New York.

1874. First venture in stock speculation.

1874–1876. Member of Travelers' Club and of Seventh Regiment, National Guard; interest in boxing; vacations in the Adirondacks; took in J. B. Livingston as partner and firm became E. H. Harriman & Co.

1876. Founded Boys' Club on Tompkins Square, New York.

1877. First venture in field of transportation; purchase of steamer Twilight.

1879. Married Mary W. Averell, of Ogdensburg, New York.

1880. Entrance into railroad field; elected a director of the Ogdensburg & Lake Champlain Railroad Company.

1881. Acquired interest in Lake Ontario Southern Railroad.

1881–1883. Reorganized Lake Ontario Southern under the name of Sodus Bay & Southern, bought it, rebuilt it, and sold it to the Pennsylvania Railroad Company; established Sodus Bay Elevator Company.

1883. Elected a director of the Illinois Central Railroad Company.

1885. Retired from firm of E. H. Harriman & Co.; bought the Parrott farm in Orange County, New York, gave it the name of "Arden" and made it his summer home.

1887. Began contest with J. P. Morgan for control of the Dubuque & Sioux City Railroad Company; elected vice-president of the Illinois Central.

1888. Acquired great influence in Illinois Central; extension and improvement of that road.

1889. Acted as president of Illinois Central during absence of Stuyvesant Fish in Europe.

1893–1894. Acquired interest in Erie Railroad Company; contest with J. P. Morgan over plan of reorganization.

1896. Supported financially Erie Canal work of the Furnaceville Iron Company. Organized Horse and Road Improvement Association of Orange County, New York.

1897. Opposed but afterward promoted reorganization of the Union Pacific Railroad Company; elected a director of that company December 6.

1898. Elected chairman of executive committee of Union Pacific in May.
Made first trip of inspection over the road and called for an appropriation of $25,000,000 for betterments.

1899. Began reconstruction of Union Pacific. Reorganized and began to rebuild Chicago & Alton. Organized and conducted scientific expedition to Alaska. Elected chairman of executive committee of Kansas City & Southern. Elected a Director of the Baltimore & Ohio Railroad Company and coöperated with F. D. Underwood in financing betterments.

1900. Tried to secure control of Chicago, Burlington & Quincy Railroad Company by organizing a pool to purchase its stock.

1901. Acquired control of Southern Pacific Railroad Company, and on September 26 was elected president of it.

Put up new building for the Boys' Club.

Elected a director of the Equitable Life Assurance Society.

Bought stock of the Northern Pacific Railroad Company to the amount of $79,000,000 with a view to securing control.

Northern Pacific "corner" and panic.

Coöperated with Morgan and Hill in organization of the Northern Securities Company.

Contest with Senator Clark over the building of the San Pedro, Los Angeles & Salt Lake Railroad.

1902. Began contest with James R. Keene for control of the Southern Pacific Railroad Company.

Coöperated with Kuhn, Loeb & Co. in organizing Union Pacific preferred stock pool.

Made trip to the City of Mexico and secured concession from President Diaz for a railroad to Mazatlan and beyond.

1903. Elected a director of the Erie Railroad Company and afterward a member of its executive committee.

1904. Began a contest with the Atchison, Topeka & Santa Fé Railroad Company for control of the Gila Cañon route.

Purchased $30,000,000 of Santa Fé stock.

United States Supreme Court ordered dissolution of the Northern Securities Company.

Began contest with James J. Hill over distribution of Securities Company's assets.

1905. Became a member of the Frick Committee to

investigate management of Equitable Life Assurance Society.

Made trip to the Far East for the purpose of securing railroads in Manchuria and Siberia and establishing a round-the-world transportation line.

Began erection of new Arden House.

Saved Erie Railroad Company from great loss on its purchase of the Cincinnati, Hamilton & Dayton Railroad.

1906. Invested $130,000,000 of Union Pacific money in stock of various railroad companies.

Contest with Stuyvesant Fish and removal of the latter from the presidency of the Illinois Central.

Work in San Francisco after the earthquake and fire.

Accused of improper stock speculation in connection with increase of Union Pacific dividend rate to ten per cent.

Began fight with the Colorado River for the preservation of the Imperial Valley.

Friendly relations with President Roosevelt broken off.

1907. Interstate Commerce Commission began investigation of the Harriman lines.

Attack of "Harriman Extermination League."

Spent summer at Pelican Bay Lodge, Klamath Lake, Oregon.

Bought Central Railroad of Georgia and turned it over to the Illinois Central.

1908. Saved Erie Railroad Company from bankruptcy by taking $5,500,000 of its notes.

1909. Finished erection of new Arden House.

Made trip to Mazatlan to inspect Mexican extension of Southern Pacific.

Gave $1,000,000 and 10,000 acres of land to the State of New York for the creation of a public park on the Hudson River.

Went to Europe in June for rest and medical advice.

Returned hopelessly ill in August and died September 9th in Arden House.

INDEX

of, 362, 363; strikes on, 367, 368;
the Cincinnati, Hamilton & Dayton episode, 368–77; threatened
with serious embarrassment, ii,
312; meeting to consider means of
rehabilitating, 313–17; Harriman
comes to the relief of, 315–21;
results of Harriman's action, 321–
25.

Erie & Jersey R.R., i, 362, 363.

Evarts, Maxwell, present at interview between Sherman and Harriman, ii, 198–202; statement of,
regarding interview, 203–09; statement of, regarding his advice to
Roosevelt, 218, 219; statement of,
regarding Harriman's attempt to
get interview with Roosevelt,
223–26.

Evarts, Sherman, i, 30, 34.

Farm lands in the West, i, 145–47,
176.

Farragut, Loyall, i, 48.

Farrer, Gisbart, ii, 364.

Felton, S. M., ii, 233, 235, 256.

Fernow, Professor, i, 188.

Field, Marshall, ii, 232 n.

"Financial World," quoted, ii, 321.

Fink, President, ii, 245, 246, 254,
258.

Fish, Stuyvesant, i, 18; of the Chicago, St. Louis & New Orleans
R.R., 69; and Fitzgerald-Schiff
committee, 125; dissatisfaction
with his administration of the
Illinois Central, ii, 42–61; concerning loan made by Harriman
to, 45–48, 64 n.; deposed from
presidency of Illinois Central, 61,
65.

Fisher, N. C., i, 30, 34.

Fisher, Dr., i, 188.

Fitzgerald, General Louis, i, 121,
122, 224.

Fleming, Robert, on the Alton transaction, ii, 307, 308.

Foraker, Senator, i, 352.

Ford Motor Car Company, ii, 251.

Fordyce, Samuel W., i, 224.

French, Lord, ii, 25.

Frick, H. C., of the Santa Fé board,
i, 385; chairman of investigating
committee of insurance companies, 412, 419; director of Union
Pacific, ii, 84, 87.

Furnaceville Iron Co., the, i, 105.

Gannett, Henry, i, 188.

Gates, John W., on condition of
Union Pacific, 166; and the Kansas City Southern, 219–24.

Genesee River R.R., i, 362, 363.

Gifford, R. Swain, i, 188.

Gila flood of 1905, the, ii, 124, 127.

Gila Valley, i, 379–85.

Gilbert, G. K., i, 188.

Glaciers, i, 195–97, 200, 212.

Goelet, Robert W., ii, 5, 52.

Goschen, i, 103, 104.

Gould, George J., i, 119, 137 n.; and
the Kansas City Southern, 224;
and the Union Pacific, 290; in
syndicate to reorganize the Chicago & Alton, 233, 234.

Gould, Jay, i, 113.

Great Northern R.R., and the Burlington, i, 286–310; and the Northern Securities Company, 324–333;
stock of, a bonanza, 394–97.

Great Salt Lake, Lucin cut-off
across, i, 246–48.

Greely, General A. W., his account
of San Francisco earthquake, ii, 68.

Greene, Thomas L., quoted, ii, 253.

Grinnell, George Bird, i, 188.

Grinnell, William Morton, ii, 49.

Griscom, Lloyd C., supports Harriman's Far-Eastern plans, ii, 1, 6,
10–13.

Gross, Louis, i, 20.

Grover, Mr., i, 389 n.

Grunsky, C. E., ii, 123.

Hackstaff, A. G., of Illinois Central,
i, 89, 90.

414